GW00339139

DEPARTMENT OF STATE
UNITED STATES OF AMERICA
24
THE HOUSE SPECIAL SUBCOMMITTEE'S
FINDINGS AT CTU

01:22 01:25 01:27 01:29 01:30 01:31 01:33 01:
1:39 01:41 01:43 01:44 01:45 01:47 01:49 01:50 0
01:56 01:57 01:58 01:59 03:01 03:04 03:06 03:09
03:14 03:15 03:17 03:20 03:21 03:22 03:25 03:2
3:31 03:33 03:35 03:37 03:38 03:39 03:41 03:
03:47 03:49 03:50 03:52 03:53 03:54 03:56 03:5
04:01 04:03 04:04 04:06 04:09 04:11 04:13 04:1
04:20 04:21 04:22 04:25 04:27 04:29 04:30 04:3
04:37 04:38 04:39 04:41 04:43 04:44 04:45
4:50 04:52 04:53 04:54 04:56 04:57 04:58 04:59 06
06:06 06:09 06:11 06:13 06:14 06:15 06:17
06:22 06:25 06:27 06:29 06:30 06:31 06:33 06
06:39 06:41 06:43 06:44 06:45 06:47 06:49 06:5
6:54 06:56 06:57 06:58 06:59 07:01 07:03 07
7:11 07:13 07:14 07:15 07:17 07:20 07:21 07:22 07
07:30 07:31 07:33 07:35 07:37 07:38 07:39 07:4
07:45 07:47 07:49 07:50 07:52 07:53 07:54 07:
07:59 10:01 10:03 10:04 10:06 10:09 10:11 10:
10:17 10:20 10:21 10:22 10:25 10:27 10:29 10:30
10:35 10:37 10:38 10:39 10:41 10:43 10:44 10:
0:50 10:52 10:53 10:54 10:56 10:57 10:58 10:59 1
14:06 14:09 14:11 14:13 14:14 14:15 14:17 14:2
14:25 14:27 14:29 14:30 14:31 14:33 14:35 14:37
14:41 14:43 14:44 14:45 14:47 14:49 14:50 14:5
4:56 14:57 14:58 14:59 15:01 15:03 15:04 15:06 1
15:14 15:15 15:17 15:20 15:21 15:22 15:25 15:2
5:31 15:33 15:35 15:37 15:38 15:39 15:41 15:43 1
15:49 15:50 15:52 15:53 15:54 15:56 15:57 15:
8:03 18:04 18:06 18:09 18:11 18:13 18:14 18:15 1
18:22 18:25 18:27 18:29 18:30 18:31 18:33 18:3
18:39 18:41 18:43 18:44 18:45 18:47 18:49 18:50
8:54 18:56 18:57 18:58 18:59 20:01 20:03 20:0
20:11 20:13 20:14 20:15 20:17 20:20 20:21 20:
0:29 20:30 20:31 20:33 20:35 20:37 20:38 20:
20:44 20:45 20:47 20:49 20:50 20:52 20:53 2
20:58 20:59 23:01 23:03 23:04 23:06 23:09 23:
23:15 23:17 23:20 23:21 23:22 23:25 23:27 23
3:33 23:35 23:37 23:38 23:39 23:41 23:43 2

24
THE HOUSE SPECIAL SUBCOMMITTEE'S
FINDINGS AT CTU
By Marc Cerasini
With Alice Alfonsi
BOXTREE

24: The Official Investigation
The House Special Subcommitee's Findings at CTU

First published 2003 by Boxtree,
an imprint of Pan Macmillan Ltd
Pan Macmillan, 20 New Wharf Road, London N1 9RR
Basingstoke and Oxford
Associated companies throughout the world
www.panmacmillan.com

ISBN 0 7522 15639

First published in the United States by Harper Collins Publishers Inc,
10 East 53rd Street, New York, NY 10022.

9 8 7 6 5 4 3

A CIP catalogue record for this book is available from the British Library.

Design by Timothy Shaner

Printed by Bath Press

The authors would like to thank the following people for helping us to unlock the secrets of CTU: Our editor, HOPE INNELLI of HarperEntertainment . . . for her ideas, her professionalism, and her dedicated persistence at getting to the truth. GEORGE R. CAPALDO, M.D., for lending his expertise in forensic pathology to this project. GRACE A. ALFONSI, M.D., for lending her expertise in family-practice medicine to this project. VIRGINIA KING of 20th Century Fox for her guidance and enthusiasm. VIRGIL WILLIAMS of *24* for patiently reviewing the text and offering his insights and ideas from the very beginning through to the very end. And to J. J. PIERCE for his continued encouragement.

CONTENTS

01:25 01:27 01:29 01:30 01:31 01:33 01:35
01:41 01:43 01:44 01:45 01:47 01:49 01:50 01:52
01:57 01:58 01:59 03:01 03:04 03:06 03:09
03:15 03:17 03:20 03:21 03:22 03:25 03:27
03:33 03:35 03:37 03:38 03:39 03:41 03:43
03:49 03:50 03:52 03:53 03:54 03:56 03:57
04:03 04:04 04:06 04:09 04:11 04:13 04:14
04:21 04:22 04:25 04:27 04:29 04:30 04:31
04:38 04:39 04:41 04:43 04:44 04:45
04:52 04:53 04:54 04:56 04:57 04:58 04:59
06:09 06:11 06:13 06:14 06:15 06:17
06:25 06:27 06:29 06:30 06:31 06:33 06:35
06:41 06:43 06:44 06:45 06:47 06:49 06:50
06:56 06:57 06:58 06:59 07:01 07:03 07:04
07:13 07:14 07:15 07:17 07:20 07:21 07:22 07:25
07:31 07:33 07:35 07:37 07:38 07:39 07:41
07:47 07:49 07:50 07:52 07:53 07:54 07:56
10:01 10:03 10:04 10:06 10:09 10:11 10:13
10:20 10:21 10:22 10:25 10:27 10:29 10:30
10:37 10:38 10:39 10:41 10:43 10:44 10:45
10:52 10:53 10:54 10:56 10:57 10:58 10:59
14:09 14:11 14:13 14:14 14:15 14:17 14:20
14:27 14:29 14:30 14:31 14:33 14:35 14:37
14:43 14:44 14:45 14:47 14:49 14:50 14:52
14:57 14:58 14:59 15:01 15:03 15:04 15:06 15:09
15:15 15:17 15:20 15:21 15:22 15:25 15:27
15:33 15:35 15:37 15:38 15:39 15:41 15:43 15:44
15:50 15:52 15:53 15:54 15:56 15:57 15:58
18:04 18:06 18:09 18:11 18:13 18:14 18:15
18:25 18:27 18:29 18:30 18:31 18:33 18:35
18:41 18:43 18:44 18:45 18:47 18:49 18:50
18:56 18:57 18:58 18:59 20:01 20:03 20:04
20:13 20:14 20:15 20:17 20:20 20:21 20:22
20:30 20:31 20:33 20:35 20:37 20:38 20:39
20:45 20:47 20:49 20:50 20:52 20:53 20:54
20:59 23:01 23:03 23:04 23:06 23:09 23:11
23:17 23:20 23:21 23:22 23:25 23:27 23:29
23:35 23:37 23:38 23:39 23:41 23:43 23:44

By Marc Cerasini,
Investigative Journalist

You hold in your hands a classified document leaked to this reporter by an anonymous source. Not since the *New York Times*'s publication of *The Pentagon Papers* has such a raw glimpse of misconduct within the most powerful agencies of our government been made available to the public.

Created exclusively for members of the House Special Subcommittee, this report provides the transcript of testimony answering the many questions surrounding two attempts on the life of Senator, now President-elect, David Palmer, in one twenty-four-hour period on the day of the California primary.

In ferreting out details from various witnesses, the subcommittee documents a number of startling revelations: collusion between elected officials and paramilitary organizations; extortion of the political process; evidence of an internationally wanted political prisoner secretly held by the U.S. government; the existence of a clandestine prison system operated by the Department of Defense; and the vulnerability of the Central Intelligence Agency's Counter Terrorist Unit to espionage, corruption, and extortion from within.

The eye of this geopolitical storm appears to be Special Agent Jack Bauer of the CIA's Counter Terrorist Unit. As the subcommittee's principal witness, Bauer testifies that his Delta Force operation in the Balkans two years ago, known as "Operation Nightfall," failed on many levels. Every man on his covert mission was lost, and his target escaped.

It was Bauer's target—Victor Drazen, the infamous "Butcher of Belgrade"—who put into motion a complicated scheme of revenge that involved kidnapping Bauer's wife and daughter as a means of forcing him into two assassination attempts against the life of presidential hopeful Senator David Palmer.

With the help of publisher HarperCollins, this reporter and his staff have attempted to provide insight into the subcommittee's transcript of testimony by consulting with Beltway pundits, policy analysts, and a variety of anonymous sources, who have contributed appropriate commentary as well as documentation from their files. As a result, you will find in these pages not only Special Agent Jack Bauer's sworn testimony and David Palmer's interview statements but also autopsy records, profiles of international criminals involved in the kidnapping and attempted assassination of Palmer, photographs of key witnesses, screen grabs from security cameras, previously sealed files on U.S.-sanctioned paramilitary activities in Central Europe, and more.

Perhaps the most shocking revelation of this entire report is the level of corruption exposed within the Counter Terrorist Unit itself. The report discloses the identity of not one but two moles who were operating freely within this elite, clandestine unit, where they had access to some of the most sensitive intelligence records in the Central Intelligence Agency's top secret database. The testimony of witnesses that follows confirms the depths of betrayal reached in these bizarre and ominous events.

At the end of this report, the subcommittee's chairman officially closes these matters. Yet one must ask: Are all the questions raised in this report truly answered? Or will the release of this report create a public outcry that will demand more answers, more verifications, and possibly even reverse some or all of Chairman Fulbright's conclusions?

Right now, this reporter can only speculate. In the end, only time and the opinion of the general public will tell.

KEY PLAYERS

The following individuals are featured in this publication. Their brief biographies are valid for the time period covered in this report and are updated in the section entitled "Subcommittee's Conclusions."

JACK BAUER is the special agent in charge of the Los Angeles Counter Terrorist Unit (CTU), a domestic unit of the Central Intelligence Agency.

TERI BAUER is the wife of Jack Bauer and the mother of Kimberly Bauer. She is a homemaker and a freelance interior designer.

KIMBERLY BAUER is the daughter of Jack and Teri Bauer and a sophomore at Santa Monica High School.

JANET YORK is a friend of Kimberly Bauer's and a sophomore at Santa Monica High School. Her father is Alan York.

NINA MYERS is the assistant special agent in charge of the Los Angeles CTU. She primarily serves as chief of staff to director Jack Bauer.

TONY ALMEIDA is an intelligence agent assigned to the Los Angeles CTU.

JAMEY FARRELL is a computer programmer assigned to the Los Angeles CTU.

RICHARD WALSH is the administrative director of the Los Angeles CTU.

GEORGE MASON is the assistant administrative director of the Los Angeles CTU.

RYAN CHAPPELLE is the regional division director of CTU.

ALBERTA GREEN is an assistant regional division director of CTU.

ROBERT ELLIS is a senior intelligence operative and adviser for the Central Intelligence Agency and an adviser to the U.S. Senate Intelligence Committee.

DAVID PALMER is a U.S. senator running for election in the presidential primaries. He is expected to become the first African-American president. Members of Palmer's staff include Mike Novick (chief of staff), Carl Webb (political adviser), Patty Brooks (campaign manager), and Elizabeth Nash (advance team staffer).

SHERRY PALMER has been married to David Palmer for twenty-five years. Their children are Keith Palmer and Nicole Palmer.

VICTOR DRAZEN is an international war criminal. He is charged with committing atrocities in the Balkans.

ANDRE DRAZEN is the son of Victor and the older brother of Alexis. He is well trained in special forces tactics. His associates include European and American mercenaries and Ted Cofell, who launders the Drazens' money.

ALEXIS DRAZEN is the son of Victor and the younger brother of Andre. Alexis is trained in special forces tactics.

IRA GAINES is a mercenary hired by the Drazens to implement a revenge plan against David Palmer and Jack Bauer for their key involvement in a mission known as Operation Nightfall, which resulted in the accidental deaths of Victor Drazen's wife and daughter. Gaines's many associates include Kevin Carroll, Greg Penticoff, Rick Allen, Dan Mounts, and Eli Stram.

CHAIRMAN JAYCE FULBRIGHT (D-Calif.) is a U.S. congressional representative from the state of California. He chairs the twelve-member House Special Subcommittee convened to investigate CTU and the events surrounding the attempt to assassinate David Palmer on the day of the California primary.

PAULINE P. DRISCOLL (D-Conn.) is a U.S. congressional representative from the state of Connecticut. She is one of the two most vocal members of the twelve-member House Special Subcommittee.

ROY SCHNEIDER (R-Tex.) is a U.S. congressional representative from the state of Texas. He is one of the two most vocal members of the twelve-member House Special Subcommittee.

LIEUTENANT COLONEL KEVIN JASON NEWTON is a judge advocate in the United States Army, attached to the office of General Donovan C. Henderson, Defense Intelligence Agency, director of the Special Unit for Counterintelligence Initiatives.

KEY EVENTS AT A GLANCE

2 Years Before Super Tuesday

- **Operation Nightfall.** A Delta team led by Jack Bauer attempts to assassinate Balkan war criminal Victor Drazen. The attempt fails. The secret operation was authorized by Senator David Palmer.
- Victor Drazen is secretly captured and imprisoned in the United States.

Super Tuesday

- **Midnight–1 A.M.:** Jack Bauer and his wife, Teri, discover their daughter, Kim, is missing. Jack is called into CTU and learns of an assassination plot against presidential candidate David Palmer.
- **1 A.M.–2 A.M.:** Richard Walsh gives Jack a CTU key card filled with encrypted information on the Palmer assassination plot. Teri is contacted by Alan York, who claims his daughter, Janet, is out with Kim.
- **2 A.M.–3 A.M.:** Following Walsh's instructions, Jack gives the key card to CTU programmer Jamey Farrell to decrypt. Kim realizes she's been kidnapped.
- **3 A.M.–4 A.M.:** Agent Tony Almeida reports Jack's erratic behavior and CTU is placed on lockdown. Jack goes to an address revealed on the encrypted key card. Janet York is critically injured.
- **4 A.M.–5 A.M.:** After a shootout, Jack follows his suspect to a police station, frees him from LAPD custody, and follows him to a corpse wrapped in plastic in the trunk of a car. Janet York is taken to a hospital. Kim is still missing.
- **5 A.M.–6 A.M.:** Jack joins Teri at St. Mark's Hospital, where Janet is undergoing surgery. Ira Gaines tells Jack that Kim is his hostage.
- **6 A.M.–7 A.M.:** Under Gaines's orders, Jack returns to CTU to retrieve the incriminating key card. Nina Myers confronts Jack and he must take her out of CTU at gunpoint. Teri Bauer is kidnapped.
- **7 A.M.–8 A.M.:** Controlling Jack with threats of harm to his wife and daughter, Gaines orders him to smuggle a sniper rifle into a breakfast rally for Palmer and to deliver it to a waiting assassin. Jack thwarts the first assassination attempt, but the Secret Service mistakenly thinks Jack is the assassin.

- **8 A.M.–9 A.M.:** Jack is taken into custody. Jamey Farrell is revealed to be a mole helping Ira Gaines. Teri and Kimberly are terrorized on Ira Gaines's compound.
- **9 A.M.–10 A.M.:** Alberta Green takes over Jack's office. One of Jamey's e-mails reveals a lead—the name Ted Cofell. With Nina Myers's help, Jack evades the authorities and confronts Cofell.
- **10 A.M.–11 A.M.:** Jack questions Cofell and sees a possible connection to Operation Nightfall. An associate appears and leads Jack to Gaines's compound.
- **11 A.M.–12 NOON:** Jack drives to Gaines's compound and gains entry. Dr. Ferragamo, a former therapist of Palmer's son, Keith, dies in a suspicious gas explosion. Palmer suspects his political adviser, Carl Webb, and a group of powerful financial backers are responsible for the death of Ferragamo, who had been threatening to reveal incriminating news about Keith.
- **12 NOON–1 P.M.:** Jack rescues Teri and Kim and turns himself in to Alberta Green of CTU. Tony Almeida learns about a secret bank account in the name of Jamey's mother. CTU traces payments from an account in the Balkans.
- **1 P.M.–2 P.M.:** CTU discovers another assassination plan against Palmer. New shooters have arrived in Los Angeles. Teri and Kim are examined at Grace Clinic.
- **2 P.M.–3 P.M.:** With the help of Robert Ellis, Palmer and Jack review Operation Nightfall files and discover that Victor Drazen's wife and daughter were killed in the attempt to assassinate Drazen. Teri and Kim are moved to a CTU safe house.
- **3 P.M.–4 P.M.:** Palmer discovers that a member of his staff, Elizabeth Nash, has been lured into an affair with one of the shooters sent to kill him, Alexis Drazen, Victor Drazen's youngest son. Jack asks Elizabeth to plant a tracking device on the man. The CTU safe house is assaulted and Teri and Kim flee. Palmer's son, Keith, tape-records Palmer's political adviser, Carl Webb, confessing to a blackmailing scheme linked to Dr. Ferragamo's death.

KEY EVENTS AT A GLANCE

- **4 P.M.–5 P.M.:** Teri and Kim are separated. Teri becomes disoriented. Elizabeth fails to help CTU dupe Alexis, but a call on Drazen's cell phone gives Jack a new lead.
- **5 P.M.–6 P.M.:** Jack's lead is a meeting with a power company worker. An address in Saugus, California, is revealed. An assassin attacks Teri. Kim is trapped in a drug dealer's house.
- **6 P.M.–7 P.M.:** Jack and George Mason arrive at the Saugus address to find a deserted field and a power generator. Palmer makes a nationally televised speech revealing his son Keith's involvement in the coverup of an accidental death seven years before and the blackmailing scheme by Palmer's political adviser and key financial backers.
- **7 P.M.–8 P.M.:** In the Saugus field, Jack stumbles upon a secret underground DOD prison. Victor Drazen is transported to the prison by helicopter. Jack interrogates Victor.
- **8 P.M.–9 P.M.:** Victor Drazen's eldest son, Andre, and a strike team attack the prison. Jack is captured and informs Victor that his younger son, Alexis, is in CTU custody. Victor contacts George Mason and attempts to negotiate a swap: Jack for Alexis. Palmer wins the Super Tuesday primary election.
- **9 P.M.–10 P.M.:** Mason can't make the deal with Victor because of red tape. Nina Myers contacts Palmer, who helps Jack by calling Mason and urging him to make the deal anyway. Alexis is swapped for Jack.
- **10 P.M.–11 P.M.:** Victor has recaptured Kim and uses the threats against her to make Jack do his bidding. Palmer's life is put in direct jeopardy a second time.
- **11 P.M.–12 MIDNIGHT:** Jack uncovers the identity of another mole in CTU and suffers a tragic personal loss.

1 01:22 01:25 01:27 01:29 01:30 01:31 01:33
01:38 01:39 01:41 01:43 01:44 01:45 01:47 01:4
01:53 01:54 01:56 01:57 01:58 01:59 03:01 03:0
09 03:11 03:13 03:14 03:15 03:17 03:20 03:21
25 03:27 03:29 03:30 03:31 03:33 03:35 03:37
39 03:41 03:43 03:44 03:45 03:47 03:49 03:50
53 03:54 03:56 03:57 03:58 03:59 04:01 04:03
04:09 04:11 04:13 04:14 04:15 04:17 04:20 04:2
25 04:27 04:29 04:30 04:31 04:33 04:35 04:37
3 04:41 04:43 04:44 04:45 04:47 04:49 04:50
04:54 04:56 04:57 04:58 04:59 06:01 06:03 06:0
06:11 06:13 06:14 06:15 06:17 06:20 06:2
25 06:27 06:29 06:30 06:31 06:33 06:35 06:37
9 06:41 06:43 06:44 06:45 06:47 06:49 06:50 06:5
4 06:56 06:57 06:58 06:59 07:01 07:03 07:04
07:11 07:13 07:14 07:15 07:17 07:20 07:21 07:2
07:29 07:30 07:31 07:33 07:35 07:37 07:38 07:3
43 07:44 07:45 07:47 07:49 07:50 07:52 07:53
56 07:57 07:58 07:59 10:01 10:03 10:04 10:06
10:13 10:14 10:15 10:17 10:20 10:21 10:22 10:2
29 10:30 10:31 10:33 10:35 10:37 10:38
10:43 10:44 10:45 10:47 10:49 10:50 10:52 10:5
10:57 10:58 10:59 14:01 14:03 14:04 14:06 14:0
3 14:14 14:15 14:17 14:20 14:21 14:22 14:25 14:2
30 14:31 14:33 14:35 14:37 14:38 14:39 14:41
44 14:45 14:47 14:49 14:50 14:52 14:53 14:54
14:58 14:59 15:01 15:03 15:04 15:06 15:09 15:1
14 15:15 15:17 15:20 15:21 15:22 15:25 15:27
15:31 15:33 15:35 15:37 15:38 15:39 15:41 15:4
45 15:47 15:49 15:50 15:52 15:53 15:54 15:56
15:59 18:01 18:03 18:04 18:06 18:09 18:11 18:1
18:17 18:20 18:21 18:22 18:25 18:27 18:29 18:3
18:35 18:37 18:38 18:39 18:41 18:43 18:44 18:4
18:50 18:52 18:53 18:54 18:56 18:57 18:5
01 20:03 20:04 20:06 20:09 20:11 20:13 20:14
7 20:20 20:21 20:22 20:25 20:27 20:29 20:30
33 20:35 20:37 20:38 20:39 20:41 20:43 20:44
7 20:49 20:50 20:52 20:53 20:54 20:56 20:5

THE HOUSE SPECIAL SUBCOMMITTEE'S

FINDINGS AT CTU

DECLASSIFIED - E.O 14367, Sec. 4.8
With PORTIONS EXEMPTED
E.G. 16842, Sec. 2.1(a) (2)

BQ 02-25, #1 NSC 6/10/02

By TSS , NARA, Date 8/26/02

~~TOP SECRET~~/SENSITIVE (XGDS)

DECLASSIFIED

01:43 01:44 01:45 01:47 01:49 01:50 01:52
01:57 01:58 01:59 03:01 03:04 03:06 03:09 03:11
03:17 03:20 03:21 03:22 03:25 03:27 03:29
03:35 03:37 03:38 03:39 03:41 03:43
03:50 03:52 03:53 03:54 03:56 03:57 03:58
04:04 04:06 04:09 04:11 04:13 04:14 04:15
04:22 04:25 04:27 04:29 04:30 04:31 04:33
04:38 04:39 04:41 04:43 04:44 04:45 04:47
04:53 04:54 04:56 04:57 04:58 04:59 06:01
06:09 06:11 06:13 06:14 06:15 06:17 06:20
06:27 06:29 06:30 06:31 06:33 06:35
06:43 06:44 06:45 06:47 06:49 06:50 06:52
06:57 06:58 06:59 07:01 07:03 07:04
07:14 07:15 07:17 07:20 07:21 07:22 07:25
07:33 07:35 07:37 07:38 07:39 07:41 07:43
07:49 07:50 07:52 07:53 07:54 07:56
10:03 10:04 10:06 10:09 10:11 10:13 10:14
10:20 10:21 10:22 10:25 10:27 10:29 10:30 10:31
10:37 10:38 10:39 10:41 10:43 10:44 10:45
10:53 10:54 10:56 10:57 10:58 10:59 14:01
14:09 14:11 14:13 14:14 14:15 14:17 14:20 14:21
14:29 14:30 14:31 14:33 14:35 14:37 14:38
14:44 14:45 14:47 14:49 14:50 14:52 14:53
14:58 14:59 15:01 15:03 15:04 15:06 15:09
15:17 15:20 15:21 15:22 15:25 15:27 15:29
15:35 15:37 15:38 15:39 15:41 15:43 15:44
15:50 15:52 15:53 15:54 15:56 15:57 15:58
18:06 18:09 18:11 18:13 18:14 18:15 18:17
18:25 18:27 18:29 18:30 18:31 18:33 18:35 18:37
18:43 18:44 18:45 18:47 18:49 18:50
18:57 18:58 18:59 20:01 20:03 20:04
20:14 20:15 20:17 20:20 20:21 20:22
20:30 20:31 20:33 20:35 20:37 20:38 20:39
20:47 20:49 20:50 20:52 20:53 20:54
23:01 23:03 23:04 23:06 23:09 23:11
23:20 23:21 23:22 23:25 23:27 23:29
23:37 23:38 23:39 23:41 23:43 23:44

DECLASSIFIED

OPENING REMARKS

by Special Subcommittee Chairman,
Representative **Jayce Fulbright**, (D) California

Before we begin this hearing, I have a few things I would like to say. I am shocked, appalled, dismayed, and confounded at the nature of the events we are assembled here to examine. The apparent egregious and flagrant violations of procedure within the Counter Terrorist Unit confirm for me that humans have not become any more greedy or corrupt than in generations past but have simply found more avenues by which to express such greed and corruption.

This Special Subcommittee hopes to untangle and sort out a long list of elaborate charges largely manifested in one twenty-four-hour period on the day of the California presidential primary—among them:

- A disgruntled CTU computer programmer, dealing on a daily basis with vital national security information, apparently traded the lives of a colleague and his family along with her country's security for a monetary bribe.
- A special agent in the CTU, again one of our country's most sensitive intelligence agencies, after being lured into the bed of an international spy who had previously established herself as a CTU special agent, apparently violated dozens of agency protocols and aided a terrorist twice in the attempted assassination of a presidential candidate.
- And finally, a senator running for the office of president of the United States illegally sanctioned a covert mission involving the assassination of a foreign national.

Members of this committee, myself included, quite rightly wish to point fingers at the responsible parties and send heads rolling accordingly. I fear, however, that the task at hand is much larger.

To avoid a crisis of confidence in this country, a crisis of trust in our government's ability to protect and deal honestly with its own citizens, we need to do everything in our power to preserve the ethic that has made us so strong. As long as there are members of our military risking their lives outside our borders, all members within the agencies set up to serve them must be willing to give the full measure to ensure justice and protection for us all. There is no room for government employees who will not risk so much as their next pay-grade review to protect their fellow Americans.

We must adhere ever so strongly to the principles of this nation if we are going to effectively deter terrorism. We must maintain proper moral authority and a code of ethical conduct. Manifestations of lax governance are largely symptoms of forgetting. But none of us in public service, on any level, can afford to forget our sacred oath. We can never forget that the word *government* is just another word for our communities, our neighbors, and our families.

The charges we are here to examine raise a multitude of questions, including questions that go far beyond public policy: What, for example, are the duties we have as citizens to protect one another? To protect our leaders, our colleagues, our families? And how far do we dare go in ensuring that protection?

I am particularly interested in the forthcoming testimony of CTU Special Agent Jack Bauer, who appears to be sitting at the very heart of this tangle of violence and corruption.

Mr. Bauer, we can create all the laws and agencies, all the bureaus and divisions and regulations in the world, but in the end morality and integrity are the responsibility not of the state but of every individual man and woman.

I and my twelve distinguished colleagues sitting here with me on this Special Subcommittee now ask you, Mr. Bauer, for that integrity and responsibility to manifest itself through honest testimony.

Due to the amount of sensitive information we anticipate will be presented to this Special Subcommittee, we have closed this hearing to the public and the press and deemed all information in any subsequent reports classified, but never once forget that we, as congressional representatives, represent the American people, the people you serve, and the Constitution you have sworn an oath to uphold.

Now, as my colleagues are eager to begin hearing testimony and have all exercised their option to waive opening remarks, let us begin by officially swearing in our first and principal witness—Special Agent Jack Bauer

PRESENTATION OF KEY TESTIMONY AND EVIDENCE

OPERATION NIGHTFALL

01:27 01:29 01:30 01:31 01:33 01:35
01:43 01:44 01:45 01:47 01:49 01:50 01:52
01:58 01:59 03:01 03:04 03:06 03:09 03:11
03:17 03:20 03:21 03:22 03:25 03:27 03:29
03:35 03:37 03:38 03:39 03:41 03:43
03:50 03:52 03:53 03:54 03:56 03:57 03:58
04:04 04:06 04:09 04:11 04:13 04:14 04:15
04:22 04:25 04:27 04:29 04:30 04:31 04:33
04:38 04:39 04:41 04:43 04:44 04:45 04:47
04:53 04:54 04:56 04:57 04:58 04:59 06:01
06:09 06:11 06:13 06:14 06:15 06:17 06:20
06:27 06:29 06:30 06:31 06:33 06:35
06:41 06:43 06:44 06:45 06:47 06:49 06:50 06:52
06:57 06:58 06:59 07:01 07:03 07:04
07:14 07:15 07:17 07:20 07:21 07:22 07:25
07:33 07:35 07:37 07:38 07:39 07:41 07:43
07:49 07:50 07:52 07:53 07:54 07:56
10:03 10:04 10:06 10:09 10:11 10:13 10:14
10:20 10:21 10:22 10:25 10:27 10:29 10:30 10:31
10:37 10:38 10:39 10:41 10:43 10:44 10:45
10:53 10:54 10:56 10:57 10:58 10:59 14:01
14:11 14:13 14:14 14:15 14:17 14:20 14:21
14:29 14:30 14:31 14:33 14:35 14:37 14:38
14:44 14:45 14:47 14:49 14:50 14:52 14:53
14:58 14:59 15:01 15:03 15:04 15:06 15:09
15:17 15:20 15:21 15:22 15:25 15:27 15:29
15:35 15:37 15:38 15:39 15:41 15:43 15:44
15:50 15:52 15:53 15:54 15:56 15:57 15:58
18:06 18:09 18:11 18:13 18:14 18:15 18:17
18:25 18:27 18:29 18:30 18:31 18:33 18:35 18:37
18:43 18:44 18:45 18:47 18:49 18:50
18:57 18:58 18:59 20:01 20:03 20:04
20:14 20:15 20:17 20:20 20:21 20:22 20:25
20:30 20:31 20:33 20:35 20:37 20:38 20:39
20:47 20:49 20:50 20:52 20:53 20:54
23:01 23:03 23:04 23:06 23:09 23:11
23:20 23:21 23:22 23:25 23:27 23:29
23:37 23:38 23:39 23:41 23:43 23:44

CHAIRMAN FULBRIGHT: Special Agent Bauer, please rise and raise your right hand.

SPECIAL AGENT JACK BAUER: Yes, Mr. Chairman.

FULBRIGHT: Do you solemnly swear that the testimony you are about to give this subcommittee is the truth, the whole truth, and nothing but the truth so help you God?

BAUER: I do.

FULBRIGHT: Mr. Bauer, you may consider yourself under oath. Please be seated. For the record, state your name and occupation.

BAUER: My name is Jack Bauer, At the time of the twenty-four-hour period under investigation by your subcommittee I was the special

JACK BAUER
AGE: 36
BIRTHPLACE: Santa Monica, California

CTU MISSIONS
- Team Leader, Operation Proteus, 2000
- Section Captain, Hotel Los Angeles attack, 1998

EXPERIENCE
- CTU - Special Agent in Charge, Los Angeles Domestic Unit (Deactivated)
- Los Angeles Police Department - Special Weapons and Tactics Team

EDUCATION
- LASD - Basic SWAT School
- Master of Science, Criminology and Law, University of California (Berkeley)
- Bachelor of Arts, English Literature, University of California (Los Angeles)
- Special Forces Operations Training Course

MILITARY
- U.S. Army Combat Applications Group
- U.S. Army First Special Forces Operational Detachment Team, Delta

PERSONAL
Married - Teri Bauer (deceased)
Daughter - Kimberly Bauer

~~TOP SECRET~~/SENSITIVE (XGDS)
NARA, Date 8/26/02

agent in charge of the Los Angeles Division of the Central Intelligence Agency's* Counter Terrorist Unit.* I'm also a reserve officer in the First Special Forces Operational Detachment, also known as Delta.*

FULBRIGHT: What was your military rank in the Delta reserve?

BAUER: Captain.

FULBRIGHT: And your status now?

BAUER: I'm currently inactive, sir.

FULBRIGHT: Thank you, Agent Bauer. Now let's begin at the beginning. Your involvement with a Delta Force assassination attempt on Victor Drazen's life seems to be the ignition point of this particular bonfire. Please summarize your participation in this classified special operation.

BAUER: Yes, Mr. Chairman. But, sir, before I begin, is this subcommittee aware of the events that led to the direct-action mission I'm about to describe? Are you all fully aware of the extent of Victor Drazen's crimes?

FULBRIGHT: Yes, Mr. Bauer, this subcommittee has reviewed the background briefing prepared by the State Department on Drazen's connection to the atrocities in the Balkans, as well as the United Nations list of charges against him. We'll include the State Department's briefing in this subcommittee's final report. Start with Operation Nightfall, please.

BAUER: Yes, Mr. Chairman. Three days before Operation Nightfall was launched I was reactivated by Delta Force for a special operation inside Kosovo. I was ordered to report to the Joint Special Operations Command (JSOC)* at Fort Bragg, North Carolina, for a Delta Force premission briefing.

REP. PAULINE P. DRISCOLL, (D) CONN.: Excuse me, Agent Bauer, but not all of us here in the Congress are intimate, let alone *comfortable*, with military procedure. Enlighten us. Is a reactivation like yours unusual?

BAUER: No, ma'am. A reactivation like mine was not unusual at all. I had gone into Kosovo in direct action missions on three previous occasions, and twice I'd gone to Belgrade. Each time I had been placed on temporary active duty.

FULBRIGHT: Tell us, Special Agent Bauer, what were your orders?

(The following is an excerpt from a report released by the U.S. Department of State, Washington, D.C.)

EXECUTIVE SUMMARY DOCUMENTING THE ABUSES

This document was compiled from thousands of reported violations of human rights and humanitarian law since the withdrawal of the Kosovo Verification Mission—which prior to its departure had been regularly issuing human rights reports.

Serbian military, paramilitary, and police forces in Kosovo have committed a wide range of war crimes, crimes against humanity, and other violations of international humanitarian and human rights law. This report reviews seven categories of such crimes: forced expulsion of Kosovars from their homes; looting and burning of homes, schools, religious sites, and health care facilities; detention, particularly of military-age men; summary execution; rape; violations of medical neutrality; and identity cleansing. . . .

. . . The regime of Slobodan Milosevic is conducting a campaign of forced migration on a scale not seen in Europe since World War II. Milosevic's general Victor Drazen and his eldest son, Andre, have trained and financed an elite paramilitary force of Serbian nationalists who have aided Milosevic's regime in the following crimes. . . .

1. **FORCED EXPULSION:** More than 90 percent of all ethnic Albanians have been expelled from their homes in Kosovo. Yugoslav Army and Special Police units have joined with recently armed Serb civilians to expel their neighbors from almost all towns and villages in Kosovo. . . .
2. **LOOTING AND BURNING:** Some six hundred residential areas have been at least partially burned, including over four hundred villages, according to overhead imagery. Houses and apartments as well as mosques, churches, schools, and medical facilities have been targeted and destroyed. Many settlements have been totally destroyed in an attempt to ensure that residents do not return.
3. **DETENTION:** Serbian forces are separating military-age men from their families in a systematic pattern. At the time of this writing, their fate is unknown.
4. **SUMMARY EXECUTION:** Refugees have provided accounts of summary executions in at least eighty-five towns and villages throughout Kosovo. In addition to random executions, Serbian authorities are targeting intellectuals, professionals, and community leaders.
5. **RAPE:** Ethnic Albanian women are reportedly being raped in increasing numbers. Refugee accounts indicate systematic and organized mass rapes in Dakovica and Pec.
6. **VIOLATIONS OF MEDICAL NEUTRALITY:** Serbian authorities have looted and destroyed dozens of medical facilities, murdered Kosovar Albanian physicians, expelled ethnic Albanian patients and care providers from hospitals, and used large numbers of health facilities as protective cover for military activities.
7. **IDENTITY CLEANSING:** Refugees report that Serbian authorities have confiscated passports and other identity papers and even removed license plates from departing vehicles as part of a policy to prevent returns to Kosovo. Reports of identity cleansing are prevalent in refugee camps in Macedonia and Albania.

BAUER: I was ordered to assemble a six-man operation team. We were to infiltrate Kosovo by air, eliminate the threat posed by Victor Drazen, and move to a distant exfiltration point where we would be extracted by a Pave Hawk* helicopter.

DRISCOLL: *Eliminate the threat?* What does that mean in plain English?

BAUER: Our orders were clear, ma'am. We were to end the threat Victor Drazen posed through direct action. In laymen's terms, that meant assassination. We were ordered to take him out.

VICTOR DRAZEN
AGE: 62
BIRTHPLACE: Požarevac, Serbia

EXPERIENCE
- Commander, Black Dogs* (Slobodan Milosevic's secret police organization)
- Serbian National Liberation Front* (Serbian nationalist paramilitary organization banned in 2001)
- Member, Kosovo/1389* (Serbian nationalist paramilitary organization banned in 1986)

EDUCATION
- Master of Science, Engineering, University of Belgrade
- KGB Antiespionage/Covert Action Training Program

MILITARY
- Federal Republic of Yugoslavia Military Command, Deputy Director of Intelligence
- Commander, Serbian Army Special Operations Unit

PERSONAL
Married - Vesna Drazen
Sons - Andre Drazen, Alexis Drazen
Daughter - Martina

DRISCOLL: And you had no qualms about this mission? These orders did not trouble you?

BAUER: No, ma'am, they did not. In the premission briefing I learned that Drazen was living alone in an old manor house along the banks of the Erenik River, on the outskirts of the city of Dakovica. NATO intelligence sources later confirmed Drazen's location.

FULBRIGHT: And do you know why Drazen was in Dakovica?

BAUER: Dakovica was a good place for him to hide. Victor Drazen's wife was born there, and he had both in-laws and sympathizers in the region. More importantly, Dakovica was close to the border of Albania. JSOC's concern was that Drazen, his son Andre, and their private army could bribe border officials and slip into the North Albanian Alps, where NATO forces might never track them down. Other Serbian officers had done just that, and have so far eluded prosecution by the United Nations war crimes tribunal.

FULBRIGHT: Tell us about the mission.

BAUER: Twelve hours after I got the action order, I selected qualified and experienced personnel to take part in a six-man operational detachment team. They were all men I had worked with before. Most of them I trained. Most of them I trusted. We'd gone to Belgrade together, and that mission went quite well. I felt that with the men I selected Nightfall would go off without a hitch. The subjects were notified, and we assembled on board an army cargo plane headed for Aviano Air Base in Italy. My unit was half the size of a typical OD team—

DRISCOLL: (Interrupting) OD?

BAUER: Operational detachment team. As I said, my group was smaller than usual, but I had worked with everyone before, and I was comfortable with the mix of specialties.

I served as the OD commander. My second in command was Warrant Officer Dwayne Shelton, a former Green Beret and Gulf War veteran who joined Delta in the 1990s. We met five years before Nightfall, during SERE* training in the Rocky Mountains—

DRISCOLL: (Interrupting) And what, may I ask, is SERE training?

REP. ROY SCHNEIDER, (R) TEX.: Representative Driscoll, if we're to stop Agent Bauer to define every term, we're likely to be here for a month. Mr. Chairman, I move that terms be defined in the final written report, but otherwise, unless they have a bearing on discovery, we move on.

FULBRIGHT: Fine. That's fine. Terms will be asterisked in the transcript and defined in an appendix to this report. But if Congresswoman Driscoll needs clarification, she has every right to ask the witness. Go on, Agent Bauer.

BAUER: Just to answer Congresswoman Driscoll's question, sir, SERE training has to do with what we must know to endure capture and torture. We also learn tactics of escape and evasion.

FULBRIGHT: Fine. Go on with your mission details.

BAUER: As I said, Warrant Officer Dwayne Shelton, a former Green Beret, was my second on every mission into Kosovo. He was a pro, and I trusted Shelton with my life and the lives of my team.

First Sergeant Brice Gardener was weapons officer, and he was talented in a range of specialties, from demolition to hand-to-hand combat. During a previous mission, Brice held off a Serbian armored car with an automatic weapon while the rest us escaped by helicopter. Brice walked out of the woods ten days later, dragging three prisoners with him.

First Sergeant Haj Illijec was the communications officer. Haj was an Army Ranger who served in Somalia. His parents were born in Yugoslavia, and he spoke Serbian like a native. I'd been in the field with Sergeant Illijec twice, and he performed well in both operations.

First Sergeant Gary Graham was the medical officer. Graham was a former Green Beret and a physician—a graduate of McGill University. Graham learned trauma medicine by treating gunshot victims in a Watts emergency room before joining Delta. Graham was to be married that June, and was leaving Delta Force. Nightfall was supposed to be his last mission.

Technical Sergeant Roger Voss was our Air Force Special Operations* combat controller. Though we wouldn't see him until the mission was over, Roger was officially a part of our team. In Operation Nightfall, Voss was parachuted in many hours ahead of the main force, to establish a secure exfiltration zone where our escape helicopter could land.

Master Sergeant Fred Peltzer was our intelligence specialist. Everyone called him "Peltz." Peltzer knew Kosovo like the back of his hand—in fact, he swore he would write a Lonely Planet travel guide about Serbia after the war. He also knew every member of the Drazen family on sight, which was another plus. Peltz was older than the rest of us, and did double duty as team sergeant—which made Peltzer the guy responsible for assembling the gear we would need to accomplish the mission. On the flight over to Italy, it was Peltzer's job to refamiliarize me and the other team members with the proper techniques of HALO* jumping—

DRISCOLL: (Interrupting) Please explain HALO jumping, Special Agent Bauer. Despite Representative Schneider's concern for expediency, I do wish to understand you.

BAUER: HALO means High Altitude, Low Opening. The OD team jumps out of aircraft flying at a very high altitude. Wearing masks and breathing oxygen, the team free-falls for several minutes until opening parachutes at a predetermined altitude that is very close to the ground. The aircraft we jump from is too high to alarm Serbian antiaircraft defenses, and the OD team open their chutes too low to be visible to Serbian radar.

DRISCOLL: You took a lot of care not to be seen, Special Agent Bauer. Were such efforts really necessary? After all, NATO controlled the skies above Kosovo—why not ride into the combat zone on a Black Hawk helicopter?

SCHNEIDER: Pauline, I'm impressed. You suddenly know what a Black Hawk is? (Pause) You saw that movie, didn't ya?

DRISCOLL: As a matter of fact, Roy, I did.

FULBRIGHT: Let's not get off the subject. Agent Bauer, answer the congresswoman's question. Why the special operation theatrics?

BAUER: Because our mission was technically illegal, in that it violated the terms of the United Nations resolution concerning military action in Kosovo, Operation Nightfall was to remain a secret—even from our allies. We used HALO jumping techniques because we were hiding from NATO radar, too.

And there was another reason for using such a covert insertion method. Victor Drazen's bodyguards had stolen lots of equipment from the Serbian Army, including a Soviet-made portable radar array, two BOV-3 self-propelled antiaircraft guns, and a Praga armored truck suited with a 30-millimeter antiaircraft cannon. The radar made constant sweeps of the airspace around Drazen's compound, and the vehicles were placed in strategic locations. By the time we located him at Dakovica, the compound was surrounded by an effective antiaircraft screen. Drazen's army had the capability to detect and shoot down a helicopter, or even a jet aircraft—which was another reason we opted for the HALO jump.

Once we arrived at Aviano, we had a few hours to rest before the final briefing. At 0300 hours—3:00 A.M. local time—we boarded an Air Force Special Operations MC-130 Combat Talon,* which took us over the drop zone at an altitude of 27,000 feet. One hour and twenty-two minutes later—at 0422 hours—our OD team jumped from the loading ramp into the dark skies above Kosovo.

By 0500 hours we had assembled on the ground just northwest of our target, buried our parachutes and HALO gear, secured our weapons, and were moving along the banks of the Erenik River. The terrain was fairly mountainous, but we stuck to the river valley, so movement was easy. It was late April, so there were still patches of snow on the ground. We avoided them when possible, leaving no footprints. We were to avoid all contact, so we steered clear of any farms or settlements. There were also NATO ground forces in the region, so we maintained complete radio silence until it was time to contact Hammer One—

FULBRIGHT: (Interrupting) Contact whom?

BAUER: I'm sorry, Mr. Chairman. I should have mentioned that the radio call* sign for our OD team was "Anvil." When we located Victor Drazen, we were to call down "Hammer One"—the code name for the F-18 Hornet* that was going to make the air strike against Drazen's compound, once our ground team firmly established he was present and painted the target.

DRISCOLL: (Interrupting) *Painted the target?* I'm sure that particular term has nothing to do with a trip to Home Depot. Please explain.

BAUER: It's a shorthand term for marking the target. Every member of the Nightfall team had an AN/PEQ-2 Infrared Aiming Laser attached to the rail of his M4A1 Carbine.* Once we established the whereabouts of Victor Drazen, we were to illuminate the target with the lasers. The precision-guided bomb—an AGM-84E Standoff Land-Attack Missile fired from Hammer One—would follow our projected beam right down to the marked or "painted" target.

DRISCOLL: Explain something else to me, then, Agent Bauer. If you were going to blow Drazen up with a bomb anyway, why not just drop one on his house? Why risk placing a special operations team on the ground?

BAUER: JSOC wanted to guarantee that our target was neutralized and that collateral damage was kept to a minimum—

DRISCOLL: (Interrupting) Well, things didn't quite turn out that way, did they, Agent Bauer?

BAUER: No, ma'am, they did not.

FULBRIGHT: Please continue, Agent Bauer.

BAUER: At 0800 hours we arrived at a narrow dirt road that led to Victor Drazen's compound. After establishing a primary and secondary path of withdrawal and two separate rendezvous points, we split our forces. Warrant Officer Shelton, along with Gardener and Graham, were to circle around Drazen's compound to locate and then neutralize the antiaircraft guns so Hammer One could approach the compound safely.

Sergeants Illijec and Peltzer accompanied me on a reconnaissance run of the house and barn. Both units were in constant contact through our short-range helmet radios, and reconnaissance was complete by 0900. We established that the compound consisted of two structures circled by a low stone fence.

The larger structure was the manor house, which appeared to be unoccupied. The other structure was a barn, but was not used as living quarters for Drazen's security detail. Our OD team counted eleven men inside the compound, with six more manning the antiaircraft guns and the portable radar station camouflaged in a copse of trees about half a klick behind the compound—excuse me, that's half a kilometer, Congresswoman Driscoll.

DRISCOLL: Thank you, Agent Bauer, I appreciate the thought.

BAUER: All of Drazen's men were heavily armed, with a mix of Russian-made weapons, including AK-47s, rocket-propelled grenades, and several light machine guns.

Fortunately, discipline was lax, which indicated that Drazen was *not* at this location. After securing the area, we hunkered down among the trees and watched the approach to the compound, waiting for Victor Drazen to show up. Meanwhile Shelton's team prepared to neutralize the radar station and antiaircraft guns at the first sign of our target.

It didn't take long for Drazen to show his face.

At 1111 hours we spotted movement on the unpaved road. A

moment later we heard the sound of an engine. It was a Serbian armored car with a driver and a single passenger. Peltz watched the approach through binoculars and verified the passenger's identity. It appeared to be Victor Drazen. We both watched as he entered the house. Then we gave Shelton, Brice, and Graham a heads up and called Hammer One.

The pilot alerted us that his ETA to the target zone was under six minutes.

I never blinked once for the three hundred and sixty seconds it took Hammer One to arrive. There was no indication that anyone but Drazen was inside that building, and when I painted the target with my infrared illuminator, I was convinced that Victor Drazen—and only Victor Drazen—was going to die.

Courtesy of the Department of Defense

Ten seconds before the final ETA, Hammer One indicated that he had a positive lock on the laser beam. At that second an explosion signaled that Shelton, Graham, and Gardener had neutralized the antiaircraft guns. I refused to let the blast distract me and continued to aim the laser. Three seconds later the pilot launched the SLAM missile and veered away.

We never saw or heard the aircraft.

I watched the house until a yellow streak rushed over our heads seven seconds later. There was a second explosion—much larger than the first. The missiles had entered a small window near the door. The house was completely destroyed. There was no possibility of survivors.

I wanted to get my team out of the area while Drazen's men were still in shock, but it didn't happen that way. I keyed my radio and ordered Shelton's team to meet us at the first rally point—a ditch close to the unpaved road where we first separated. But as Peltz, Illijec, and I moved out of the woods, we heard the shots. Something had gone wrong.

I keyed the radio for a situation update, but it didn't work. I turned to Sergeant Illijec, but he just tapped his earphones and shook his head—his radio wasn't working either. Peltz cursed and tore his helmet off.

"I think we're being jammed," he said.

Which should have been impossible. We were using encrypted ASTRO SABER* digital radios—anyone who tried to jam us would need to know the precise frequency we were using as well as our encryption codes. Our radios were preprogrammed at JSOC, and the only people who should be able to interfere with them were the people who programmed those radios in the first place.

I ordered Peltz and Illijec to move to the rally point, while I doubled back to find Shelton, Brice, and Graham. As I moved through the trees and entered the compound, I could hear Drazen's men calling to one another from among the trees. They had gotten over their shock pretty quickly, and now were spreading out through the woods in a concerted effort to locate us. They were out for blood.

I hopped the stone fence and entered the compound. The heat from the house was intense. I could smell cordite and burning flesh. As I approached the barn, the door burst open and one of Drazen's men stumbled out. He was as surprised to see me as I was to see him. As he fumbled with his AK-47, I gave him a double tap and moved on—

DRISCOLL: (Interrupting) Excuse me again, but I'd like you to define for the record a *double tap*.

BAUER: Two shots to the head in quick succession. It's the fastest way to drop a man so he won't get up again.

FULBRIGHT: That's fine. Please continue.

BAUER: I moved to the rear of the compound, hopped the back fence, and approached the copse of trees where the antiaircraft guns had been. They were still burning, their crews dead. Brice had done a good job putting the guns down, but there was no sign of him, nor of Graham or Shelton. I doubled back through the woods and found the road. I could hear Drazen's thugs clumping through the forest, but they were heading away from me. The shooting had stopped.

Seven minutes later I arrived at the rally point. Peltz and Illijec were there, but there was still no sign of Shelton, Gardener, or Graham. I pleaded with Illijec to get the radios working again, but nothing he did seemed to help. Then we heard shots coming from the northeast—AK-47s first, then the sound of an M4A1 automatic weapon. I knew Shelton's team had run into more trouble.

There was also another group of soldiers approaching from the south—the Serbs were trying to surround us, and I wondered how they knew where we were. I told Peltz and Illijec to follow the banks of the Erenik to the exfiltration point while I covered their retreat. When they were gone, I took off after Shelton's team.

As I approached the woods, there was an explosion that knocked me off my feet. Smoke billowed around me as I rolled with the force of the blast. Crouching between two trees, I spotted figures moving through the forest. I tested the radio again but couldn't raise Shelton. Someone must have seen or heard me and opened fire. I fired back, dropping two men.

FULBRIGHT: In all that chaos, how did you know you weren't shooting at Shelton's team?

BAUER: Munitions manufactured in the former Soviet Union give off green traces. NATO munitions give off a red trace. The Serbs used munitions made in the former Soviet Union, and the bullets flying at me were tracing green.

FULBRIGHT: I see.

BAUER: I found the men I'd shot. They were part of Drazen's entourage—I recognized one of them as the armored car driver. A few minutes later I found Shelton, Gardener, and Graham. . . . I found their bodies. . . .

FULBRIGHT: (After a pause) Agent Bauer? (Muffled voices) Do you need a moment, Agent Bauer? (Muffled voices) Take some water, son. Take a moment.

BAUER: As I was saying, I found my men. They were dead, along with five of Drazen's men. Shelton's team had been ambushed. Shelton and Graham had been shot repeatedly—and Brice had detonated the last of his explosives to finish off the Serbs and to buy us some time. There wasn't much left of him.

DRISCOLL: Were the remains of your teammates recovered and returned to their families?

BAUER: Yes, ma'am, they were.

DRISCOLL: I'm glad to hear that.

BAUER: It was time to move on. I set out through the forest, using my GPS* system to follow the terrain. I knew Illijec and Peltz were moving parallel with the river. All I had to do was catch up with them. I was alone, and moving through unfamiliar territory, so I was happy to hear the radio crackle and the sound of Peltz's voice.

"Did Haj get the radio working?" I asked.

"No, the jamming stopped," said Peltz. Then it hit me. When I tried to use the radio in the woods, Drazen's men vectored in on me. Shelton, Gardener, and Graham were probably trying to communicate with us when they were hit.

"Get off the net," I shouted. "The Serbs are using our radio frequency to locate us."

But my warning came too late. I heard shots, and the sound of grenades. I started running, down a hill toward the river. I could see the dark, sluggish water through the trees. I hit a patch of snow and slipped, just as a green tracer whizzed over my head and struck a tree behind me. I raised my carbine and pumped off some shots—hitting one of Drazen's men as he rose from cover to fire again.

Then I jumped to my feet and kept shooting as I ran toward the water. I kept shooting until I was sure I'd killed all of Drazen's men. But I was too late again. By the time I got to the river's edge, Peltz was dead, and Sergeant Illijec's body was floating in the middle of the river, facedown. I knew I had to move, I knew the Serbs wouldn't give up until all of us were dead. And I was running out of time.

I was afraid to use the radio to contact Tech Sergeant Voss, but I kept moving toward the extraction zone anyway. I had nowhere else to go. Finally I got to the designated exfiltration point. (Pause) Roger Voss was dead. The Serbs ambushed him too—cut him to pieces. He never had a chance. Voss must have been trying to raise me on the radio when the Serbs vectored in on his transmission. I found the Phoenix transmitter in Roger's pocket and called in the Pave Hawk. The helicopter arrived forty minutes later.

I got out—but my team didn't.

FULBRIGHT: It was a tragic mission, Special Agent Bauer, but I commend you on your resourcefulness in the face of tough odds. And I am sorry for the loss of your men.

BAUER: Not as sorry as I am, Mr. Chairman.

FULBRIGHT: I understand. Would you like a short recess, Agent Bauer?

BAUER: No, sir, I am prepared to answer more questions.

FULBRIGHT: Good. Now, Special Agent Bauer, you began your description of Operation Nightfall by saying that you were reactivated. Who exactly reactivated you? Who authorized this mission?

BAUER: I was approached by NSA floating agent Robert Ellis—

FULBRIGHT: Ellis? Ellis? I don't recognize that name. Excuse me, Agent Bauer. (Muffled voices) Sam, why is he not on our witness list?

BAUER: Excuse me, Mr. Chairman—

FULBRIGHT: A moment, Agent Bauer, while I consult with my staff—

BAUER: Mr. Chairman, he's deceased.

FULBRIGHT: Who's deceased?

BAUER: Ellis, sir. Robert Ellis was murdered in New Orleans on the day of the California primary.

FULBRIGHT: That's why he's not on our witness list. (Pause) I'll want to hear more about that, but right now let's address the question. Who authorized Ellis to authorize you to conduct Operation Nightfall?

ROBERT ELLIS
AGE: 46
BIRTHPLACE: Brownsville, Texas

COVERT OPERATIONS
- Operation Pinstripe, 2001, Adviser
- Operation Proteus, 2000, Adviser
- Classified Special Operations in Haiti, Kosovo, Cuba, and Nicaragua

EXPERIENCE
- CTU, Adviser
- National Security Agency, Special Operative
- Senate Special Defense Appropriations Committee, Adviser
- Senate Intelligence Committee, Adviser
- Department of Defense, U.S. Army Senior Civilian Intelligence Coordinator

EDUCATION
- Master of Science, Criminal Psychology, Georgetown University
- Bachelor of Arts, Theology, Fordham University

MILITARY
- U.S. Army Special Forces
- U.S. Army First Special Operational Detachment Team, Delta

PERSONAL
- Twice Divorced - Amber Kay Ellis, Consuela Reyes-Ellis

BAUER: The Special Defense Appropriations Committee of the United States Senate.

FULBRIGHT: Excuse me again, Special Agent Bauer. (Muffled voices) Sam, call Senator Card's office and get a copy of the paperwork for the final report. All right, let's resume. Connect the dots for me, Agent Bauer. Operation Nightfall failed. Correct?

BAUER: Correct.

FULBRIGHT: But Victor Drazen's body is in a U.S. government morgue, correct?

BAUER: Correct.

FULBRIGHT: And he wasn't killed in Kosovo but at a dock at the Port of Los Angeles—

BAUER: I put the bullets in him myself, Mr. Chairman.

FULBRIGHT: I see, but—

BAUER: And I was glad to do it.

FULBRIGHT: Agent Bauer, I did not ask how you felt about shooting Victor Drazen. What I asked, and what I still do not understand, is how the man ended up at a Los Angeles dock!

OFFICE OF SENATOR DAVID PALMER

MEMORANDUM

TO: Agent Robert Ellis, NSA
FROM: Senator David Palmer
RE: Victor Drazen
DATE: [redacted]

CLASSIFIED

The Senate Special Defense Appropriations Committee has concluded its review of the evidence gathered by the State Department against Victor Drazen and the on-site intelligence your agency has gathered about his illegal activities, and we concur with the State Department and the intelligence community that Drazen poses a threat to the stability of the emerging Balkan states and to the national interest of the United States in that region's stability and must be dealt with swiftly and efficiently with a minimum of collateral damage.

Therefore the appropriation for the execution of Operation Nightfall is hereby approved. The funds for your mission [redacted] e [redacted]

Good luck and God speed.

DECLASSIFIED

SENATOR DAVID PALMER

EXPERIENCE
- United States Congress, Senator (Maryland)
  - Senate Appropriations Committee, Member
  - Senate Special Defense Appropriations Committee Chairman
  - Senate Commerce Subcommittee, Member
- United States Congress, Representative (Maryland)
  - House Ethics Committee, Chairman
  - House Ways and Means Committee, Member
  - House National Security Subcommittee, Member
- Maryland State Congress, Representative (Baltimore)
- Fidley, Barrow & Bain, Attorneys at Law

EDUCATION
- Juris Doctorate, University of Maryland School of Law
- Bachelor of Arts, Political Economy, Georgetown University

HONORS
- NCAA All-American, Men's Basketball
- Big East Conference Defensive Player of the Year
- *Sporting News* College Player of the Year
- Wooden Award for Player of the Year

PUBLISHED PAPERS
- *The New York Times*, Op-Ed Page, "Serb Intransigence and European Destabilization"

PERSONAL
- Married — Sherry Palmer
- Son — Keith Palmer
- Daughter — Nicole Palmer

BAUER: With all due respect, Mr. Chairman, I can connect *some* of the dots for you, but not others. Some trail off into oblivion.

FULBRIGHT: Don't answer me with riddles, Agent Bauer, I haven't the patience—

BAUER: I don't know how Drazen was captured and brought to the United States, sir, but he was. When this was done is fairly obvious. It had to have happened the same week, if not the same day, my team and I eliminated his decoy. Otherwise, intelligence reports would have confirmed that he was still walking around in good health.

If I were a betting man, which I am not, I'd lay odds that Operation Nightfall was set up to fail from the start. Once we killed Drazen's decoy, I was supposed to have died along with my men. That would have ensured the rest of the world's belief that Drazen was dead. There were to be no witnesses.

FULBRIGHT: Set up, you say?

BAUER: They knew the types of radios we were using and the frequencies. How else can that be explained?

FULBRIGHT: Set up by whom?

BAUER: I'd like to know myself, sir. Believe me. In fact, I'd like you to find the son of a bitch and leave me alone in a room with him for five minutes.

FULBRIGHT: Calm down, Agent Bauer. Take a moment. (Muffled voices) Let's keep this simple. If you and your team didn't kill Drazen in Kosovo, and you didn't capture him and bring him to the United States, then who did?

BAUER: I don't honestly know, sir. What I do know is that he was being held in a Department of Defense prison. A secret prison, sir, one I stumbled upon during my investigation. If I were you, I'd ask the Department of Defense.

FULBRIGHT: A secret prison. A *secret* prison?

BAUER: Yes, sir, that's what I said.

FULBRIGHT: Do you mean to tell me that within the borders of this United States, there are prisoners being held without trial in facilities unknown even to an intelligence agent with a high security clearance like yourself?

BAUER: And you, too, sir.

FULBRIGHT: Jesus God. (Muffled voices) Please tell me, if you can, why this was not in any of the briefs previously submitted to this subcommittee by George Mason at CTU?

BAUER: I can only speculate, sir.

FULBRIGHT: Then do so, damn it.

BAUER: George Mason doesn't like to ruffle feathers. Your subcommittee is investigating CTU. I'm sure he felt it would be better to stick to that subject and avoid the can of worms I've just opened.

FULBRIGHT: And you don't care about opening the can, I take it?

BAUER: I do not.

FULBRIGHT: I see. Thank you, Agent Bauer. I intend to get to the bottom of this so-called secret prison system operated by an extension of the executive branch of our government. Let's adjourn for lunch. (Muffled voices) Sam, get Martin on his cell phone. Now.

DEPARTMENT OF DEFENSE TESTIMONY:
* SECRET HOLDING OF VICTOR DRAZEN * COVERT PRISON SYSTEM

REPORTER'S NOTE:
Following Agent Jack Bauer's initial sworn testimony, the subcommittee's chairman contacted the office of the Secretary of Defense and demanded that a witness appear as soon as possible to answer questions regarding Agent Bauer's claim that Victor Drazen had been held in a secret prison system operated by the Defense Department of the United States. Lieutenant Colonel Kevin J. Newton appeared that afternoon before the subcommittee. The following is an abridged version of his testimony.

CHAIRMAN FULBRIGHT: Lieutenant Colonel Kevin J. Newton, please rise and raise your right hand. Do you solemnly swear that the testimony you are about to give this subcommittee is the truth, the whole truth, and nothing but the truth so help you God?

Lt. COL. KEVIN J. NEWTON: I do.

FULBRIGHT: You may consider yourself under oath. Please be seated. For the record, state your name and occupation.

NEWTON: My name is Kevin J. Newton. I am a lieutenant colonel in the United States Army.

FULBRIGHT: Where do you currently serve, and who is your commanding officer?

NEWTON: I serve the Defense Intelligence Agency* as a judge advocate attached to the office of Donovan C. Henderson, a two-star general in the United States Army. General Henderson is the DIA's director of the Special Unit for Counterintelligence Initiatives.*

Lieutenant Colonel Kevin Jason Newton, Judge Advocate, United States Army
AGE: 31
BIRTHPLACE: Richmond, Virginia

MILITARY EXPERIENCE

- Judge Advocate, Office of General Donovan C. Henderson, Defense Intelligence Agency, Director of the Special Unit for Counterintelligence Initiatives
- Assistant Judge Advocate General, U.S. Army Capture Management Program, Albania 2001
- Staff Judge Advocate, U.S. Army, I-FOR, Kosovo, 1998-2000
- Assistant Judge Advocate, Center for Law and Military Operations, 1994-1997
- First Lieutenant, 10th Mountain Division, Somalia, 1993

EDUCATION

- Law and Special Operations Program, John F. Kennedy School of Special Warfare, Fort Bragg, North Carolina
- Master of Arts, Law and the Military, Georgetown University
- Bachelor of Arts, Military History, Carlisle Military College

PERSONAL

- Divorced — Cheryl Ann Clemson-Newton
- No children

REP. PAULINE P. DRISCOLL, (D) CONN.: So you're General Donovan's lawyer, correct?

NEWTON: I am a lawyer, Congresswoman, but I am here today only as a spokesman. The general is out of the country on a national security mission, and your subcommittee requested that someone appear to answer your questions. My department wants to cooperate fully in this investigation.

FULBRIGHT: And we thank you for your cooperation. Begin by telling us why the military targeted Victor Drazen.

NEWTON: Two years ago, Drazen had not yet been charged with war crimes. Though he had already been dubbed the "Butcher of Belgrade" in the international press, the United Nations was still building a case against him. However, time was running out. Drazen's activities had become detrimental to the peace process in the Balkan states, and there was evidence of his participation in other nefarious activities that had the potential to pose asymmetric threats to the United States and our allies—

DRISCOLL: (Interrupting) Excuse me, Lieutenant Colonel, but what exactly is an *asymmetric threat*?

NEWTON: Asymmetry—or the lack of symmetry—in warfare is the use of hostile military force in unanticipated or nontraditional ways. The intent of an asymmetric threat is to reduce the conventional military superiority of the United States by exploiting a perceived weakness in our defenses.

The DIA works to identify such threats and to develop a new mind-set for assessing potential asymmetric threats while also developing effective measures for combating them.

DRISCOLL: Have you ever wrestled with Jell-O, Lieutenant Colonel?

NEWTON: Ma'am?

DRISCOLL: You're slipping around the question—answering without answering. Please address the question again—this time in plain English.

NEWTON: If you insist. Victor Drazen posed what's known as an operational asymmetric threat—meaning that he attempted to undermine our capabilities, Congresswoman. It was determined by our intelligence sources that Drazen's activities could endanger the security of the United States.

DRISCOLL: (Loudly) Enlighten me, Lieutenant Colonel—just how could a two-bit Serbian thug endanger the security of the United States of America?

NEWTON: I'm sure I don't need to remind you, ma'am, that Osama bin Laden is a two-bit thug, too, and that his nontraditional use of power—his asymmetric threat activities—managed to damage our country and murder thousands of our citizens. Remember also that Victor Drazen nearly assassinated a United States presidential candidate on the day of the California primary. Frankly, the value in holding him captive seems quite clear to me. Drazen had hundreds of known criminal associates. If he gave up any one of them, we could make a significant dent in the terrorist threat against the United States. Surely, Congresswoman, you don't have a problem understanding that?

FULBRIGHT: Let's take the acrimony down a notch, shall we. All right, Lieutenant Colonel, what I believe Congresswoman Driscoll would like to hear, as would I, are *specifics.*

NEWTON: Yes, Mr. Chairman. Let's start with . . . (papers shuffling) the fact that our sources inside Germany's GSG9* revealed that Drazen had been negotiating certain deals with known criminal and terrorist organizations in various parts of the world.

To be *specific,* the Drazens had been funneling money to high-ranking members of the Russian mob; they were also employing former members of the KGB in clandestine operations and bribing current members of the Russian intelligence service, including the FSB* and SVR.* Victor Drazen had even made contact with several antigovernment militia groups inside the United States. Our own intelligence data clearly suggested that Drazen was using his money to influence some very dangerous people—people who were and are quite clearly a *threat* to the *security* of the *United States.*

FULBRIGHT: Lieutenant Colonel, you began your testimony today by stating that your department wants to cooperate fully in this investigation, but your tone suggests that *you* do not. May I remind you that you're speaking to the representatives of the *people* of the United States right now. You might show them—and us—a little respect by checking that attitude of yours.

NEWTON: (After a pause) Point taken, Mr. Chairman.

REP. ROY SCHNEIDER, (R) TEX.: Ah, Lieutenant Colonel Newton, would you mind telling me exactly *where the hell* Victor Drazen got the *money* for all these so-called payoffs?

NEWTON: We know some of the Serbian Army officers involved in ethnic cleansing* have become very rich—usually by stealing property from their victims. These are the same tactics the Nazis used to amass wealth during World War II.

Victor Drazen was no exception. What was different about the Drazens was that they were using their money to buy influence with criminal organizations—in Russia, in Europe, and in the United States. The pattern of his spending suggested that Drazen was in the process of creating a new international terrorist organization.

Two years ago, Drazen transferred the bulk of his assets—approximately two hundred and twenty-five million dollars in United States currency—to an offshore bank account. Moving money was usually the first step taken by a Serbian war crimes suspect before he bolted.

The State Department, National Security Agency, and DOD's Defense Intelligence Agency were concerned that Drazen might escape the region before charges could be brought and NATO forces could catch up to him. From a secure location, Drazen had the potential to continue wreaking havoc on the peace process while escalating his other criminal activities.

Because of these developments, NSA Agent Robert Ellis brought the idea of neutralizing Drazen to the attention of Senator, now President-elect, David Palmer. As I understand it, Ellis and Palmer had worked together many times before when Palmer had served as a member of the House National Security Subcommittee.

Ellis knew that Palmer would be a strong congressional advocate for neutralizing both Slobodan Milosevic and Victor Drazen—the man Milosevic relied on to carry out many of his genocidal activities. It was then Senator Palmer, in his capacity as a member of the Senate Appropriations Committee, who secured the funds and the Senate's approval for the Delta operation called Nightfall.

FULBRIGHT: But the Delta action, as it turns out, was directed at Drazen's *decoy*—and resulted in the deaths of six U.S. soldiers.

NEWTON: And in the deaths of Drazen's wife and daughter as well.

FULBRIGHT: Yes, that is clear from the after-action report.* Both women were in the building a Delta team had targeted—although the team's only survivor, Special Agent Jack Bauer, claims he had no idea those civilians were present.

NEWTON: That's acceptable collateral damage, in my estimation.

FULBRIGHT: In your estimation, Lieutenant Colonel, but *not* in Victor Drazen's.

NEWTON: In any event, once General Henderson's intelligence sources discovered that the decoy was killed and not Drazen himself, General Henderson arranged to capture Drazen in a *second* covert mission, conducted by personnel from the DIA's Special Unit for Counterintelligence Initiatives, under his command.

FULBRIGHT: Then you are stating—and I remind you that you are under oath—that your commanding officer did not *intentionally* set up Jack Bauer and his Delta team to fail so that he could grab Drazen for his own purposes? You are testifying *under oath* that General Henderson did not provide Drazen's forces with the Delta team's radio frequencies so that they could jam their transmissions and vector in on Bauer's men?

NEWTON: Even such a suggestion is reckless and preposterous.

SPECIAL AGENT JACK BAUER: (From the back of the room) Answer the question!

FULBRIGHT: Special Agent Bauer, this is no place for outbursts. Remain silent or I'll have you removed from this hearing. (Muffled voices)

SCHNEIDER: Lieutenant Colonel Newton, tell me something: if it was so important for this Drazen to be "neutralized," and all the plans approved by the Senate and NSA were to have him "neutralized," then why the hell did your boss suddenly decide to take him prisoner—and then not bother to *inform* the Senate, the NSA, or the rest of the whole damned world? I don't recall, from my own service as an officer in the Marine Corps, that the DOD ever changed its mind about an action plan once that plan had been approved.

NEWTON: Congressman, I do not appreciate your veiled accusation that General Henderson set out to dupe the Senate, the NSA, and the rest of the international community—

DRISCOLL: (Interrupting) Yet that is exactly what General Henderson did! He captured Drazen, brought him to the United States, and imprisoned him without trial—and all of it was done covertly, without the knowledge or approval of his superiors in the

Congressional Intelligence Oversight Committee. Am I not correct?

NEWTON: There is no admission here. Nor is there an admission that we set up a Delta Force team for murder. We categorically *deny* any such charges.

FULBRIGHT: Your denial is so noted. (Shuffling papers) Let's move on to the subject of the covert prison system, which as I understand from a statement given to us by the office of the secretary of defense falls under your boss's area of responsibility.

NEWTON: That's correct. You are referring to the DOD's facilities for Mobile Underground Detention and Detainment.*

DRISCOLL: MUDD?

NEWTON: Yes, Congresswoman. MUDD is the military acronym for our Level 3 Detention Centers.

SCHNEIDER: As in *mud*. As in the prison facilities are about as easy to see through as *mud*. I see the DOD has finally developed a sense of humor.

NEWTON: (Incomprehensible response)

DRISCOLL: Excuse me, Congressman, but may I say there's nothing amusing about a prison system operated covertly within the borders of a nation that believes in basic human rights like trial *before* imprisonment. It goes against everything this country stands for.

NEWTON: Might I point out that the prisoners detained by the Captivity Management Department are not, and never have been, citizens of the United States. Might I also point out that many of our prisoners have been convicted in absentia for crimes against humanity.

SCHNEIDER: Lieutenant Colonel, just how many MUDD facilities does your department operate?

NEWTON: Because that question is not relevant to the current investigation, I am not at liberty—

SCHNEIDER: Son, you look like a smart lawyer. Well, hell, I'm a smart lawyer, too. And we're both smart enough to know that you either answer my question today, or we'll get answers from your commanding officer after we subpoena him.

NEWTON: Yes, sir. (Shuffling papers) There are twenty-seven Level 3 Detention Centers scattered across the continental United States. To ensure the highest level of security, prisoners are periodically moved within the system. All of the facilities are former Strategic Air Command antiaircraft sites abandoned in the 1960s—

SCHNEIDER: Nike sites? You converted old Nike sites? Well, I'll be damned.

NEWTON: The facilities are suitable for our purposes. All are located underground in rural areas, and the costs for conversion were minimal.

DRISCOLL: How many prisoners are you currently holding?

NEWTON: Eleven, ma'am. As I stated before, none of them are U.S. citizens.

FULBRIGHT: Who are these eleven prisoners, Lieutenant Colonel?

NEWTON: Mr. Chairman, to reveal the identities of these prisoners could jeopardize national security—

DRISCOLL: (Interrupting) You stated that some of your prisoners had been found guilty of crimes against humanity? That's a tall statement, Lieutenant Colonel. Surely you can back it up with a name or two.

NEWTON: (Shuffling papers) I know the identities of only four of the prisoners, Mr. Chairman. I am not apprised of all the sensitive information in my department—

FULBRIGHT: Answer the question, Lieutenant Colonel.

NEWTON: To the best of my knowledge, MUDD is currently holding Liam O'Shea, Abdullah Ahmed Al-Adel, Ichiro Nakada—

DRISCOLL: (Unintelligible) Irish Republican Army—

FULBRIGHT: (Muffled voices) Al-Adel! The Israelis would be furious if they knew—

SCHNEIDER: Nakada! He's wanted for that sarin gas attack on the Tokyo subway. Hell, I just met the Emperor of Japan two weeks ago. If I had known this—

FULBRIGHT: All right, I'm going to close this line of inquiry right now and advise that the Joint Congressional Intelligence Oversight Committee be convened to continue this line of investigation. Lieutenant Colonel Newton, if I were you, I'd get on your cell and tell your commanding officer to expect an official invitation from Capitol Hill.

We're adjourned for today.

DECLASSIFIED

Drazens' "Eye for an Eye" Revenge Plan Uncovered

REPORTER'S NOTE: The next witness called before the subcommittee was Darinka Brankovich. Ms. Brankovich is a CTU analyst and translator based in Washington, D.C. As an expert in Eastern European languages, including Serbian, she was able to translate and lend insight into the evidence recovered from Alexis Drazen's handheld personal digital assistant (PDA) and Andre Drazen's laptop computer, which was found in the trunk of his Mercedes sedan.

The Drazen computer files listed names, places, and other information that-once explained in later testimony from Jack and Kim Bauer, among other sources-clearly linked both Alexis and Andre to the two attempts on Senator David Palmer's life, the kidnapping of Jack Bauer's wife and daughter, and the attempt to free their father, Victor Drazen, from his imprisonment in the United States two years to the day after their mother and sister were killed during Operation Nightfall. The following are her translation notes submitted as evidentiary documentation.

Translation of Contents from Alexis Drazen's Handheld PDA

(Asterisks indicate identical key files found in Andre Drazen's laptop.)

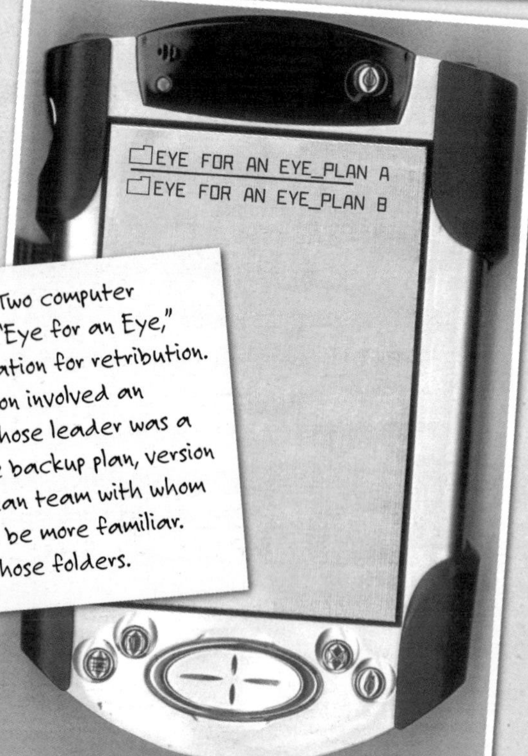

TRANSLATOR'S TESTIMONY: Two computer folders were found labeled "Eye for an Eye," which appears to be an operation for retribution. The A version of this operation involved an almost all American team whose leader was a man named Ira Gaines. The backup plan, version B, involved a smaller European team with whom Andre and Alexis appear to be more familiar. Here are the contents of those folders.

EYE FOR AN EYE_PLAN A

CONTACTS

■ Gaines, Ira: JPG photo; cell #XXX-XXX-XXXX; wire transfer operational budget through Cofell; Cayman account #XXX-XX-XXXX-XXXXX; General notations—Ex-N Seal; was very good on Marseilles job. Led team on stinger operation. Known addresses L.A., N.Y., London; no wife/children; sister Ohio, U.S.; elderly father Ohio, U.S.

■ Carroll, Kevin: JPG photo; cell #XXX-XXX-XXXX; wire transfer operational budget through Cofell; U.S. bank account #XXX-XXXXXX; General notations—Ex-DEA. Known addresses L.A., Miami; ex-wife, 2 children, Miami, Fla.

■ Farrell, Jamey: JPG photo, CTU (turned by Gaines), wire transfer payoff through Cofell; mother to receive payments in chunks; Erika Vasquez U.S. bank account #XXX-XXXXXX; son Kyle; ailing father, mother and son live in L.A., Calif. Ex-husband, Derek Patrick Farrell, remarried, living in Seattle, Wash.

■ ? "Jonathan" aka "Eric" aka "Heinrich Raeder": wire transfer payment through Gaines; General notations—Sniper expertise. Known addresses Berlin, Munich, Paris, Rome; mother and sister in Munich. Plastic surgery completed Berlin.

■ ? "Mandy" aka Miranda Stapelton: General notations—Nothing on this one. Unacceptable. Ask Yelena for background/ID search. Payment notations: wire transfer payment through Gaines. Cofell notes a late complication required additional unscheduled $1 million transfer. Done on condition of one-hour loan only. Swiss account used for this one. Final note: Money repaid within hour as promised.

■ Gaines compound, JPG map, North Valley, Calif.

■ Belkin, Martin: JPG photo, Flight 221, Berlin-New York-Los Angeles. Mojave Desert execute approx. 1 A.M. local, Yelana to provide IFF code for airliner. Andre to relay to Gaines and his people.

■ Yelana: cell #XXX-XXX-XXXX. USE YELANA ON NEED-TO-KNOW BASIS. UNDER NO CIRCUMSTANCES IS YELANA'S COVER TO BE REVEALED TO GAINES OR HIS PEOPLE. ALL COMMUNICATION THROUGH ANDRE ONLY.

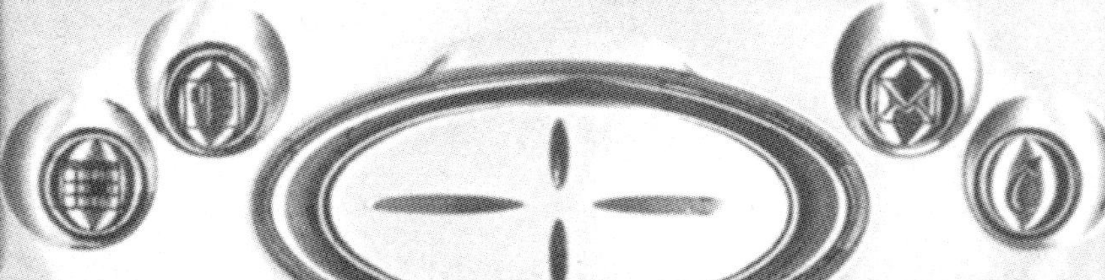

EYE FOR AN EYE_PLAN B

CONTACTS

- Myovic, Jovan: cell US #XXX-XXX-XXX, 500,000 DEM via Cofell, plus we promised him some names from Alexis's PLAYTIME files.
- Suba, Misko: cell US #XXX-XXX-XXXX, 500,000 DEM via Cofell, but remind him he lost his bet and owes us 3 M9 Berettas with mags.

MAPS

Downloads

- Berlin.jpg
- Prague.jpg
- WashingtonDC.jpg
- LosAngelesCounty.jpg
- SantaClarita.jpg
- SaugusWildLifePreserve.jpg
- Nevada.jpg

BAUER, JACK

INFO

TRANSLATOR'S SUMMARY: Information in this file was lengthy, very detailed, and similar to a private investigation report. It covered the personal life of Jack Bauer, his wife, Teri Bauer, and their daughter, Kimberly Bauer. All known addresses and phone numbers were listed as well as details on where Teri worked and where Kim attended high school. Their typical schedules were included along with names of friends and associates and their addresses.

PALMER, DAVID

INFO

TRANSLATOR'S SUMMARY: As with the Bauer file, the Palmer file was also lengthy, very detailed, and similar to a private investigation report. It covered the personal life of David Palmer, his wife, Sherry Palmer, and their children, Nicole and Keith Palmer. All known addresses were listed, including those in Washington, D.C., and Palmer's home state of Maryland. This folder also contained extensive profiles on his staff members and details on his speaking engagements the week of the California presidential primary. The most detailed file had to do with the senator's breakfast rally held at the Santa Clarita power plant the morning of the primary. Extensive information was listed on the building's personnel, including names of several supervisors. Blueprints of this power plant as well as Palmer's Los Angeles hotel were also found in this folder.

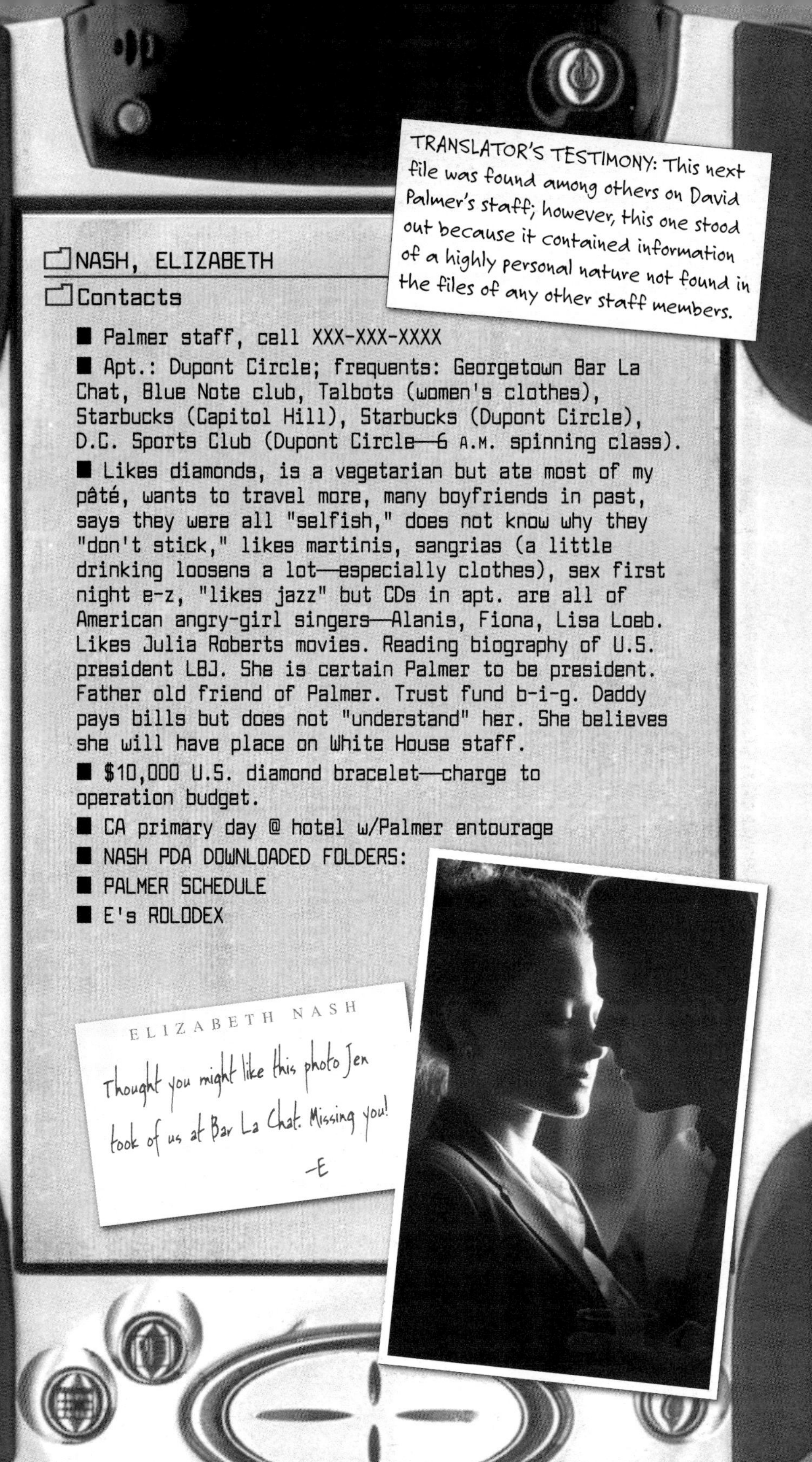

TRANSLATOR'S TESTIMONY: This next file was found among others on David Palmer's staff; however, this one stood out because it contained information of a highly personal nature not found in the files of any other staff members.

NASH, ELIZABETH

Contacts

- Palmer staff, cell XXX-XXX-XXXX
- Apt.: Dupont Circle; frequents: Georgetown Bar La Chat, Blue Note club, Talbots (women's clothes), Starbucks (Capitol Hill), Starbucks (Dupont Circle), D.C. Sports Club (Dupont Circle—6 A.M. spinning class).
- Likes diamonds, is a vegetarian but ate most of my pâté, wants to travel more, many boyfriends in past, says they were all "selfish," does not know why they "don't stick," likes martinis, sangrias (a little drinking loosens a lot—especially clothes), sex first night e-z, "likes jazz" but CDs in apt. are all of American angry-girl singers—Alanis, Fiona, Lisa Loeb. Likes Julia Roberts movies. Reading biography of U.S. president LBJ. She is certain Palmer to be president. Father old friend of Palmer. Trust fund b-i-g. Daddy pays bills but does not "understand" her. She believes she will have place on White House staff.
- $10,000 U.S. diamond bracelet—charge to operation budget.
- CA primary day @ hotel w/Palmer entourage
- NASH PDA DOWNLOADED FOLDERS:
- PALMER SCHEDULE
- E's ROLODEX

ELIZABETH NASH

Thought you might like this photo Jen took of us at Bar La Chat. Missing you!

-E

FATHER

THE ROSE OF KOSOVO.PDF

The Rose of Kosovo

A true Serb, a man who shares Serbian blood,
Willingly pours out his life onto the rich soil of Kosovo,
For all Serbs share the legacy of the bloodred rose.
We come, we fight, we bleed on the field of honor,
And roses spring from the sodden earth.

The sword of our enemies slash,
The arrows of our enemies strike,
And the scarlet rose of death blooms on our armor.
We fall in battle, but we do not die,
For Kosovo endures.

TRANSLATOR'S TESTIMONY: Both Drazens carried within their computer files a fragment of a Serbian poem called "The Rose of Kosovo," one of dozens of poetical works written around 1389, the same period that the famous epic poem, "The Battle of Kosovo," was composed to commemorate the clash between a Serbian prince and the Ottoman Turks. The Serbs were defeated in that battle, which ushered in four centuries of Ottoman/Muslim domination. In 1989, as part of a celebration to commemorate the anniversary of this decisive battle, Yugoslav president Slobodan Milosevic used "The Battle of Kosovo" to rally the Serb people to resist surrendering that beleaguered region. Milosevic's intransigence ultimately led to the 1999 NATO air attacks.

It appears that Victor Drazen used "The Rose of Kosovo" in much the same way that Milosevic used "The Battle of Kosovo"—as a piece of propaganda to rally support around his own political organization, the dreaded secret security force called the Black Dogs. Both Alexis and Andre Drazen kept this fragment from "The Rose of Kosovo" within folders titled simply FATHER. Victor Drazen often quoted this verse in interviews and speeches as part of his political ideology aligning himself with Milosevic's struggle.

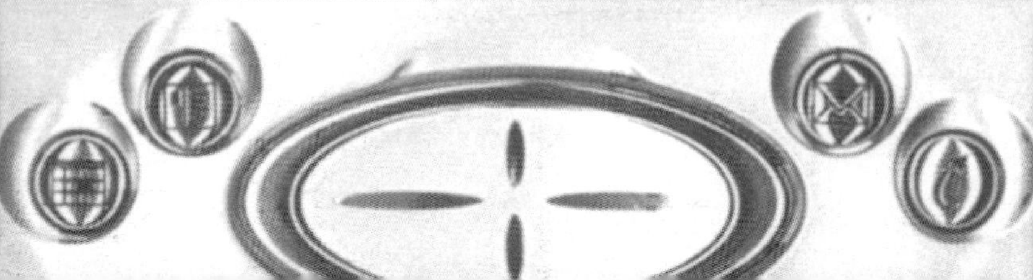

MOTHER AND MARTINA

- JPG photo—female middle-age "MOTHER"
- JPG photo—female early twenties "MARTINA"
- "Dagger" payment $1 million. U.S. wire transfer to Cayman bank
- PDF FILE "RECOVERED ELLIS FILE_FROM DAGGER":

TRANSLATOR'S TESTIMONY: A file labeled "MOTHER AND MARTINA" contained what appears to be a classified U.S. government memorandum from NSA agent Robert Ellis to then Senator David Palmer. In the memorandum, Jack Bauer's name is mentioned along with the details of Operation Nightfall and the bombing of Drazen's compound. This document clearly links Bauer to Senator, now President-elect, Palmer, as well as the questionable and disastrous special operation called Nightfall.

This report was part of the larger file that Robert Ellis discovered was missing from his Operation Nightfall folder shortly before his murder in a New Orleans bar men's room. Obviously the Drazens knew the details of this file.

The source of obtaining this file appears to be a mole of some sort with the code name DAGGER.

The deaths officially reported in this file include Victor Drazen's, which eventually proved to be inaccurate. The other casualties included "two unidentified women." CTU has since recovered Ellis's complete Nightfall report. Additional memos, filed much later than this stolen file, subsequently identify the women as Drazen's wife, Vesna, and daughter, Martina.

In addition to the attached memorandum, the missing Ellis file also contained an extensive list of surveillance notations. The dates and locations showed Victor Drazen's movements in the months prior to Operation Nightfall. The last entry in the file was made two weeks after Nightfall. The entry was an address in Saugus, California, 21911 Kipling.

This address was later linked to one of the underground prison facilities where the captured Victor Drazen would be held.

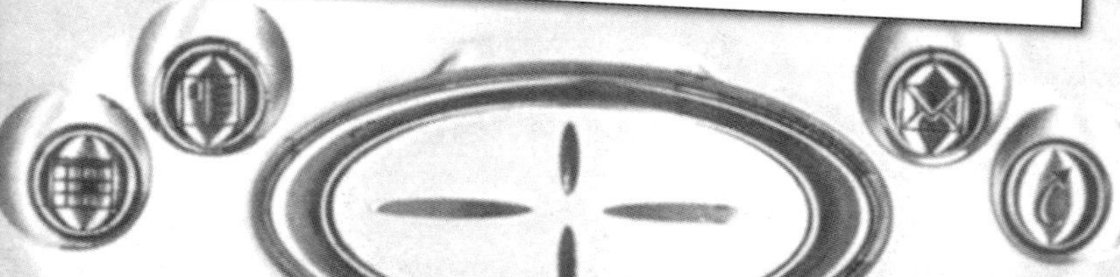

CHAIRMAN DP/SAC EYES ONLY

FILE: ΠΣΧΔΔΦφ

MEMORANDUM

Date: XXXXXXXX
From: Robert Ellis
To: David Palmer, Chairman, Senate Appropriations Committee
Subject: OPERATION NIGHTFALL (This follow-up memo to verify mission results. See primary AAR-09787 for preliminary details/rules of engagement/mission parameters.)

SOURCE: DIA and DOD intelligence

(Getting this intel out of the bastards was like pulling teeth with pliers—something I haven't done since Haiti!)

Nine days ago a seven-man direct-action infiltration team was HALO-dropped in the vicinity of the Serbian Army installation at Dakovica, in Kosovo, Victor Drazen's primary area of operations since the beginning of NATO air operations.

DA team—code name ANVIL—was led by operative 324-XXXX-262.

DA team targeted Victor Drazen at his secure compound on the banks of the Erenik River, approximately (4) kilometers northwest of the city of Dakovica. Up to twenty (20) Serbian regulars were already based in the compound and in two antiaircraft gun emplacements in the surrounding forest.

Victor Drazen arrived with entourage at 1115 local time. Entered main building.

DA team neutralized antiaircraft emplacements and painted target for attack plane. Compound destroyed at approximately 1119 local time by AGM-64 precision-guided missile launched by F-18 Hornet attack plane, code name HAMMER.

Immediately thereafter, Captain Bauer's DA team was subject to jamming that successfully disrupted their communications and prevented their safe exfiltration. Source of this jamming is still being investigated. Because of radio interference, Serbian forces were able to vector in on DA team and inflict six KIAs of DA team Anvil.

MISSION ASSESSMENT:

Victor Drazen was eliminated in the explosion, along with two members of his inner circle:
Mislov Pajalik, Serbian arms dealer
Vassili Tupelov, ex-head of the KGB in Belgrade.

COLLATERAL DAMAGE:

I regret to report there was also collateral damage. Two women—identities unknown—were killed in the bombing. Jack Bauer's DA team had no knowledge these civilians were inside the house when they targeted it, and Captain Bauer—the only survivor of the DA team—has not been informed.

KIA:

Warrant Officer Dwayne Shelton, U.S. Army First Special Operations Detachment—Delta
First Sergeant Brice Gardener, U.S. Army First Special Operations Detachment—Delta
First Sergeant Haj Illijec, U.S. Army First Special Operations Detachment—Delta
First Sergeant Gary Graham, U.S. Army First Special Operations Detachment—Delta
Master Sergeant Fred Peltzer, U.S. Army First Special Operations Detachment—Delta
Technical Sergeant Roger Voss, Combat Controller, U.S. Air Force Special Operations

SEE ATTACHMENT 0-—Δ987π FILE NOT FOUND (Attachment Missing)

REPORTER'S NOTE:
The operative referred to as 324-XXXX-262 is of course Captain Jack Bauer, United States Army, First Special Forces Operational Detatchment--Delta.

DECLASSIFIED

TRANSLATOR'S TESTIMONY: Folders were also recovered from Alexis Drazen's PDA. Although many appear to be unrelated to the investigation, they do give some insight into Alexis Drazen's leisure activities. The FBI* and CIA are conducting follow-up interviews with all contacts listed.

DOWNLOADS

- e-books: *Tactical Use of Small Arms in Urban Guerrilla Warfare* (nonfiction—Serbian publication); *Valley Green* (fiction—Serbian publication); *Rainbow Six* by Tom Clancy (fiction—Serbian edition); *Black Hawk Down* by Mark Bowden (nonfiction—English edition)
- Balkanmusic.com music files: Enix, Energija, Trik Fx, Milik Vukasinovic

PLAYTIME

- Susie Q. cell XXX-XXX-XXXX, expensive but worth it
- Natasha cell XXX-XXX-XXXX, likes to party, bring X-tras
- Cee-Cee cell XXX-XXX-XXXX, cheap and wild
- Margot cell XXX-XXX-XXXX, pretty but yawn, more Andre style—set him up

File: GIRLS (BERLIN)
File: GIRLS (BARCELONA)
File: GIRLS (PRAGUE)

TRANSLATOR'S NOTE: Many more files of a similar nature were found.

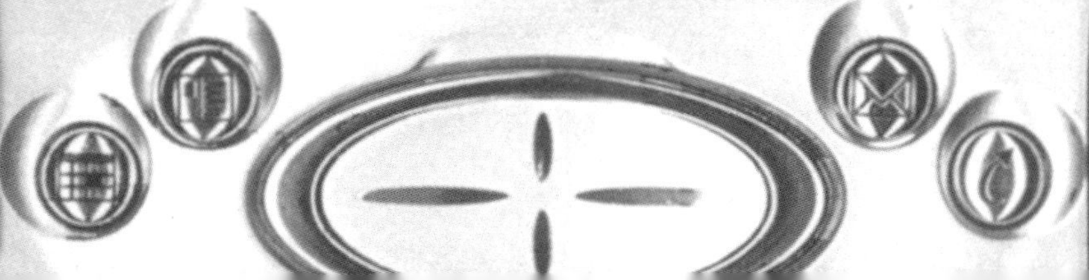

HOUR-BY-HOUR TESTIMONY OF EVENTS

MIDNIGHT—1:00 A.M.

REPORTER'S NOTE:
The following testimony by federal agent Jack Bauer covers the events that occurred between midnight and 1:00 A.M. on the day of the California presidential primary.

SPECIAL AGENT JACK BAUER: We all have our weak moments, our times when we think that just a little cheating won't hurt. Some of us even tell ourselves we're entitled to it, and that we're in total control of anyone finding out, of any damage it may cause. But the truth is we compromise that control the second we compromise our principles.

During my years at CTU, I had turned in colleagues for breaking rules and taking bribes. It's not a popular thing, turning in your coworkers, but I believed that if you looked the other way just once, it made it easier to compromise the next time, and pretty soon you'd just start thinking that's the way it's supposed to be. It was the philosophy I had lived by—never compromise your principles. Not even once.

After everything that's happened, I can see now that I should have followed my own philosophy. But I strayed from it—and because of that, I failed my wife and my daughter. I failed them long before any of these events began. I put my family in danger because I allowed myself to be compromised. As a result, I've been played like a chess piece: Worked on. Handled. Manipulated into position.

I guess the chess analogy comes to mind because that's what my daughter and I were doing the night they put their plan into action, the night they grabbed Kim and put her through hell . . . and my wife, Teri . . . and me. . . .

It was late for a school night, but Kim was still awake. She's a natural strategist and she had just read a new chess book, so we started playing after dinner and the time got away from us. I was happy to be home, just beginning to feel comfortable again, but there was still tension in the house. I had been separated from Teri for about six months and had just moved back a few weeks before.

Teri was the one who asked me to move out, but I never blamed her. After I came back from Nightfall—after losing every man, apologizing to their families, and attending their funerals—I'd been having problems adjusting. I couldn't talk to Teri about the mission, and I had a lot of trouble concentrating on just about anything else. Nothing seemed to matter anymore. I felt as if I just didn't have a right to be happy.

Teri saw my withdrawal as a symptom of marital problems and felt that some time apart might help. Kim only saw her mother asking me to leave—she was too young to understand that I had pushed Teri away first. So she blamed her mother and continued to give her attitude even after I'd moved back in.

That night, after Kim said good night to me, she gave Teri the brush-off. It upset me. I didn't like seeing her treat Teri that way. So Teri and I had a discussion about her behavior, and we decided to talk with Kim right then, together. But when we went into her room, Kimberly was gone—she had sneaked out.

It was hard to take, Kim's lying to us like that. The Kim I knew before I moved out would never have done something like that. At the time, I tried to tell Teri it was just a teenage rebellion thing, but now that I look back, I realize it was something much deeper. Teri and I had broken our trust with Kim when we split, so she felt entitled to break her trust with us.

While Teri and I began searching Kim's room for some clue to where the hell she'd gone, Nina Myers, my chief of staff at CTU, called to inform me that Special Agent Richard Walsh, a high-ranking officer within the division, had summoned everyone into headquarters for a briefing.

REPORTER'S NOTE: According to the separate testimony of Jack's daughter, Kimberly Bauer, which was submitted to the subcommittee as a videotaped statement, a friend of hers, seventeen-year-old Janet York, had asked her to come out to party with two young men, whom they were to meet at a furniture shop in the San Fernando Valley. According to Kim Bauer, Janet York had first met one of the boys at a local mall the previous week. The boy, whose name was Dan, claimed to be a sophomore at San Diego State and to be employed at the furniture shop where the teens would ultimately meet that night.

RICHARD WALSH

AGE: 49

CTU MISSIONS

- Administrative Director, CTU, Los Angeles Domestic Unit
- Administrative Director, Operation Pinstripe, 2001
- District Commander, Operation Toreador, 2000
- District Commander, Operation Proteus, 2000 (Special Commendation)
- Team Leader, Operation Jump Rope, 1999
- Team Leader, Hotel Los Angeles attack, 1998
- Section Captain, Operation Farmhouse, 1997

EXPERIENCE

- Administrative Director, Counter Terrorist Unit
- Deputy Director of Psychological Operations, Central Intelligence Agency
- Council for the Nonproliferation of Nuclear Weapons, Chief Adviser
- John F. Kennedy School of Special Warfare, Instructor
- County of Los Angeles Department of Juvenile Justice, Youth Counselor

EDUCATION

- Master of Science, Criminology and Law, Stanford University
- Master of Science, Psychology, Brown University
- Bachelor of Arts, Sociology, University of Pittsburgh
- U.S. Army Special Forces Operations

MILITARY

- U.S. Army Rangers
- U.S. Army Special Forces, SPARTAN Program, Assistant to the Director

PERSONAL

- Married — Madeline Walsh
- Daughters — Victoria Walsh, Veronica Walsh

DECLASSIFIED

Among our other recent assignments, CTU had been helping to provide intelligence to the Secret Service* for the protection of Senator David Palmer. Since the next morning was Super Tuesday,* I assumed Walsh's briefing had something to do with Palmer. The senator was the first African-American with a real shot at winning the presidency, making him the target of some credible assassination threats.

I told Teri I would probably be home in an hour. I promised her that if Kim wasn't home by then we would go out and look for her together. On the way to CTU I called Kimberly's ex-boyfriend Vincent O'Brien, but he swore he didn't know where she was. Then I called Nina again to see what more I could find out about the briefing. She didn't know anything more than when she first called me. She sensed some tension in my voice, but I avoided any questions before she could ask. I told her I was minutes away from the command center and hung up.

In the CTU parking lot, I called Teri once more and tried to reassure her about Kim. I knew she felt abandoned, and I hated the idea of her thinking I was starting to pull away again, but I had to report in. It was my job.

After I arrived, Nina told me she'd activated the satellite uplink. About a half-dozen people were already in CTU's command center, including Tony Almeida, one of my best information analysts. Our civilian computer programmer had also arrived, Jamey Farrell. She was dressed like she'd just come from a club—

REP. PAULINE P. DRISCOLL, (D) CONN.: Agent Bauer, I'm sorry to interrupt. I know I'll have more questions for you about your staff, especially Nina Myers, but right now I'd like to ask you about this Jamey Farrell. At that time, did you trust her?

BAUER: I did. Jamey was clean when she was hired. She'd had the proper security clearances, no record at all, but I trusted her most because she had been recommended to us by a man I greatly respected, a man to whom I owed my life: Special Agent Richard Walsh.

Walsh was a former member of the Green Berets. He had earned a degree in psychology, so twice a week he counseled gifted inner-city teenagers. These were kids who weren't in trouble yet, but who could easily go that route given their environment. He met Jamey in one of his sessions, recognized her brilliance, and helped her to make it into college by the age of sixteen. Just after college, Jamey had run into some troubles at her Microsoft job and she needed a new one. Walsh got her the civilian slot at CTU. Until that night, Jamey Farrell had been an exemplary employee.

At that point I suggested that perhaps Senator Palmer was the reason Walsh had called us in, and asked everyone to start pulling together information on the candidate. Tony Almeida was resistant to the idea—he didn't feel it was politically correct to assume we had to

JAMEY FARRELL

AGE: 26

EXPERIENCE

- CTU Programmer, Los Angeles Domestic Unit
- Recruited for CTU by Richard Walsh after she was fired from Microsoft for creating open source software for intelligence gathering
- Microsoft Corporation, Security Specialist
- MIT Artificial Intelligence Lab, Staff Hacker (brief stint)

EXPERTISE

- Infoserve technologies; detailed understanding of network security; proficiency in Python, Java, C/C++, Perl, LISP, and HTML

EDUCATION

- Bachelor of Science, Applied and Computational Mathematics, University of California (Riverside)
- UC Linux user group

PERSONAL

- Single
- Child — Kyle Farrell

pay special attention to the senator because he was African-American. I overrode Tony's objections. It wasn't our job to worry about how things looked—it was our job to protect the senator's life.

As we waited for Walsh, I had trouble focusing on the problem at hand. I was still worried about Kim, so at approximately 12:14 I called an old friend, Fred Kirowan, from the LAPD Tactical Squad and asked him to lend a hand looking for my daughter.

Then Special Agent Walsh arrived and the briefing began. In attendance were myself, Nina Myers, Tony Almeida, and Jamey Farrell. Walsh informed us that the CIA had reason to believe that there would be an attempt on David Palmer's life before the end of the day and that a well-funded shooter was coming from overseas.

Walsh was of the opinion that the people who hired the assassin were members of a domestic hate group, and ordered us to check the backgrounds of everyone close to Palmer and then cross-check those backgrounds with our database of known terrorists. The meeting was called after that, but Walsh pulled me aside.

He informed me confidentially that he suspected there was an element inside the Agency involved in the hit on Palmer. He ordered me to do what I could to find out more. I told Walsh that because of my past in busting corrupt agents, I was the last person he should be asking to ferret out a mole. No one like that, I thought at the time, would ever give me reason to suspect them.

Walsh claimed I was the only person he could trust. We both knew how serious the situation really was—if Senator Palmer was assassinated, it would tear the country apart. So I told Walsh I would do what I could. He then

REPORTER'S NOTE: An anonymous source consulted about this testimony claims that Special Agent Bauer was referring here to his activities in the aftermath of the arrest and conviction of a man caught laundering money for a ring of overseas terrorists. Bauer was instrumental in making a case against three CTU agents who had taken bribes from this man in exchange for intelligence information that would have allowed him to escape capture. Teddy Hanlin, the partner of one of those agents, would cause some real troubles for Special Agent Bauer later in the day. See testimony between the hours of 5:00 P.M. and 6:00 P.M.

informed me that George Mason was on his way to CTU to provide a more detailed briefing.

At approximately 1225 hours Nina approached me. She was concerned about not being included in a meeting with District Director George Mason. I told her Walsh had ordered me to meet with Mason privately. She spotted the lie immediately. I felt bad excluding her, but at that point I felt I had to shield Nina from what I was about to do.

I was glad to have the interruption of Teri's call, even though she told me she had found marijuana in Kim's desk. I suggested she check Kim's e-mail account, but Teri needed to know her password.

I returned to my office to prepare for the meeting with George Mason. He arrived at my office at 1227 hours. Mason claimed the suspected shooter was European—probably German—and that he was either in Los Angeles already or was arriving today. Then Mason handed me a disk he claimed would give me access to secured data nationwide, but refused to tell me the source of the disk, saying he wasn't "authorized" to reveal it.

I found this ridiculous and was immediately suspicious. Mason had to know that I couldn't do a *thorough* cross-check of the data if I didn't know its source, and he responded in a way that made me even more suspicious: he brought up Palmer's *politics*, insinuating that the man was "no friend of the Agency's," and CTU would be eliminated should Palmer become president.

I got the distinct impression that Mason wanted me to go along with running a substandard cross-check. Was that because he didn't want Palmer's assassin to be tracked down? Maybe.

Maybe Mason wanted Palmer to feel the heat of an assassin getting close so that he'd appreciate the worth of the Agency. Or maybe Mason's target wasn't Palmer at all. Maybe it was me. Maybe he was looking to set me up for some blame later on. Given my past whistleblowing actions, I didn't exactly have friends around every corner at CTU anymore. It doesn't matter what it was. Given Walsh's warning to me that someone in the Agency was in on the Palmer hit, I decided to test him.

I insisted Mason call his boss, Regional Director Ryan Chappelle, and ask if I could get "clearance" as to the source of the info on the disk. Mason "agreed," so I left him alone in my office to make the call. Pretending to go for coffee, I actually went to the command center's first floor and had Nina patch me into his line. Mason had lied; he had placed a call to hear the correct time. That's when I loaded the tranquilizer gun—

CHAIRMAN FULBRIGHT: Excuse me, Agent Bauer—the *what*?

BAUER: The tranquilizer gun, Congressman—it's a gun that shoots a tranquilizer dart. I had to buy some time to put the pressure on Mason, so I told Nina to keep everyone out of my office, then I shot him in the leg. The sedative worked in seconds.

While Mason was out, I told Nina to call up the Darcet file. Philippe Remy Darcet was a heroin smuggler and arms dealer. He was captured in Barcelona, extradited to the United States, and convicted in federal court of helping to fund and equip the failed terrorist attack on the United States embassy in Cairo in 1999.

REPORTER'S NOTE: Photo of George Mason after having been shot with a tranquilizer gun as taken by the surveillance cameras at CTU.

I gave her Mason's disk. If it truly allowed access to secured data nationwide, then we'd be able to access all the transactions that had been made dealing with the Darcet account at the Bank of Barcelona.

I had always suspected that George Mason had skimmed off a couple of hundred grand from Darcet's account for himself. Here was my chance to prove it, and maybe get Mason to talk. We had a half hour or less before Mason woke up.

Nina was nervous about blackmailing a superior, but I persisted and she agreed to speak with Agent Tony Almeida about cracking the Darcet encryption. She and Tony had formed an intimate relationship, and I knew he'd do what she asked without questioning it.

DRISCOLL: Excuse me, Agent Bauer, but since you've brought up the subject, let's be clear on this: Nina Myers was sleeping with Tony Almeida at that time, is that right?

BAUER: That's correct.

DRISCOLL: And this was only a few months after she'd been sleeping with you, is that correct?

BAUER: (After a pause) I'm sorry to say it is.

DRISCOLL: Thank you. Go on with your testimony, please.

BAUER: I didn't want to finger another CTU agent, ruin another career. But I had to do my job, no matter what that job entailed. After I'd shot Mason, I did try to reach Richard Walsh to inform him of my actions, but I got his voice mail instead. I was troubled by my assignment, bothered by what I might be forced to do. I was also still worried about helping Teri find our daughter.

At approximately 12:36 hours, my wife received a phone call at home. The call was from a man who identified himself as Alan York. He said he was the father of Kimberly's friend Janet, and was looking for his daughter, who was also missing.

At 12:40 hours I locked my office and approached Jamey Farrell at her workstation. I asked her to trace the password for Kimberly's e-mail account. I called Teri and told her that Kimberly's password was (pause) LIFESUCKS.

Teri accessed Kimberly's e-mail account and found an address where the girls might have gone. At that point, Teri was beside herself—she'd left a number of messages on Kim's cell phone, but Kim hadn't responded. I'm sure Teri was feeling desperate with me not there and Kim missing, and she had no reason to suspect that Alan York was anyone but who he appeared to be. So she called the man claiming to be York, and together they decided to try to track down the girls.

BAUER: Back at CTU, Tony Almeida finally cracked the Bank of Barcelona's encryption code and accessed the Darcet account. Tony sent the information to the terminal in my office, and sure enough I found an unexplained wire transfer of two hundred thousand dollars to an unidentified account in Aruba. There was no evidence it was Mason's, but I knew it looked bad enough to scare him.

REPORTER'S NOTE: According to Kim Bauer's testimony, around this same time, approximately 12:50 A.M., she checked her cell phone and saw the many messages from her mother. Rather than calling her mother back, she asked Dan and his friend to drive her home. They agreed, and the group climbed into Dan's van and left the furniture store.

I woke Mason, showed him what I'd uncovered, and suggested the account might be his. Mason denied it, but I threatened to send it to Chappelle, and the tactic worked: he gave me the information I needed to proceed with my investigation. He typed out the name of the source of the information on my screen and left.

The source was Victor Rovner, a CIA informant and freelance operator who does most of his work out of the Czech Republic. He had transmitted an encrypted message to the Counter Terrorist Unit at midnight L.A. time and 4:00 A.M. local time in Kuala Lumpur, Malaysia.

Rovner is a dealer in arms, drugs, and information. He claimed that a shooter—a professional assassin—was on his way to Los Angeles, and that the assassin's target was David Palmer.

At 12:57 Tony informed me that International Flight 221, on its way to Los Angeles from Berlin, had exploded over the Mojave Desert and that preliminary reports indicated the airliner was probably brought down by a bomb. It was a potential Stage One terrorist incident, and CTU had to investigate. I wanted to find my daughter, but I could not leave—I had to remain at my post.

and the FAA's investigation found in its review of the Mojave Desert crash, in which 257 people, mostly citizens of Eastern European nations, lost their lives, that the commercial airliner had been destroyed by a bomb. Evidence suggested that a door of the jet was blasted open, depressurizing the passenger compartment mere seconds before a plastic explosive detonated, tearing the fuselage in half and sending the wreckage careening 27,000 feet to the earth below.

REPORTER'S NOTE: Subsequent testimony before the subcommittee revealed this crash to be part of the Drazens' elaborate revenge scheme. Their target appeared to be an internationally known photojournalist named Martin Belkin. Belkin had been hired by "Lifestyle" magazine to photograph Senator David Palmer on the day of America's Super Tuesday primaries. Since Senator Palmer had never met Belkin before, the Drazens planned to send someone else in his place, but first Belkin had to be disposed of.

CTU investigators later discovered a telling inconsistency at the airport that led them to these conclusions. Despite the fact that several passengers were turned away at the gate because Flight 221 was overbooked, the passenger manifest the airlines provided to the authorities indicated that there was an empty seat in first class. This discrepancy was later explained among materials recovered at the North Valley compound of Ira Gaines, the man hired by the Drazens to conduct the day's operation.

It appears as if an airline employee was paid off to doctor the manifest to look as if no one occupied the seat when in fact Martin Belkin did. In addition, records at the compound indicate that a shadowy international assassin using the name Miranda Stapleton had obtained the seat next to Belkin. She had, according to plan, lured Belkin into having sex in the airplane's first-class rest room, stealing his passport and identification papers during the act.

"Mandy" then escaped the plane by detonating small charges on the door of the plane. She parachuted to the floor of the desert minutes before a larger charge exploded within the plane itself.

A check of Belkin's cell phone account reveals that a call had been placed from the airport just prior to boarding time for Flight 221. The call was to Patty Brooks, Senator David Palmer's campaign manager and speechwriter. Brooks recalled that Belkin had placed the call to confirm a breakfast meeting with the senator for that morning at 7 A.M. However, Brooks said he'd made no mention of the flight he was about to board, and she had no reason to be suspicious of Belkin or anything associated with him at that time.

1:00 A.M.–2:00 A.M.

REPORTER'S NOTE: The following testimony by federal agent Jack Bauer covers the events that occurred between 1:00 A.M. and 2:00 A.M. on the day of the California presidential primary.

SPECIAL AGENT JACK BAUER: Military battles are won or lost before the first shot is fired. Victory lies in the planning, the strategy, and the surprise. By the time an attack begins, it's often too late for the defender. He's lost the initiative, and he may never get it back.

From the moment my administrative director, Richard Walsh, pulled me aside, told me about the mole in CTU, and warned me to trust no one—not even my own staff—I knew I was in trouble. I didn't have a plan. All I was doing was reacting—to what Walsh told me, to the threat against Palmer, to the explosion aboard the commercial airliner.

I had to regain control of the situation and get back my initiative, which meant I needed allies. But given Walsh's comments, I wasn't sure who I could count on.

From the beginning, I decided it wasn't Tony Almeida. He challenged my leadership five minutes after George Mason walked out the door. In front of the whole command center staff Tony announced in an accusatory tone, "George Mason comes in, disappears into your office for half an hour, then limps out of here. What's that all about?"

When the staff looked at me with suspicion, I found myself *reacting* yet again.

Thankfully, Nina Myers, my chief of staff, came to my rescue with a smooth, elaborate bluff about how Mason had made some nasty accusations about me and other people in the office because of past actions of mine that he didn't like.

Rather than see me own up to the truth—that I'd blackmailed a possibly innocent district director—Nina jumped in and made it appear as if I'd just heroically defended myself and my staff's honor against a superior's unfounded accusations.

I could see Tony didn't buy that explanation for a second, but the staff did. Nina's bluff was so coolly delivered, I almost bought it myself. So Tony had no choice but to back off.

DECLASSIFIED

NINA MYERS

AGE: 34

BIRTHPLACE: Boston, Massachusetts*

CTU MISSIONS

- Division Leader, Operation Proteus, 2000

EXPERIENCE

- CTU, Assistant Special Agent in Charge (Chief of Staff), Los Angeles Domestic Unit
- Department of State, Special Assistant to the Secretary, Bureau of Intelligence and Research
- RAND Corporation, Research Analyst
- United Nations Security Council, Policy Analyst

EDUCATION

- Master of Arts, Criminal Investigative Psychology, John Jay College of Criminal Justice
- Master of Arts, Law and Diplomacy, Fletcher School of International Relations, Tufts University
- Bachelor of Arts, (double major) Middle Eastern Studies and History, Harvard University

PUBLISHED PAPERS

- Center for Defense Information, *The Role of Intelligence in Rooting Out Terrorism*
- Cato Policy Report, *The Rogue State Doctrine and National Security*
- The Brookings Institution, *Metropolitan Readiness in the Face of a Global Threat*

PERSONAL

- Single

* NOTE: Biographical information prior to college years is highly suspect and now under investigation by CTU and FBI.

DECLASSIFIED

At the time, I saw Nina's lie as an act of loyalty, proof that I could rely on her as my ally. Now I look back at that incident with new eyes. After everything that's happened, it's impossible not to see things differently. . . .

CHAIRMAN FULBRIGHT: Differently, Agent Bauer? I'm not sure I understand what you're saying.

BAUER: I mean it wasn't the first time Nina Myers had come up with a smooth, elaborate lie inside of three seconds. She was a pro at it, yet I never materially questioned it. I chose to see it as a highly developed mark of our trade. In retrospect I realize that when I cover quickly, I do it consciously. With Nina, it seems more natural—more like a reflex action. Something practiced . . . what you do when you're playing both sides.

REP. PAULINE P. DRISCOLL, (D) CONN.: Can you give us another example?

BAUER: A few months before, when Nina and I were first getting involved, we wanted to keep our relationship private. We usually left CTU in separate cars to avoid raising any eyebrows.

The Agency frowns on fraternizing. I was her superior, and we both knew it wouldn't look good to be seen together. So I would take a circuitous route to her place, where she was waiting.

One Sunday evening we were out having dinner. She and I both got separate calls on our private cell phones to come into the command center for an urgent meeting. The radio warned of some major tie-ups en route to her place, so she told me not to waste time taking her home to get her car. She suggested that we just go straight to CTU. I did, hoping no one would notice our arrival in the same car on a Sunday evening.

Unfortunately, George Mason was getting out of his car in the underground parking garage around the same time we drove up together in my car. He stood there and watched us get out. As we passed him, he gave us a smug look and asked in a mildly sarcastic tone if there was something wrong with Nina's car.

"No," she told him without even a second's pause. "Jack and I were following an unofficial lead on an Al-Adel associate. Gee, George, guess it's been a while since you did fieldwork if you think using two cars on a tail doesn't make you twice as likely to be spotted."

She said this with such a cool head and such perfect disdain that Mason looked away, obviously embarrassed that he'd made the insinuation in the first place. I myself was dumbfounded.

DRISCOLL: Dumbfounded or *impressed*?

BAUER: At the time, I admit, I was impressed. I told myself then, as I did the day of the California primary, that her lies were okay because they were protecting me.

DRISCOLL: And now?

BAUER: Now I know better.

FULBRIGHT: Please continue.

BAUER: While all this was going on at CTU, I was still worried about my daughter, who had sneaked out of the house. And I was worried about my wife, too, who was now driving around looking for Kimberly with a man I didn't know.

My cell phone rang and I expected it to be Teri, but it was Administrative Director Richard Walsh. He was under fire and asked for my help. I wanted to call for backup, but Walsh insisted that I didn't. He still didn't know who to trust. Despite the danger, he asked me to come alone.

He'd gone downtown to Dunlop Plaza for a secret meeting with a CTU security systems analyst named Scott Baylor. Baylor, I found out later, had been enlisted by Walsh to help track down the mole in CTU.

FULBRIGHT: Tell us more about Baylor. What exactly did your administrative director ask him to do?

BAUER: About a week before Super Tuesday, Walsh sent around his assistant to abruptly collect every CTU employee's key card. He claimed it was a security system upgrade and that all cards would be destroyed once they were turned in. He also said that new cards would be issued through supervisors. But this was a ploy. Walsh didn't destroy the cards. Instead, he secretly put Baylor in charge of analyzing the old key cards. Baylor was supposed to be running cross-checks on time clocks, looking for red flags.

REP. ROY SCHNEIDER, (R) TEX.: What sort of red flags?

BAUER: Anything out of the ordinary. Patterns of entry by personnel that didn't make sense given their work schedules. Or a pattern of entry into secure areas where they otherwise would have had no business.

SCHNEIDER: And what did he find?

BAUER: Baylor found something even more incriminating. The magnetic strip on one of the key cards contained more than just the minor bit of coding that allowed access to buildings and secure areas. Someone had embedded a file with a great deal of data on this card. It was ingenious. Having that information on a key card would have allowed a mole to smuggle classified intel out of a restricted area without ever being questioned.

DRISCOLL: And whose key card was it?

BAUER: Well, that was the problem. Baylor didn't know. Any identifying information had already been erased from the card. And the remaining information had been encrypted. He could only partially read the data. But it was clear from what he was able to read that much of the information concerned David Palmer.

Obviously, the person who embedded information onto that card was taken by surprise the day Walsh announced the key card revocation. Wiping the ID info was easy, but the encrypted data couldn't be as readily removed. It was locked in. He or she was obviously forced to hand in the card before the data could be properly wiped, too. Since Walsh announced the cards would be destroyed, and since no one knew about Walsh's plan anyway, the person must have reasoned that *not* handing it in would draw a lot more unwanted attention.

As far as decoding the encrypted data, Baylor needed many more man-hours to complete the job, but by that time, Baylor wanted out.

DRISCOLL: Why? He agreed to help Walsh, didn't he?

BAUER: Baylor never knew *why* Walsh wanted the cross-checks. The key card information made it clear to Baylor that he was about to finger a mole in CTU associated with a hit on Palmer. It was too much for him.

Baylor was an analyst, not a field man. He'd never so much as *fired* a weapon. It wasn't as if he'd signed on for hazardous duty or anything. So the moment he discovered the incriminating key card, he put his wife and two children on a plane to Canada and called Walsh for a final meeting. His plan was to hand over the key card,

SCOTT BAYLOR
AGE: 32
BIRTHPLACE: Seattle, Washington

EXPERIENCE
- CTU, Security Systems Analyst, Los Angeles Domestic Unit
- CompuShield Advanced Security Systems, Consultant

EXPERTISE
- Advanced proficiency in security software technologies and encryption protocols; holds five patents on original firewall, virus detection, and encryption software programs; proficient in Infoserve technologies, Python, Java, C/C++, Peri, LISP, and HTML

EDUCATION
- Doctoral program candidate, Computer Science, Software Theory, Stanford University (incomplete)
- Master of Science, Computer Science, Software Theory, Stanford University
- Bachelor of Science, Mathematics, Cornell University

PERSONAL
- Married
- Wife — Sarah Schiffer-Baylor
- Son — Jacob Baylor
- Daughter — Jacqueline Baylor

resign, and get on a plane himself. He never got that far. Baylor was shot and killed during his meeting with Walsh.

SCHNEIDER: And that's when Walsh called you?

BAUER: Yes, Congressman. I phoned Nina for the entry code into the Dunlop Plaza garage and she gave it to me. I found Walsh alive but wounded. He suspected there might still be shooters loose in the building. As we tried to escape, we managed to kill one of the men.

I wanted to ID the man, but there were no papers on him, and I wasn't about to carry his body with me, so I cut off his thumb, wrapped it in a handkerchief, and headed out with Walsh—

DRISCOLL: Excuse me, you cut off his *what*?

BAUER: I cut off his thumb, ma'am, so I could ID the man through a print.

Before we could get to my car, though, Walsh was shot again. He was wounded very badly this time, and I couldn't get to him. A shooter or shooters had pinned me behind a concrete wall.

I told Walsh to lie still. If he played dead, he wouldn't draw fire. But Walsh was bleeding to death and he knew it. He didn't want to lose consciousness without giving me the information that Baylor had given to him, so he showed me the key card and told me to have Jamey Farrell decode it.

"Take it to Jamey," he told me. "She'll match it to a computer. Find the computer, you've got the dirty agent."

I already knew Walsh trusted Jamey. He'd been the one to recruit her in the first place. And he also made a point of telling me that Baylor trusted her, too, which made sense, since Baylor had been one of the people who'd helped to train Jamey in how our systems worked.

After Walsh told me this, he moved to throw me the card. The movement attracted the attention of the shooters. Walsh knew it would. He didn't care. He knew he was acting to save the life of the man likely to be our next president.

So Richard Walsh moved . . . and they shot him again. . . . That shot finished him. . . .

FULBRIGHT: (After a pause) Agent Bauer? (Pause) Agent Bauer, would you like a short recess?

BAUER: Yes, if you don't mind.

FULBRIGHT: Not at all. Let's take fifteen minutes.

FULBRIGHT: Special Agent Bauer, are you ready to resume your testimony?

BAUER: Yes, I am, Mr. Chairman.

REPORTER'S NOTE: An anonymous source consulted about this testimony commented that Special Agent Jack Bauer and Administrative Director Richard Walsh had been close personal friends for many years.

Walsh had initially recruited Jack Bauer into CTU. Additionally, Walsh had received a commendation for risking his life to save Bauer's during a highly classified CTU operation known as "Proteus," which took place in 2000. This reporter could uncover no further details about that operation.

FULBRIGHT: Then continue, if you please. Pick up with the key card.

BAUER: In my car, I put the key card into my mobile scanner and sent the information to our programmer, Jamey Farrell. I asked her to tell me whose computer had encoded the card. The scan came back with a name: Nina Myers.

I remember reading that name on the screen in front of me and feeling physically sick. I told myself there *had* to be some explanation—

Nina had defended me, she'd gone out on a limb to help me countless times. I trusted her—and as I said, at the time I was desperate for allies.

Now that Walsh was dead, I didn't want to believe Nina was dirty. I resolved to confirm the information with Jamey the moment I returned to the command center. And if it was true, I would confront Nina.

In the meantime, during this same hour, my daughter was being driven around in a van, kidnapped by two punks. And my wife, Teri, was driving around looking for her with a man claiming to be Alan York, the father of my daughter's friend.

Since York claimed his daughter had received an e-mail about a meeting at an address in Van Nuys, Teri agreed to accompany him there. It turned out to be a furniture store, Paladio Furniture, and a work schedule there included the name Dan on it.

Dan was the name of the boy who had become involved with Janet and arranged the rendezvous.

When Teri arrived at the shop with York, they found Janet's car parked in the lot, but the girls were gone.

REPORTER'S NOTE:

According to the separate testimony of Jack's daughter, Kimberly Bauer, between the hours of 1:00 A.M. and 2:00 A.M., Dan and his friend Rick refused to take Kim or Janet home or to set them free.

At approximately 1:56 A.M., Dan pulled the van over to the side of the road and ordered Kim to step out. When she would not, he assaulted her, dragging her out himself and throwing her to the ground. Dan then ordered Kim to call her mother on her cell phone and say that she was at a party and would be home in a few hours.

According to Kim Bauer's testimony, which was submitted to the subcommittee as a videotaped statement, this is what happened next:

KIMBERLY BAUER
AGE: 15
BIRTHPLACE: Santa Monica, California

EDUCATION
- Santa Monica High School (currently enrolled, second year)
- Freshman Year GPA: 4.0
- Sophomore Year GPA: 2.4

SCHOOL CLUBS/ACTIVITIES
- Girls Volleyball Team
- Chess Club

SMHS VICE PRINCIPAL'S NOTE

Kim's first year at Santa Monica High was outstanding. She maintained a GPA of 4.0 while actively participating in a wide range of student activities including Pep Club, Yearbook, Photography Club, and Chess Club. She also joined the Tennis, Swimming, and Girls Volleyball teams. Her teachers' evaluations were all complimentary of her classroom performance and cheerful attitude.

Kimberly's second year at SMH showed a marked decline in her scholarly performance. In addition, she abruptly dropped out of all clubs but Chess and all teams but Girls Volleyball. Her record now reflects six detentions and one warning notice of failure in Algebra.

PERSONAL
- Parents — Teri (deceased) and Jack Bauer
- Ex-boyfriend — Vincent O'Brien

KIMBERLY BAUER: I refused to call home and pretend everything was okay. I knew the longer I was out, the likelier my dad was to send the police looking for me. So I told Dan to go to hell. He looked like he was going to slap me, but I didn't care. I was so pissed!

Then Rick said, "Gaines told us not to hurt her, remember?"

I didn't know who Gaines was, but it sure worked on Dan—it scared him real bad because he backed right off. I thought for a minute that Janet and I were going to be okay.

Like I said, Rick was sticking up for me, which made me feel

REPORTER'S NOTE: "Rufie" is street slang for the drug Rohypnol, also known as "rope" or "ropies" on the street. Rohypnol depresses the body's central nervous system, slowing respiration and heart rate and lowering inhibitions. On the street, the drug is also known as the "forget me" drug because it boosts the black-out/amnesia effect of alcohol. Ten times more potent than Valium, rufies typically take the form of small white tablets and are considered one of the most common "predator" or "date rape" drugs. Many colleges routinely warn young women about the possibility of being "slipped" one unknowingly in a social situation.

safer. It was clear that Dan was the boss, you know? So Rick wasn't that bad a guy. It was Dan who was the creep.

Anyway, the three of us were standing there beside the van, and Janet was in the passenger seat.

Dan just went and yanked Janet's arm out of the window so it hung down next to the van door. She didn't even notice. Dan had given her something earlier—I thought it was a rufie, you know, because she'd been totally out of it for the past hour.

So Dan held up a crowbar and looked at me like if I didn't call he would smash Janet's arm up.

Well, Rick had *just said* we weren't supposed to be hurt. So I didn't think he'd do it, but he did. He completely crushed it! He broke her arm right there in front of me!

Janet started screaming and crying, and I was completely terrorized. I called my mom's cell right away and told her I was at a party and I'd be home soon. I did my best to pretend I was going along. Then I said "I love you" at the end.

With all the bad karma between us for the last few months, I knew my mom would know that was a signal something was wrong. Normally, "I love you" is like the *last* thing I would ever say. . . .

2:00 A.M.–3:00 A.M.

REPORTER'S NOTE: The following testimony by federal agent Jack Bauer covers the events that occurred between 2:00 A.M. and 3:00 A.M. on the day of the California presidential primary.

REP. PAULINE P. DRISCOLL, (D) CONN.: Agent Bauer, I'm curious about that man's thumb. Were you still carrying it around?

SPECIAL AGENT JACK BAUER: Yes, ma'am. I dealt with it after I scanned the key card. I switched my mobile scanner from magnetic to optical and sent the thumbprint to a tech at CTU's data services.

DRISCOLL: And what did they find?

BAUER: They found nothing on record for the shooter, which was pretty nearly impossible. Given the extensive international databank available to us, and given the tactics the shooter used to covertly track, then ambush Baylor and Walsh inside a secure facility, it seemed logical to me that the man would have a record somewhere—as an ex-law enforcement employee, government agency worker, or as a criminal with priors . . . *something.* But there was nothing.

The only possible explanation was that his file had been erased, which meant that someone with high-level clearance had manipulated the data systems to protect his identity—and that was pretty unsettling.

DRISCOLL: You have his body, don't you? Can you ID him now?

BAUER: My understanding is that there is still no ID on the man. He's a John Doe.

CHAIRMAN FULBRIGHT: And the other shooter or shooters at Dunlop Plaza? Can you speculate about their identities?

BAUER: My best guess, looking back, sir, is that they were Ira Gaines's men. Gaines had access to CTU security camera images, and eventually he had Jamey slow the decoding process on the card.

It's possible Gaines found out about Baylor's having the card, then supplied the shooters to tail and kill Baylor—and anyone else they suspected he might have informed.

I have to say, I honestly don't think Jamey knew Scott Baylor or Richard Walsh were ever in danger. Baylor had helped train her. And Walsh had been a real mentor and friend to her.

When I got back to the command center and informed her that

Walsh had been murdered along with Baylor, her reaction was genuine. She appeared truly shocked and disturbed.

DRISCOLL: So whose key card was it?

BAUER: Well, the ID information was wiped, and someone, we don't know who, disposed of the remaining cards the night Scott Baylor was murdered. So discovering the card's owner wasn't even possible by a process of elimination. However, if I had to speculate, I'd say the key card was Jamey Farrell's all along.

DRISCOLL: What makes you think so? You said the embedding had taken place on Nina Myers's computer? Jamey had shown you evidence of that, correct?

FULBRIGHT: Excuse me—I'm sorry to interrupt you, Pauline, but I think it's important that we hear about the events in order, as they happened. That way we'll be able to understand what was in Agent Bauer's mind as he took the various actions he did that day. Agent Bauer, please pick up with what you did next during that hour.

BAUER: Let's see . . . (papers shuffling) after I scanned the key card and thumbprint, I began driving back to the command center when my cell phone rang. It was Teri with good news. Kim had phoned to say she was at a party.

I felt such relief. I was convinced that all Teri had to do was pick up Kim and the family crisis would be over. But apparently Kim told Teri she didn't know where the party was and then hung up before Teri could get anything else out of her except the words *I love you.* Frankly, those words raised a red flag for both Teri and me. It had been a long time since Kim had said "I love you" to her mother.

I tried to tell myself it would be okay. At least Teri had heard from Kim, and her friend Janet was still with her. I assumed we'd just have to keep it together and wait until she came home or called Teri again. But I'm a father, and I couldn't help it—I continued to worry.

FULBRIGHT: Agent Bauer, after your wife's call, did you return to CTU's command center?

BAUER: Yes, I returned at approximately 2:15 A.M. By that time, I was working hard to control my emotions. I wanted to grab Nina and shake the truth out of her. But I knew I couldn't. Not without absolute proof.

REPORTER'S NOTE: Kimberly Bauer testified that between the hours of 2:00 A.M. and 3:00 A.M., she and her friend Janet attempted to escape from Dan and Rick, fleeing on foot through back alleys in an area of North Hollywood.

They managed to elude the two young men long enough for Kim to place another call on her cell phone to her mother, verifying that she was in fact in danger. She gave the name of an auto body store she saw nearby, but she was forced to hang up when the two young men found and recaptured her.

Janet York, on the other hand, attempted to flee and was hit by a car. The young men then left Janet for dead on the street, carrying Kim back with them to their van.

Kim also testified that before the escape attempt, she witnessed Dan talking seriously on his cell phone. She assumed the conversation was with the person who had hired Dan and Rick to kidnap her and Janet.

Phone records show that Ira Gaines had in fact called Dan about that time. Later notations found in an encrypted log kept by Gaines—apparently meant to be used for an after-action report for the Drazens—revealed that his plan was running late.

After "Mandy"—the suspected assassin aboard International Flight 221—had blown the plane to pieces and parachuted her way down to the Mojave Desert floor, she lit a fire, burned her clothes, and hid Martin Belkin's ID in the sand.

At approximately 1:00 A.M., one of Gaines's men picked her up by Jeep, using the light of the fire to find her, and took her to Gaines's desert house.

In the meantime, Mandy's associate "Bridgit" used a tracking device to find the ID, which Mandy had placed inside a case along with an electronic homing beacon. Bridgit was to hold the ID until Mandy had received her one million dollars in cash and signaled Bridgit to bring the ID to the desert house.

REPORTER'S NOTE: This image of Kimberly Bauer and Janet York being chased by their kidnappers was provided to the police by the owner of a local warehouse. The warehouse security system caught the pursuit on tape.

(XGDS)

Security tape courtesy of W.H.F. Warehouse

Security tape image courtesy of Larsen Parking Garage L.L.C.

"DAN"

REAL NAME: DANIEL MOUNTS
OTHER ALIASES: "TREAT"
AGE: 20
BIRTHPLACE: Los Angeles, California

EDUCATION
- Echo Park High School (never graduated, incomplete)

CRIMINAL ACTIVITIES
- Daniel Mounts has a minor juvenile record including vandalism, assault, and possession of a controlled substance (marijuana).
- One arrest on adult charge of possession of an illegal substance (Rohypnol) with intent to sell.
- Two years before the California primary, charges against Daniel Mounts were dropped in a pending federal narcotics case. The Drug Enforcement Agency case officer responsible for the prosecution was former agent Kevin Carroll.

NOTE: Subject deceased.

"RICK"

REAL NAME: Richard Marc Allen
OTHER ALIASES: "RICHIE"
AGE: 18
BIRTHPLACE: San Diego, California

CRIMINAL ACTIVITIES
- One juvenile arrest for criminal possession of a controlled substance (marijuana), probation. One arrest by undercover narcotics detectives for criminal purchase of Ecstasy (XTC) with intent to sell, case still pending.

REPORTER'S NOTE: In separate testimony given without benefit of counsel to detectives of the Los Angeles Police Department, Richard Allen confessed that he was hired by "Dan's friend Kevin" to kidnap Janet York and Kimberly Bauer and deliver them to a mysterious third party Rick identified as "some fucking psycho named Ira Gaines." Kidnapping charges dropped in exchange for full cooperation in federal investigation.

"MANDY"

NOTE ON PHOTO

- ID unverified but presumed to be operative called "Mandy" referred to in log of deceased mercenary Ira Gaines.
- Image captured by security cameras at Berlin's Tempelhof International Airport matches a description of her also found in Gaines's log.
- The name Miranda Stapleton appears on the passenger list for the downed flight. This may have been Mandy's alias. No remains recovered.

AGE/PERSONAL

Photo in Gaines's log indicates she is an attractive woman believed to be between the ages of 20 and 35.

MERCENARY/CRIMINAL ACTIVITIES

- Wanted for the bombing of Berlin to Los Angeles International Flight 221.

ASSUMED EXPERTISE

- Demolitions, skydiving, reconnaissance, counterintelligence activities.

REPORTER'S NOTE: According to the log, Bridgit arrived at the house shortly before 2:00 A.M. with only a photo of the ID, claiming she had found a new hiding place for it and declaring the new spot would not be revealed until she and Mandy had been paid an additional one million dollars. Wire transfer records show Gaines had withdrawn one million dollars from his personal bank account between 2:00 A.M. and 3:00 A.M. that day, but shortly after 3:00 A.M. the funds had been transferred right back.

CTU analysts are unclear about exactly what transpired between Gaines, Mandy, and Bridgit during that time at the desert house, but they suspect that Gaines pretended to pay the extra million to Bridgit, then killed her once she handed over the ID.

It's fairly clear that Mandy is still alive, as later entries in Gaines's log reveal she had agreed to assist him in a future job.

At the time of this writing, CTU is still working on identifying and apprehending her.

If I wrongly accused her of being dirty after all we'd been through, and all she'd done to back me up, she would never forgive me.

You see, Nina told me that I had deeply hurt her when I broke off our intimate relationship to return to my wife, but she also said she wasn't going to ask for a transfer. She prided herself on being a professional. She wasn't going to let our personal history get in the way of our working relationship.

I respected that choice. By then, I knew I didn't love her—in fact, I'm not sure I ever did love her—but I did care about her very much. I admired what I saw as her strength and dedication, and that morning I counseled myself to be careful. *I had to be sure of my judgments.* A big part of me was praying that Jamey was wrong.

From a hiding place in the hallway, I called Nina on my cell and asked her to wait for me in my office. Then I went over to Jamey, gave her the encrypted key card, and asked her to produce evidence that it had been burned on Nina's computer.

Jamey asked me to distract Nina long enough for her to access her computer files. I did. I went to my office and kept Nina occupied until Jamey called me on the phone.

She had absolute confirmation that the key card came from Nina's terminal—proving that Nina was indeed the dirty agent, because each of our terminals is locked with a personal password.

I was no longer sick about this—I was pissed. Really pissed. Nina had used me, compromised me, and was probably laughing at me behind my back.

I asked her pointedly, "How long have you been playing me?"

She denied everything, of course. I pressed, but her only responses to my accusations were anger and hurt.

I took her down to the command center floor where I asked Jamey to show us the evidence. Jamey produced a record of the line-by-line activity. It clearly showed how the intel had been gathered on Nina's computer, then burned onto the key card.

Then Nina noticed the date when the transaction apparently occurred—*January 14.*

"The second week in January, Jack," Nina whispered to me.

That's all she had to say. It was the weekend we'd gone to Santa Barbara together. Nina had been with me the entire time. There was no way she could have slipped away, driven back to L.A., and burned the information onto that card. No way.

I realized someone had hacked into her computer—or knew her password. At the time, a number of suspects raced through my mind, including Tony Almeida.

DRISCOLL: Agent Bauer, wasn't there a way to discover the truth at that time? Didn't you have security camera footage on record to see *who* had tampered with Nina Myers's computer?

BAUER: Yes, of course, we had footage. And I made a mental note to order and review the digital files for that date. But you have to understand that access to past footage is relatively easy only up to thirty days. Beyond that, the data is compressed and stored in Washington, D.C., archives.

I knew we'd have to wait as long as twenty-four to forty-eight hours for that footage to be accessed and sent to us—and before I could even think of ordering it, I had to begin damage control on Nina.

I had just accused my chief of staff and former lover of treason and betrayal, and she was furious. As I've said before, I needed allies. And my priority at that moment was making sure Nina remained one.

DRISCOLL: All right, let me understand this. You say that Nina Myers was with you on the weekend when the key card was encoded. So tell me again; who do you believe encoded it?

BAUER: It's pure speculation at this point, but I believe Jamey Farrell was the person who actually encoded the card. At the time, I didn't suspect her, of course, because both Walsh and Baylor had advised me to trust her. But she was dirty, as we later found out.

Whoever encoded that card

REPORTER'S NOTE: Additional testimony by CTU staff indicated that the digital archives of the security camera footage for the evening of January 14 had been sabotaged. The findings would have been inconclusive, even if Special Agent Bauer had ordered the footage immediately.

knew that the ID info on it didn't matter because it was something that could be wiped in a flash. The encrypted data, which was locked into the card, was the real risk because it could be matched to a personal terminal.

Jamey knew how to hack into systems and uncover passwords. And, after she agreed to help Ira Gaines, she obviously began to look for loopholes in our systems to take advantage of.

I believe Jamey used Nina's computer to burn the card on January 14 because she knew I was her alibi that weekend. Using Nina's terminal meant there would be no one to blame if the card was compromised. And that's exactly what happened: I didn't suspect Jamey because Walsh and Baylor trusted her, and I no longer suspected Nina because I had been with her when the card was burned. At the time, I was reeling—I had no idea who could have burned that card.

DRISCOLL: So you believe that Jamey Farrell knew you and Nina Myers were seeing each other? And that you would be her alibi that weekend?

BAUER: Yes. (After a pause) During this hour, Jamey made it clear to me that she had known about my affair with Nina. . . . I think it's fairly accurate to say, Congresswoman, that office romances are seldom kept private for long.

DRISCOLL: Yes, Agent Bauer, I think most office workers would agree that you don't need to be a field agent in an intelligence division to detect these things. Water coolers are usually all it takes. (Soft laughter from subcommittee members.)

FULBRIGHT: All right, okay. . . . Let's take a short recess, shall we?

3:00 A.M.–4:00 A.M.

CHAIRMAN FULBRIGHT: Let's talk about the lockdown, Agent Bauer. It occurred about 3:00 A.M., is that correct?

SPECIAL AGENT JACK BAUER: That's correct. Agent Tony Almeida had challenged me earlier in front of my staff. After that, he began to watch me very closely. Two agents had been killed since midnight. Naturally he became suspicious of my every action.

REPORTER'S NOTE: The following testimony by federal agent Jack Bauer covers the events that occurred between 3:00 A.M. and 4:00 A.M. on the day of the California presidential primary.

Although Tony didn't know why I was interrogating Nina Myers, he saw enough of it from a distance to consider it harassment. He called District Director George Mason, claiming I needed to be relieved of my command.

REP. PAULINE P. DRISCOLL, (D) CONN.: Agent Bauer, there was *personal* animosity between you and Agent Almeida, is that fair to say?

BAUER: Yes. (After a pause) Tony was sleeping with Nina Myers, and he knew I had also been involved with her. (Pause) I assure you all, I deeply regret that these personal conflicts occurred under my command. I take full responsibility for them. I can only say by way

TONY ALMEIDA
AGE: 29
BIRTHPLACE: Chicago, Illinois

CTU MISSIONS
- Operation Proteus, 2000 (Special Commendation)

EXPERIENCE
- CTU, Intelligence Agent, Los Angeles Domestic Unit
- Transmeta Corporation, Systems Validation Analyst

EXPERTISE
- Certified Instructor, Krav Maga hand-to-hand combat defense

EDUCATION
- Master of Science, Computer Science, Stanford University
- Combined Bachelor of Engineering/Bachelor of Computer Science, San Diego State University

MILITARY
- U.S. Marine Corps, First Lieutenant
- Scout-Sniper School, Third Marine Division
- Surveillance and Target Acquisition Platoon School, First Marine Division

PERSONAL
Single

~~SECRET~~/SENSITIVE (XGDS)
ARA, Date 8/26/02

of explanation that I assumed professionals could act as professionals on the job—and that private lives could remain private.

While I had always been confident that Nina and I could act professionally, I guess I never expected her to become involved so quickly with another man in our command center after we split. It's understandable how her new lover could become overprotective of her and overly wary of me.

Now, of course, I look back and clearly see why she needed to become involved so quickly with another man at CTU: she needed a malleable ally for her own purposes.

DRISCOLL: Thank you for your honesty, Agent Bauer. Please go on. What happened when District Director George Mason arrived and called for the lockdown?

BAUER: By the time Mason arrived, I was already on my way out. And I just kept on going.

DRISCOLL: But doesn't a lockdown mean no one can leave?

BAUER: A presidential candidate's life was at stake. Two agents had already been murdered attempting to uncover information regarding the assassination plot, and I wasn't going to let what I saw as petty personal issues get in the way of following my only lead.

FULBRIGHT: Back up a bit. What lead was that?

BAUER: Jamey Farrell claimed it would take her many hours to decode the intricately encrypted data on the key card. The only thing she said she was able to find was an address on the key card: 18166 San Fernando Road.

DRISCOLL: I assume, then, that she set you up? Sent you to that address with a shooter waiting?

BAUER: That's a fair assumption—although the evidence is pretty much circumstantial. Scott Baylor may have already decoded the address when he started looking at the encryption on the card, and at that point there was nothing Jamey could do to hide it from us.

Wherever it came from, though, that address was our only thread. I left CTU and drove to 18166 San Fernando Road. The location was a large abandoned warehouse in a desolate industrial park complex. After seeing a sliver of light through an open door, I went in with my weapon drawn.

A man was waiting inside. He was lighting a cigarette, and I seemed to have surprised him. He fired at me, but missed.

Outside, a policewoman named Jessie Hampton heard the gunfire and called for backup. She saw the shooter run off, but she stopped me. I showed her my badge and asked for her help. We pursued the shooter as a team into the warehouse. I made a point of telling Jessie that I needed the shooter alive for questioning.

Police backup arrived in the form of a helicopter. The chopper's searchlight caught me in its glare, and I dove for cover to avoid the shooter's gunfire. Unfortunately, the shooter captured Jessie and held her at gunpoint.

He warned me to drop my weapon or he'd kill her. She was very brave. She yelled for me not to do it or he'd shoot both of us.

I took a chance that the shooter didn't know Spanish, and I called to her in that language, telling her to *move* the second my weapon hit the ground.

I dropped my weapon. She moved, and I charged the shooter. I got him, but he had already discharged his gun and Jessie caught the bullet. He'd killed her.

When the police arrived, the patrolmen were visibly furious to see that a fellow officer had been gunned down. The shooter, whose name was Greg Penticoff, was pretty disturbed. He knew my name, which alarmed me. Then he told me if I let the police take him, he was dead.

At first I thought he was talking about the wrath of the officers, but he wasn't. He said he was afraid of someone else getting to him and killing him. I wanted to know who, but he wouldn't talk until he knew he wasn't going to be arrested.

I wanted to take Penticoff into my custody, but the police refused. As they hauled him off, Penticoff yelled to me, "If you ever want to see your daughter again, get me out of this!"

I followed the squad car sick with the idea that Penticoff was telling me the truth. And he was. It was my first clue that there was a link between Palmer's hit and Kim's disappearance.

REPORTER'S NOTE:

According to Kimberly Bauer's testimony, during this same time period she was recaptured by her two abductors, tied up with duct tape, and driven to a secluded spot, where Ira Gaines pulled up in a separate sedan.

Before taking her into his charge, Gaines looked hard at Kim with eyes she called "dead cold." And then, in a voice she described as chillingly matter-of-fact, he said: "You're with me now. Be good, you'll be back at the mall in a day or two. Be bad, you won't. Clear?"

Kim nodded and heard Gaines ask Dan and Rick about the whereabouts of her friend, Janet York. According to Kim Bauer, Dan and Rick lied to Gaines "in nervous voices" about Janet, telling him they killed her and hid her body.

Meanwhile, 911 records verify that an emergency call for help was placed by a passing motorist in North Hollywood who saw what looked like an injured woman on the street. An ambulance was dispatched, and paramedics found Janet York lying on the street in a pool of blood shortly thereafter. She was transported, alive, to St. Mark's Hospital.

4:00 A.M.–5:00 A.M.

REPORTER'S NOTE: The following testimony by federal agent Jack Bauer covers the events that occurred between 4:00 A.M. and 5:00 A.M. on the day of the California presidential primary.

SPECIAL AGENT JACK BAUER: George Mason's only reason for the lockdown at CTU was to question me. Once he heard my name on the police frequency, he knew where to find me, so at approximately 4:00 A.M. he ended the lockdown and drove to the Van Nuys police station.

I had followed the squad cars there earlier. When Mason walked in, I was in the middle of trying to convince the desk sergeant to let me question Greg Penticoff, who was about to be booked for the murder of Police Officer Jessie Hampton—

REP. ROY SCHNEIDER, (R) TEX.: (Interrupting) Excuse me, Agent Bauer, but you must know that George Mason's written statements about your actions during this general period are highly critical. He states that in the previous hour you assaulted an agent who was guarding an exit during his lockdown. And in this hour, he accuses you of helping Penticoff escape. Is that true?

BAUER: Please try to understand the bigger picture, Congressman—because that's what I was considering. I wasn't concerned with protocol, pleasing headquarters, or getting a bigger office. I did what I did because I was trying to *save David Palmer's life*—and by then it appeared that my own *daughter's* life was at stake, too.

On my way to the Van Nuys station, my wife called to tell me that our daughter had been in touch again. Kim had confirmed that she was in trouble. She managed to get away from her abductors, but she was still in imminent danger. She was being chased down somewhere in North Hollywood. Meanwhile Kim's friend, Janet York, was fighting for her life in a nearby hospital because she'd been hit by a car.

So *no*, I didn't play it safe. I didn't play by the rules. Because if I had, I would have given up the only link we had to the Palmer assassination attempt and to my daughter's fate.

And frankly, as far as Mason's criticism of my actions, you might want to consider the source. For as long as I've known him, George Mason has been a man preoccupied with power and pay-grades. It's always been about the ladder for Mason, about covering his (pause) political aspirations.

Do you know the only thing that got a reaction out of him during that hour? I warned him that if he *didn't* question Penticoff, he could be implicated for impeding the investigation into the assassination plot against Senator Palmer. Possible damage to his career—that's what finally got Mason interested in working the thread and interrogating the subject.

SCHNEIDER: I get the picture. But you still haven't sold me on the validity of helping a murderer escape police custody.

CHAIRMAN FULBRIGHT: Take us through the events, Agent Bauer.

BAUER: Mason said he would interrogate Penticoff himself, until Penticoff refused to talk to anyone but me. Mason had no choice. He allowed me into the interrogation room. Unfortunately, Mason and the other agents insisted on secretly watching behind a two-way mirror. I couldn't allow that. I needed to hear what Penticoff had to say in private—

REP. PAULINE P. DRISCOLL, (D) CONN.: (Interrupting) And why was that? Didn't you want their help?

BAUER: It wasn't a question of help at that point, ma'am, it was a question of trust. I was in the same position as Walsh had been just a few hours ago. I knew there was a mole, but I didn't know who it was. Two agents were already dead. I couldn't take a chance with Mason.

DRISCOLL: Yes . . . I understand your position. But . . . let me see here (papers shuffling) . . . Mason's written statement claims you "sabotaged" the interrogation. Was that the reason?

BAUER: Yes. I needed to speak to Penticoff without the possibility of dirty agents listening, so I entered the interrogation room and loudly announced to Penticoff that he wasn't just talking to me, as he'd requested, he was talking to a number of people—and I gestured to the two-way mirror covering one wall of the interrogation room. Penticoff protested, which I expected.

I then moved close and whispered so that the observers couldn't

TESTIMONY OF EVENTS

GREG R. PENTICOFF

OTHER ALIASES: "TENT," "TAPS," "BOBBY TOFF," "GARY ROBERTS"

AGE: 34

CRIMINAL ACTIVITIES

- Juvenile record includes assault, vandalism, grand theft auto, possession of an unlicensed firearm, attempted murder.
- Adult record includes six arrests, two convictions on possession of stolen goods and assault with a deadly weapon. Charges with no convictions include accessory to homicide, burglary, arson, and selling heroin and crack cocaine.
- Two years before the California primary, charges against Greg Penticoff were dropped in a pending federal narcotics case. Drug Enforcement Agency case officer responsible for both prosecutions was former agent Kevin Carroll.

NOTE: Subject awaiting trial without bail in Los Angeles County for the murder of LAPD Officer Jessie Hampton.

hear. I told Penticoff I was going to give him my cell number to call, but he needed to raise hell first, pretend as if I'd whispered a threat to him. So he did.

Penticoff shouted and got violent, and I played along, grabbing him by the hair. During the scuffle, I was able to slip a piece of paper with my cell number into Penticoff's mouth. Once the agents burst into the interrogation room and pulled us apart, Penticoff demanded his right to a phone call. *That's* how I got him to talk to me privately.

SCHNEIDER: Well, that's mighty quick thinking, son. (Chuckling) I'm sure glad you're on our side—

FULBRIGHT: Please, let's refrain from personal commentary.

SCHNEIDER: Sorry, Jayce. So what did this Penticoff character tell you?

BAUER: He claimed that the "guys" who were holding my daughter would be calling a phone on San Fernando Road. If he was not there to answer, he claimed it would be too late to save her. In effect, he said either I got him out or my daughter was dead. Congressman, what would you do?

FULBRIGHT: Agent Bauer, what Congressman Schneider would do is not the question. The question is, what did *you* do?

BAUER: What *I* did, Mr. Chairman, was try to save my daughter's life. I phoned Nina Myers back at CTU and asked her to search for phone lines at the 18166 San Fernando Road address. She found a nearby pay phone that was in service, so I asked her to set up a trace.

DRISCOLL: Without a legal warrant, is that correct?

BAUER: That's correct.

FULBRIGHT: Go on.

BAUER: At the police station, I convinced an officer named Phillips to let me into the cell holding Penticoff so I could try to question him again. The cells were locked and unlocked with access cards. The officer had one. Once we were inside the holding cell with Penticoff, I baited the officer until he became angry with me.

We struggled, and during the scuffle I got the card away from him without his knowing. Other officers rushed into the cell, and during the commotion I slipped the card to Penticoff. Once we had all cleared out of his cell, Penticoff freed himself and met me outside the station.

I drove Penticoff to the phone booth on San Fernando Road. Although Nina was tracking the pay phone, a cell phone hidden inside the booth rang instead, and Nina couldn't trace its frequency.

Penticoff took the call. It was his employer, who we later discovered was Ira Gaines. Gaines directed him to dispose of a body in the trunk of a nearby car. There were car keys inside the phone booth.

The moment I heard the words "body in the trunk," my heart stopped.

My daughter, Kimberly, was missing, this asshole claimed he was involved with people who had grabbed her, and now I heard the words "body in the trunk." I took Penticoff with me to find the car. I don't think I've ever felt as sick as I did when I opened that trunk. There was a bloody corpse wrapped in plastic. But it wasn't Kim.

The body was that of an adult Caucasian male, naked and badly mutilated. The murderer had done a professional job of slowing the ID process. The dead man's fingers were clipped, his teeth were pulled, and most of his face had been sliced. About that moment, I realized that Penticoff and I were no longer alone. George Mason and a group of agents had arrived. Using a remote link to satellite images, they had tracked me and Penticoff from the police station to the San Fernando Road location.

Mason was furious, of course, and was ready to throw the book at me, but I assure you: I never had *any* intention of allowing Penticoff to go free. I needed him to answer the phone, and he did. And now we had *another* lead—a corpse. I showed Mason the body and reminded him that this, too, was connected to the hit on Palmer.

I played Mason, hammering home what he cared about most: that if he didn't allow me to follow this lead, and something happened to Palmer, it would "look bad" for us both. I also finally admitted to Mason what Walsh had told me: that someone inside CTU was involved in the assassination attempt. I had no choice anymore, I had to trust Mason—it was either that or find myself in handcuffs and off the job.

My strategy worked—on both counts. Mason let me go. I drove

the car with the mutilated body to CTU, and Penticoff was taken back to the police station.

SCHNEIDER: Did you have any other leads to your daughter's whereabouts by then?

BAUER: Only one. My wife was still at the hospital where Janet York was undergoing surgery. By cell, I urged Teri to speak to the girl the moment she was conscious. I knew Janet was the best chance we had of finding Kim.

TERI BAUER
AGE: 34

EXPERIENCE

- Graphic Eye, Partner and Head Designer
- Click California Design, Creative Director
- L.A. Design, Graphic Artist
- Chiat/Day Advertising, Graphic Artist
- Museum of Contemporary Art, Los Angeles, Installation Assistant Curator
- Los Angeles County Museum, Consultant to Director
- Santa Monica Gallery, Assistant to Director
- Greenpeace, Advertising Art Director
- Dark Horse Comics, Colorist
- Isabella Gardner Museum (Boston), Art Conservator
- Uffizi Galleria (Florence, Italy), Restorative Assistant

EDUCATION

- Master of Fine Arts, Art Practice, University of California (Berkeley)
- Bachelor of Arts, Painting, Rhode Island School of Design

PERSONAL

Married — Jack Bauer
Daughter — Kimberly Bauer

REPORTER'S NOTE: Before the end of this twenty-four-hour period, CTU agents conducted extensive debriefing interviews with Teri Bauer. The following is an excerpt from the transcripts of Teri Bauer's taped statements. Her comments cover some of her activities during that hour and also lend insight into her relationship with her husband, Jack Bauer.

TERI BAUER: We got to St. Mark's Hospital about 4 A.M. and ran to the doors of the operating room to find Janet on the table. I waited with Alan—or the man I believed to be Alan York, and a police officer finally arrived to take down what little information we had.

Jack phoned about that time and told me the reason he *still* wasn't with me was that he wanted to question some man who might have seen Kim. He urged me to talk to Janet as soon as she got out of surgery.

I have to admit, by that point I was *furious* with Jack. For the past four hours our daughter had been missing, and he had stayed at CTU. It seemed to me he was putting his job ahead of our daughter's welfare.

Alan—or rather, the man *claiming* to be Alan—had been so supportive and helpful during those hours. He told me that his wife had left him and Janet years ago. I really felt sorry for him, being left alone like that to raise his daughter. I knew how he must have felt. When Jack and I had separated six months before, I pretty much went to pieces. It's true I had *asked* him to leave, but he had actually abandoned me first.

For months before he moved out, Jack had been a shell of his former self—there but not there. It's a terrible feeling living with someone like that, I can tell you, it's an empty, cold feeling. A part of you dies, you know? I had tried so many times to fix whatever was wrong, to draw him out, get him to open up. Over and over I tried to get him to *trust* me, *talk* to me. But he refused. To me, it felt like the most profound rejection. Then one day I decided that the dread I had of being alone couldn't possibly be any worse than the empty, devastating feeling of being rejected by a man I loved so very much. So I asked him to move out.

Since midnight, Jack's actions had started bringing back all those awful memories—the heart-wrenching feelings I had of being emotionally abandoned. All the stony silences, the distant, unresponsive moods. The "Jack Wall"—that's what I called it. When he put it up between us, there was no getting around it.

The memory was so pervasive, I began opening up to Alan, telling him about Jack and also about the problems I'd been having with Kim. She had changed so much after Jack moved out. She was so angry and rebellious. Kim is very much like her father, and these days she was acting more like him than ever, right down to her moody silences and guarded secrets.

The evening before Kim had slipped out, I found a note in the mail. It was from the principal of her school—she was failing Algebra. It was the *second* notice. When I confronted her about it, she admitted she had intercepted the first letter and destroyed it.

I was so angry, I said terrible things to her. Called her a liar, accused her of being irresponsible. I was so harsh, I realize now that I said some things I never should have. With Kim missing, every harsh word I had ever uttered came back to me with ten times the force. I began to feel as though it were all my fault—that I'd driven her out.

Alan listened sympathetically and promised to stay with me until I found my daughter. I felt my heart melt. I was so grateful to him. At the same time, I was so angry with Jack. I remember thinking that he should have been there with me. When Jack moved back in a few weeks ago, he said he loved me and he didn't want to live without me. He agreed to try harder to share his feelings with me and promised that we would start to deal with Kim's problems as a team. Together. A united front, you know?

But Jack had *deserted* me. I'd been dealing with this alone since midnight, and I was actually starting to question whether I could go through with having him back in my life again.

Around that time, Janet's heart monitor flatlined. She was in surgery, and it looked like she might not make it. I felt so helpless watching from outside the OR. A part of me was honestly worried for Janet, but another part, I have to admit, was very aware that she was our only link to Kim. For my daughter's sake, I needed Janet York to survive.

5:00 A.M.–6:00 A.M.

REPORTER'S NOTE: The following testimony by federal agent Jack Bauer covers the events that occurred between 5:00 A.M. and 6:00 A.M. on the day of the California presidential primary.

SPECIAL AGENT JACK BAUER: After I drove the car with the body in the trunk to the CTU compound, I asked Nina Myers to get started on an ID. Then I called hospital security at St. Mark's and asked them to provide guards for the patient Janet York. I boarded a CTU helicopter, which I had requisitioned by cell phone on the drive to CTU. We flew to St. Mark's and landed on the helipad—

REP. PAULINE P. DRISCOLL, (D) CONN.: (Interrupting) Excuse me, Agent Bauer, regarding that helicopter. George Mason notes here in his report that you made *personal* use of that helicopter without proper authorization.

BAUER: Oh, he says that, does he? . . . *Personal* use . . . is that right? . . . *Personal* use.

DRISCOLL: (After a pause) Agent Bauer? Do you have an answer to this charge?

BAUER: Ma'am, you don't know how deeply . . . how very *deeply* I wish that my helicopter trip had been completely *personal* and in *no way* connected to David Palmer, Operation Nightfall, or Victor Drazen. That the fate of my daughter and my wife had absolutely *nothing* to do with my work. Unfortunately, Congresswoman, I can't. It had *everything* to do with my work.

DRISCOLL: (After a pause) Yes, I see. . . . I'm sorry for the interruption. Please continue. What happened after you arrived at St. Mark's?

BAUER: I was met by Claude Davenport of hospital security who told me he'd posted a guard at each end of the corridor where Janet York was in surgery. I found my wife, Teri, waiting there. She introduced me to the man who claimed to be Janet's father, Alan York.

I had met many of Kim's friends over the years, but Janet's name was new to me. I immediately threw some questions at York. I wanted to know exactly what he knew about the boys who had abducted our daughters. But I also wanted to see how he answered my questions.

JANET YORK

AGE: 17

EDUCATION

- Santa Monica High School
- Freshman Year GPA: 2.9
- Sophomore Year GPA: 2.4

SCHOOL CLUBS/ACTIVITIES

- Cheerleading Squad (Cut when GPA fell below 2.5)
- Yearbook (Cut for nonparticipation)

SMHS VICE PRINCIPAL'S NOTE

- Though intelligent and outgoing, Janet has proved to be a discipline problem from the moment she entered high school. Teacher evaluations were mixed. Some felt she was disruptive, others believed she was only expressing a healthy adolescent disrespect for authority. Interestingly, Janet demonstrates a marked hostility toward female teachers. This evidence leads me to believe that Janet's difficulties began before she came to Santa Monica High School.
- In junior high (seventh grade), school administrators saw fit to hold Janet back a year. I believe this event did irreparable harm to Janet's self-esteem and sent her down the wrong path. This blow, coupled with her long-standing estrangement from her mother, set the stage for further confusion and rebelliousness, which only worsened in high school. Continuing the pattern established in junior high, most of Janet's hostility continues to be directed toward female authority figures.
- Janet York's record notes eleven detentions in her sophomore year—eight for tardiness, one for disrupting a classroom, and two for direct insolence to a teacher and to a member of the food service staff.

PERSONAL

- Parents — Alan and Charlotte York (Estranged)
- Note: Charlotte York lives in Sydney, Australia, and has virtually no contact with her ex-husband or daughter.

At first York seemed to purposely avoid my gaze, turning away. Then, as if he suddenly became conscious of what he was doing, he *forced* himself to meet my eyes to appear trustworthy.

In my gut, I felt that he knew more than he was saying—but my wife interrupted my questions. She objected to the interrogation. Said York had been with her, helping her, for hours, and she didn't like my suspecting him of anything. Clearly, in the few hours I had been away from my wife, this joker had duped her, won her confidence. I decided to back off and apologize to York for Teri's sake. I figured I was more than a little paranoid, and although I still didn't like the guy, I didn't want to take out my acute anxiety on a possibly harmless man.

It was around that time that I took Teri aside. I told her what I suspected. That Kim might have been kidnapped as part of a plan to assassinate David Palmer. Because I was one of the agents assigned to protect Palmer, I assumed someone was trying to get to me through her.

For the first time, my wife understood that Kim wasn't simply missing—she was in great danger, and she was very likely being held by an assassin. The news hit her hard. She broke down. . . . I did, too. . . . We held on to each other, and I remember telling Teri that I knew this was all happening because of my work (pause) because of *me*. . . .

CHAIRMAN FULBRIGHT: (After a pause) Agent Bauer?

BAUER: You have to understand where my head was at, Mr. Chairman. It was very hard for me to accept that this was happening at all, let alone because of me. When I began working for the government, I knew that I would have to deal with some of the most ruthless and brutal elements in our global society. But I had convinced myself that I was smart enough, stubborn enough, and mentally strong enough to shield my wife and daughter from it. I even thought I could protect them from the very *knowledge* of it.

For years, I had successfully put a wall up between my work and my family. Holding on to Teri for those brief moments, I finally admitted to myself, and I suppose to her, that the wall was crumbling down, and no matter what I did . . . no matter how I tried, I was afraid I couldn't do a thing to stop it.

REPORTER'S NOTE:
According to the separate testimony of Jack's daughter, Kimberly Bauer, during this same time period she was driven to a secluded compound where she witnessed a murder.

KIMBERLY BAUER: The man who took me—Gaines—he finally opened the trunk, and I sat up to see him walking over to Rick and Dan. I held my breath when he mentioned Janet's name. His words were something like "My people say someone fitting the girl's description was taken to a hospital near where you were. How do you explain that?"

Then Dan said, "Well, the thing is . . . maybe she wasn't quite dead. . . ."

Gaines was real calm. All he said back was, "Well, Dan, I'll tell you. You're either dead or you're not. There's no such thing as being sort of dead. Here. Let me show you."

Then he took out his gun and shot Dan *dead*!

I screamed even though tape was covering my mouth. I could tell Rick was stunned, too, you know. Really stunned. Gaines turned to Rick at that point and said, "You've just been promoted."

Then Gaines untied me and let me get out of the trunk. He brought me over to Rick, put a shovel in his hands, and told him to bury his friend. Then he left me there.

Of course, the first thing I thought about was how to *escape,* but I looked around and saw that the whole compound was surrounded by a high chain-link and razor-wire fence, plus there were guards with automatic rifles pacing back and forth. There was zero chance of me getting out of that place without help. So I tried to get Rick on my side. I knew he liked me, and I knew he wasn't like Dan. He'd stuck up for me, and now he had a reason to hate Gaines, too.

I told Rick, "Hey, Gaines killed your friend Dan, and he's probably going to kill you, too." I made him realize that he was in just as much danger as I was. Rick got angry, but I kept at him. I even picked up a shovel and helped him dig the grave for Dan. Eventually I wore him down and convinced him that we had to stick together and find a way to get the hell out of there.

Rick finally started to let his guard slip. He came clean with me and admitted that he thought he and Dan were only being paid to hang out with me and Janet. No one was supposed to get hurt, and he never wanted to leave Janet in the street like that.

I knew he was telling the truth. I also knew I could trust him to help me escape. It made me feel better, *stronger*, so when Gaines came to take me to the house, I wasn't afraid anymore—I was back to being *pissed*.

JACK BAUER: I heard the doctor say Janet was on her way to a full recovery. That meant I could question her about Kim. The doctor was worried about me upsetting her, but he agreed provided Janet's "father" was okay with it. I could see I had put the man on the spot. With some reluctance, he said he'd allow me to ask Janet a few questions. His only condition was that he check her first, in private, to see if she was up to it.

REPORTER'S NOTE: Around this same time, Janet York pulled through her surgery at St. Mark's Hospital and was regaining consciousness. . . .

As you might have guessed, I never got to see Janet York. My cell phone rang. It was Ira Gaines, although I didn't know that at the time. It was just a man's voice, coolly threatening to kill Kimberly if I didn't do what he said.

He told me to back away from my wife without alarming her. I did my best to smile and pretend I was having trouble with the cell reception. Then I left the hallway. Apparently Gaines was watching my every move from the hospital security cameras—federal agencies are still investigating to determine who Gaines paid off for access.

He directed me to the hospital parking lot and then into a waiting car. He gave me some more instructions, but I refused to follow any of them until I knew my daughter was safe. That's when I heard Kim's voice. She said she was okay and assured me—that they hadn't hurt her.

I knew I had no choice now. Until I could figure out their strategy, I had to do what Gaines told me to. Inside the glove compartment was an electronic earpiece. I put it inside my ear. Then Gaines ordered me to throw my cell phone out the window and drive toward the CTU office. I did.

REPORTER'S NOTE:
Teri Bauer's debriefing statements explain what happened once Jack left her standing in the hospital hallway. . . .

TERI BAUER: I watched Jack walk away from me and something seemed very wrong, you know? I remember this blackness settling over me . . . it was so disturbing . . . but I was tired and upset, and I told myself to ignore it. Jack had smiled at me as he backed away, and I told myself everything was okay, that he'd be right back. . . . But he didn't come right back.

Alan came out from seeing Janet and said he'd asked her about Kim for us. She told him that they were partying with some boys who got too aggressive. York showed me an address in Bel Air he'd written down. He said Janet told him that's where Kim was.

I was emotionally and physically exhausted, you know? And I wanted to believe it was that easy to find my daughter. So I began calling into the hospital corridors for Jack. But he was gone.

My daughter's safety was at stake, and I wasn't about to waste time. York said Janet was sleeping soundly, and he offered to drive me to that address himself. I agreed.

As we started driving, I remember seeing a bloody scratch on his wrist. I asked him about it, and he said he'd gotten the injury hours before—but it looked fresh to me, and I remember thinking *again* that something wasn't right.

Jack had told me that calling the police might endanger Kim. This whole Palmer assassination thing was beyond me, so I decided to let Jack handle the police part of things. From the car, I tried calling Jack again and again, but for some reason he wasn't picking up, so I left a message.

Then my cell rang, and it was Nina Myers at CTU. She said she couldn't raise Jack and asked me to give him a message if he called me. She said there was a murder victim that Jack had asked her to identify. I'll never forget what she said next—"Tell him the victim's name is Alan York."

I was speechless. I prayed I'd misheard her—but I hadn't. "Alan York," she repeated. "An accountant from the Valley. I'll give Jack details when I speak to him."

As I hung up I felt a tremor run through my entire body. The man driving the car—the man I'd spent the last six hours with—was *not* Alan York. We were headed into the canyons. By now the sun was coming up. My heart was racing. I knew I was in danger. I just had to get out of that car. . . .

FROM THE POLICE BLOTTER . . .

FATHER MISSING, DAUGHTER DEAD

Alan W. York, 42, an accountant with the San Fernando Valley firm of Williams and King, was reported missing yesterday afternoon by his brother, Joseph G. York, 38, of Silver Lake.

Joseph York called his older brother's Santa Monica home repeatedly when he failed to show up for their weekly golf game at 7:00 A.M. Mr. York then drove to his brother's home to find his brother's bathroom splattered with blood and no sign of either his brother or his niece, seventeen-year-old Janet York, a sophomore at Santa Monica High School. Mrs. Alan York is divorced from her husband and resides in Australia.

Joseph York notified the LAPD, whose further investigation uncovered Janet York's whereabouts. After being hit by a car in North Hollywood the night before, she had been transported by ambulance to St. Mark's Hospital for emergency surgery. Hospital records show that Ms. York pulled through the operation but expired under mysterious circumstances shortly before sunrise.

The LAPD is investigating the disappearance of a man who claimed to be her father, waited while she was in surgery, then visited with her in private once she was conscious. According to Joseph York, who spoke to Dr. Susan Y. Collier on the St. Mark's staff, the man's description was nothing like that of Janet's real father, Alan.

Wanted for questioning, this unidentified man was the last person to see Janet York alive. The LAPD later told reporters

FROM THE POLICE BLOTTER . . .

REPORTER'S NOTE:
According to a later autopsy report, Janet York was suffocated to death in her hospital bed. Tissue beneath her fingernails was later matched to Kevin Carroll, the man claiming to be her father, Alan York.

DECLASSIFIED

REPORTER'S NOTE: The following testimony by federal agent Jack Bauer covers the events that occurred between 6:00 A.M. and 7:00 A.M. on the day of the California presidential primary.

6:00 A.M.–7:00 A.M.

REP. PAULINE P. DRISCOLL, (D) CONN.: So Alan York was dead, and your wife had been driving around all night with . . . what was his name again? (Papers shuffling) I know we have some CTU profiles on the people working with Gaines—

SPECIAL AGENT JACK BAUER: Kevin Carroll. Ex-DEA.

KEVIN CARROLL

AGE: 43

CRIMINAL ACTIVITIES
- Suspected of shaking down drug gangs in South Central Los Angeles
- Implicated in 1999 shooting death of LeRoy James Tyson, street name "Chico." Never charged.

EXPERIENCE
- Special Agent, Drug Enforcement Agency, Division of the County of Los Angeles, 1998
- Federal Liaison, Drug Enforcement Agency, Dade County Drug Enforcement Task Force, 1996
- Agent, Drug Enforcement Agency, Miami/Dade County Division, 1993

EDUCATION
- Bachelor of Science, Law and Criminal Enforcement, University of South Miami

MILITARY
- Staff Sergeant, U.S. Army First Infantry Division

PERSONAL
- Divorced
- Ex-wife — Cynthia Jean Carroll
- Sons — Kevin Carroll, Jr., Brian Carroll

FROM THE DESK OF
MARC CERASINI

SUBJECT: JAMES SOFER

James Sofer, a retired Drug Enforcement Agency official, agreed to comment on Kevin Carroll for this publication. Sofer was superintendent of the Miami/Dade County Division for two years, from 1993 to 1995, and was Kevin Carroll's immediate supervisor. He remembers his former agent well, if not fondly. "There was something wrong with Carroll from the start. He was one of those guys who watched too many episodes of *Miami Vice* growing up. He thought narcotics agents all drove Jaguars, wore designer clothes, and took off on undercover assignments to Colombia and Marseilles. A lone cowboy, and a dumb one, too."

Richard Reed, a retired field agent in the Miami/Dade Division, also had some choice memories of working with Carroll. "He was always pushing to go to the guns on a raid," recalls Reed. "I probably fielded more discharged firearms reports working with him than anyone else. Kevin always did things the hard way. The trouble with Kevin was that he was never as smart as he thought he was, so he screwed up everything he got near—even his marriage to Cindy. He messed that up by screwing some Cuban stripper who worked the Dade County joints under the stage name Fuego. I don't know what happened to him after he transferred."

Repeated requests made by this reporter to the Los Angeles Division of the Drug Enforcement Agency for more information about Agent Carroll have met with dead ends. As of this writing, all federal records of Kevin Carroll's career with the DEA have been sealed.

Public records such as court documents filed in Los Angeles County reveal that while working at the Los Angeles Division of the DEA, Carroll was also recruiting low-level criminals to work for Ira Gaines, his associate in the attempted assassination of David Palmer and the kidnapping of Jack Bauer's wife and daughter.

DRISCOLL: Oh, yes. Your wife, I understand, pretended to be ill, had him pull the car to the side of the road, then tried to get away from him.

BAUER: That's correct. She dialed my cell for help, but Gaines had ordered me to ditch it. She was afraid to call the police because I'd told her it might jeopardize Kim's life. So Teri called CTU. Unfortunately, Jamey Farrell took the call. And Jamey, as we now know, was a mole for Ira Gaines.

My wife gave Jamey her location—Mulholland Drive. Jamey, of course, pretended she would be sending agents to help. Instead she contacted Gaines, who sent two thugs to abduct her, and along with Kevin Carroll, they drove her to the Gaines compound in the North Valley where they were already holding Kim.

REP. ROY SCHNEIDER, (R) TEX.: And where were you at this point, Agent Bauer?

BAUER: Gaines had forced me to drive back to CTU. His concern at that moment was the incriminating key card. He wanted me to switch it with a counterfeit card.

SCHNEIDER: And you successfully switched these cards, is that correct?

BAUER: Yes. Jamey Farrell had been stalling the decryption process on the card for hours. When I was with my wife at St. Mark's Hospital, Nina pulled Jamey off the job and called in Milo Pressman, an approved contractor.

DRISCOLL: Excuse me, a contractor, did you say? What sort?

BAUER: Milo worked for CompuShield, which recruits out of Stanford. It's a bonded company under contract with CTU for consul-

MILO PRESSMAN

AGE: 24

EXPERIENCE

- CTU, Security Systems Consultant, Los Angeles Domestic Unit
- CompuShield Advanced Security Systems, Staff Analyst

EXPERTISE

- Network security specialist; decryption specialist; proficient in Infoserve technologies, Python, Java, C/C++, Perl, LISP, and HTML

EDUCATION

- Master of Science, Computer Science, Stanford University
- Bachelor of Science, Mathematics, University of Michigan, Ann Arbor

PERSONAL

Single

tation and support personnel when needed. It's the same company Scott Baylor worked for before Walsh offered him a full-time analyst's position at CTU. Milo is an expert in encryption.

DRISCOLL: Okay, so let me get this straight. Nina Myers not only informed your wife that Alan York was dead, but she also worked to speed up the decoding of a key card that would incriminate Jamey Farrell and Ira Gaines and possibly reveal details of the Palmer assassination plan. Is that correct?

BAUER: Yes, it is.

DRISCOLL: Well, I just don't understand that! It makes no sense! I mean, if Nina Myers was working to help the Drazens, then what in the world was her motivation for these actions?

BAUER: It does make sense if you know the typical tactics that covert operatives use to achieve their goals.

CHAIRMAN FULBRIGHT: Enlighten us then, please, Agent Bauer.

BAUER: Think of the Drazen gang as a terrorist cell. Cells have many members, and each member plays a part in pulling off a terrorist attack. But only a few members in a cell know the basic plan. And only one, the leader, knows *all* the details of that plan. That way, even if one or two members of a cell are captured and reveal all they know, what each one is actually capable of disclosing is really very limited.

SCHNEIDER: You're talking about an operation where each member works on a "need to know" basis, is that right?

BAUER: That's right. Often the identities of other members are withheld—revealed only on a need-to-know basis. Only the leader may know the identities of *all* the members. Again, this is done for security purposes.

DRISCOLL: And you believe that's what happened here?

BAUER: Yes. I believe that only Victor and Andre Drazen knew *all* the details of their two plans and, with maybe a few exceptions, the identities of all the people working for them. Most of the others, including high-level operatives like Ira Gaines and Kevin Carroll—and even Nina Myers—were most likely kept in the dark regarding the bigger picture. Gaines was hired help. It's fairly clear that Andre contacted him first. Then Gaines hired Kevin Carroll, who recruited Rick and Dan to kidnap my daughter.

FULBRIGHT: So who *did* Nina Myers work for?

BAUER: She still refuses to talk, Mr. Chairman. But if you've already reviewed the report I filed about the events on this day, then you know that near the end of it, close to midnight, Nina Myers confessed to me that she did not work for the Drazens—

SCHNEIDER: It *is* possible she was lying when she confessed that.

BAUER: No. She confessed it as I held a gun to her head. She traded her life in that moment for the one thing she had—information. I believed her then, and I believe her now.

DRISCOLL: Then what is your theory on Myers?

BAUER: Nina Myers did not work for the Drazens directly. Her services as a deep-cover mole were "on loan" to Victor and Andre by her superiors, whoever they are. I think that the (pause) *creature* we call Nina Myers was trained by an intelligence service hostile to our nation—one that she claimed shared common interests with the Drazens.

SCHNEIDER: So how did Nina Myers fit into the attempt on David Palmer's life?

BAUER: Frankly, she may not have fit into that plan until much later in the day. As I said, if the Drazens were using Nina on a need-to-know basis, then it's likely that their overall plan was not known by Nina at that point. It was only *after* their first plan fell apart and Jamey was out of the picture that they turned to Nina for greater help inside CTU.

I believe that Nina was working hard to appear as if she was doing her job and doing it well. By identifying the corpse in the trunk, for example, she made us all believe that she was efficient, loyal, and on top of her duties at CTU—she was the perfect deep-cover mole. I'm sure she believed she had nothing to lose by revealing York's identity to Teri, because she was never told how that name connected with Gaines or his plan.

As for her other actions, she was mostly concerned with what *I* was working on, doing, and thinking. I get the impression she'd been asked to stay very close to me, to be aware of my every move . . . which leads me to the staged execution—

SCHNEIDER: Over Baylor's key card. Is that right?

BAUER: Yes. Jamey had already told Gaines we had the card. So Gaines ordered me to switch it with a fake one and then to leave CTU. The man was controlling me with an earpiece, so I tried to write out an SOS. But Gaines was watching from CTU's security cameras. They were everywhere in our facility, and he'd patched into them—

SCHNEIDER: Jamey Farrell set that up, right? She was the one who gave Gaines access to the cameras?

BAUER: That's right. Agent Tony Almeida heard her confess it.

FULBRIGHT: We're aware of Agent Almeida's role here. In fact, we have him scheduled to testify tomorrow. Please continue describing your own actions.

BAUER: Nina had been supervising the decryption process with Milo. After I switched the cards, the two of them quickly figured out what I had done, and she confronted me in my office. She threatened to call Division if I didn't turn the original card over. Whether she planned to sabotage the card herself or was continuing to protect her image as a good agent, I don't know. Either way, it's clear she had no idea I was acting on the orders of Drazen's man.

At that point, Gaines was watching. He assumed Nina was about to blow the whistle on me, so he kept screaming in my ear to take care of this or my daughter was dead. I knew I had no choice. I pulled a weapon on Nina. Through the earpiece, Gaines told me to get her out of the building.

At that point my mind was searching for a way to protect Nina, so I took her over to the locker in my office and slipped a jacket on her to hide the weapon I had at her back. I took the opportunity to slip an armored flak jacket on her first. I walked her outside to my car. Tony stopped us on the way. When he asked where we were headed I lied, telling him we were en route to a meeting. Gaines gave me instructions about where to go. He also had a couple of thugs waiting in another car with a remote camera pointed at me for insurance. They followed. We parked in an empty industrial area. Under Gaines's orders, I took Nina out of the car and shot her. I had no choice. He said he would end Kim's life if I didn't kill Nina. I also knew that if I didn't shoot Nina myself, the thugs in the other car *would*—and they were more likely to put a bullet in her *head.*

I was careful to hit the flak jacket. I also made sure to shoot her near the edge of an embankment and to give her a push. My hope was that when Nina fell down the ravine, the men in the second car wouldn't even bother to get out and confirm she was dead.

I was right. They didn't. Gaines believed the images he saw from their video camera and instructed me to drive away.

SCHNEIDER: Of course, we know Myers didn't die. But how did she get back to CTU?

BAUER: Tony can tell you more about that.

DRISCOLL: (After a pause) Agent Bauer, I'm sorry to belabor this, but I'm *still* confused. Gaines worked for Drazen. Nina Myers also worked for Drazen, so Myers was no threat. Gaines should have known that. Ordering Myers to be shot seems pointless.

BAUER: Not to Gaines. To Gaines, Nina appeared to be just another

CTU agent—one who had stumbled upon his plan. So he had me eliminate her. And yes, Nina Myers worked for Drazen—but only on loan. Her primary job was to supply intelligence to some other entity, some other employer. She wasn't supposed to jeopardize her position in CTU by breaking protocol or looking suspicious. *Nina's* job—at *that* point in the day—was to watch Jamey. She was Drazen's eyes inside CTU. Gaines never knew she existed.

DRISCOLL: Okay, I'm getting it. Drazen used Nina to spy on his own spy. Is that right?

BAUER: Yes. Spies and informants often have a deep-cover mole nearby watching them so they don't jump sides again and become double agents . . . so they can be eliminated before they break, like Jamey Farrell was.

It's also fairly clear that Drazen's modus operandi was to have redundancies—backup plans and reserve personnel. Nina was Drazen's insurance.

DRISCOLL: Very troubling, Agent Bauer. You describe a world of treason and back stabbing that I find perplexing.

BAUER: Unfortunately, ma'am, it's the world we live in.

DRISCOLL: I find something else troubling here—your actions. You entered CTU on false pretenses at the behest of a potential presidential assassin. You stole crucial evidence in the form of an encrypted key card from an employee. You kidnapped another employee, drove her to a remote location, and shot her at point-blank range—though I'll grant that you shot Ms. Myers after you provided her with an armored flak jacket.

BAUER: That's all true, ma'am. But I was desperate to save my family. And I also knew these same people wanted Palmer dead. I believed I could take control of the situation once I got to Gaines.

FULBRIGHT: Agent Bauer, may I remind you that you shot Nina Myers on *orders* from Ira Gaines.

BAUER: Sir, I regret most of the things I had to do in that twenty-four-hour period. But shooting Nina Myers is something I would be happy to do again.

FULBRIGHT: All right, Agent Bauer, that's enough for today. We're adjourned.

7:00 A.M.–8:00 A.M.

CHAIRMAN FULBRIGHT: Agent Almeida, please rise and raise your right hand.

REPORTER'S NOTE: The following testimony by federal agent Tony Almeida covers the events that occurred between 7:00 A.M. and 8:00 A.M. on the day of the California presidential primary.

AGENT TONY ALMEIDA: Yes, Mr. Chairman.

FULBRIGHT: Do you solemnly swear that the testimony you are about to give this subcommittee is the truth, the whole truth, and nothing but the truth so help you God?

ALMEIDA: I do.

FULBRIGHT: Agent Almeida, you may consider yourself under oath. Please be seated. For the record, state your name and occupation.

ALMEIDA: My name is Tony Almeida, I'm an intelligence agent working in the Los Angeles Division of the Central Intelligence Agency's Counter Terrorist Unit.

FULBRIGHT: Thank you, Agent Almeida. Between the hours of 7:00 A.M. and 8:00 A.M. on the day of the California primary, you contacted . . . (papers shuffling) . . . Secret Service Special Agent Aaron Pierce and warned him that Jack Bauer was a threat to Senator Palmer's life. Is that correct?

ALMEIDA: That's correct, sir.

FULBRIGHT: You also caught Jamey Farrell in the act of treason and were one of two agents who interrogated Ms. Farrell before she died, is that correct?

ALMEIDA: Yes, sir—the other agent being a traitor herself.

FULBRIGHT: Nina Myers, yes. (Pause) We understand from your written statement that you, like Agent Bauer before you, were involved with Nina Myers on an intimate level. Is that correct, Agent Almeida?

ALMEIDA: Yes, sir. I regret to say that is correct.

FULBRIGHT: And for the record, you had no idea she was a spy—

ALMEIDA: No, sir, I did not. To say it was a *shock* to find out the truth is a gross understatement, I assure you.

FULBRIGHT: Thank you. Now help us, if you can, to fill in some gaps.

ALMEIDA: Certainly.

FULBRIGHT: Agent Bauer has testified that his family was being held hostage and that he was ordered by a mercenary named Ira Gaines to shoot Nina Myers. He was then told to drive to the Santa Clarita power plant where Senator Palmer was about to give a breakfast speech. More specifically, Bauer was instructed to go to a utility closet and assemble a weapon he had smuggled into the power plant. This was to make sure Bauer's fingerprints were left on the weapon. The weapon was then given to an assassin who masked his own prints.

The assassin was able to walk into the power plant breakfast without suspicion because he'd undergone plastic surgery to look like a famous photographer by the name of (papers shuffling) . . .

ALMEIDA: Martin Belkin.

REP. ROY SCHNEIDER, (R) TEX.: Excuse me, Mr. Chairman, but I'd like to ask Agent Almeida if he knows anything more regarding the whereabouts of that unknown assassin yet?

ALMEIDA: We have yet to locate and apprehend him, sir. We have some foreign intel on him as well as leads from the Gaines compound, but that's all at the moment. I'd be happy to provide the CTU profile on him for your records.

FULBRIGHT: Thank you. Now let's go over the events of that time period.

ALMEIDA: Yes, sir. After Special Agent Jack Bauer took Nina Myers out of CTU, I became suspicious and replayed the security camera footage from Bauer's office. I saw that he pulled a weapon on Nina *and* placed a Kevlar vest on her. It was clear he'd taken her out of CTU at gunpoint.

After Jack shot Nina and left the scene, she found her way to a phone and called me. She seemed almost *desperate* to have me put Jamey Farrell on the phone. I walked to Jamey's workstation on the command center floor and overheard her lying to our encryption consultant, Milo Pressman, about Nina's whereabouts. Jamey looked me straight in the eye and told me that she'd just spoken to Nina a few minutes before.

I knew then that I couldn't trust Jamey. I walked away with the phone still in my hand, demanding that Nina tell me what was going on. I told her how Jamey had lied. Nina acted shocked by this. She hesitated and then stated that we could no longer trust Jamey. She said we were probably being watched through our own security camera system.

I sent a car to pick up Nina. By the time she returned, I made

"JONATHAN"

OTHER ALIASES
- "Eric," "Heinrich Raeder," "Dieter," "Martin Belkin"

AGE: Late twenties to mid-thirties
RACE: Caucasian
HEIGHT: 6′ 2′′
EYES: Brown or Green
HAIR: Dark or Blond

BIRTHPLACE
- Central or Eastern Europe, specific country unknown. Mother and sister reside somewhere in Munich, identity unknown.

CRIMINAL ACTIVITIES
- Assassination attempt, U.S. Presidential Candidate Senator David Palmer
- Suspect in failed terrorist attack on the Reichstag, Berlin, Germany, 1999
- Suspect in assassination of CIA operative, identity classified, Munich, Germany

MILITARY/PARAMILITARY TRAINING
- According to German antiterrorist unit GSG-9 (*Grenzschutzgruppe* 9) "Heinrich Raeder" may have trained in secret terrorist camps in Yugoslavia. Known to possess sniper skills. GSG-9 believes "Raeder" was trained by the Dutch sniper and terrorist Jan Van Loos.

MOVEMENTS SINCE PALMER ASSASSINATION ATTEMPT
- Intelligence operatives working for Interpol* believe "Jonathan" returned to Europe after the failed assassination in the United States and may be hiding in Munich, Hamburg, or in Athens, Greece.

sure the corridor and the nearby ITS room—that's the Internal Tech Support room—were dark—

REP. PAULINE P. DRISCOLL, (D) CONN.: "Dark"? What do you mean. No lights?

ALMEIDA: No, no. I mean I arranged it so that no one could observe us from a live camera. I created a ten-minute loop of an empty corridor and fed that recording into the network. Anyone who was tapping into our surveillance cameras would simply see a vacant hallway. I had effectively rendered the cameras inactive.

DRISCOLL: "Inactive." So the cameras were no longer working, is that correct?

ALMEIDA: No, not quite. If I had physically interfered with the cameras, an alarm would have gone off. So I simply relayed the actual recordings the cameras were making directly to Archives, essentially bypassing the live feed. Then I sent the phony images I had created to the live feed so that anyone tapping into our system would see what I wanted them to for that brief period of time. That's what I mean by rendering the cameras inactive. *Inactive* just means that one can't access recorded images off the live feed—they have to go directly to the archival database for them—where they would pretty much meet with a dead end, since accessing the archives requires entry codes that change frequently throughout the day.

DRISCOLL: So the cameras were still running and recording, is that right?

ALMEIDA: Yes.

DRISCOLL: Thank you for explaining that. You *do* realize why I'm asking you about these details.

ALMEIDA: Yes, ma'am. The recording of Jamey Farrell's death in the ITS room was found in our digital archives, and you want to know how. I understand.

DRISCOLL: Please go on.

ALMEIDA: Nina told me that Jack was forced to shoot her because his family was being held hostage, and the people holding Jack's family were behind the assassination plot against Palmer. Nina also said Jack was looking for a mole inside CTU and that Jamey was obviously that mole—

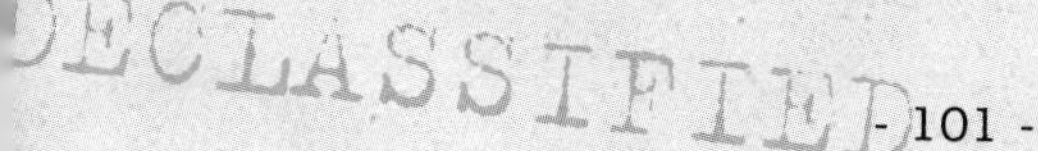

DRISCOLL: (Interrupting) In other words, Nina Myers exposed Jamey Farrell as a traitor and a spy.

ALMEIDA: Yes.

DRISCOLL: Yet apparently Nina was a spy herself and "on loan" to assist the Drazens. Can you tell us why you think she exposed Jamey, given her own apparent intention to assist the Drazens?

ALMEIDA: That's simple. She had no choice. Remember that when she first called CTU, she was desperate for me to hand the phone to Jamey. My guess is that she intended to play Jamey as best she could *without* exposing her. But I had caught Jamey in a cold lie, and I threatened Nina, telling her that she had to tell me what was going on or I would go to our regional director, Ryan Chappelle.

Nina knew I would be a witness to whatever happened next. She *had* to act the part of a trustworthy CTU agent at that point. Fingering Jamey also deflected suspicion away from *her.* Jack was looking for a mole—well *here* was the mole, Jamey Farrell. No reason to look any further.

DRISCOLL: I understand. For Nina Myers it was either give up Jamey or risk her own exposure. No honor among spies, is there, Agent Almeida?

ALMEIDA: No, ma'am. No honor.

FULBRIGHT: Agent Almeida, I understand you and Nina Myers then set a trap for Ms. Farrell. Is that correct?

ALMEIDA: It is. I returned to the command center's main floor and lied to Milo Pressman, making sure Jamey overheard. I told him we got the encrypted key card out of Jack's office, sent it to Archives to make a backup, and would have it back shortly to be fully decoded. Then I returned to the tech room to watch Jamey on the remote camera feed.

Jamey squirmed for a few minutes, then she headed for the rest room. I followed and caught her in the act of trying to communicate with an unknown party through text messaging on a handheld device.

The surveillance cameras in the rest room area are on a twenty-second rotating loop. I drew my weapon and made sure to apprehend her during the brief interval when the camera was not focused on us,

so that her employer would not know she'd been caught.

FULBRIGHT: Where did you take her?

ALMEIDA: To the tech room, where Nina was waiting to confront her. At first Jamey tried to play dumb. But Nina and I threatened her with charges of treason and murder. Richard Walsh and Scott Baylor were dead, and Jack's wife and daughter had been kidnapped. She'd played a part in all these crimes.

Jamey admitted to us that she'd been passing messages, but she would not reveal who her employer was. She then asked for Agency counsel. I was furious. By that time I had already told Secret Service Agent Aaron Pierce that Jack was compromised and that he was a threat to David Palmer. I had put Jack's family in further jeopardy. The only lead I had in helping Jack now was sitting right in front of me. I had to get Jamey to talk.

It was about that time that we noticed a loud commotion ensuing on television. We had been monitoring Senator Palmer's power plant speech, and it appeared that someone was making an attempt on David Palmer's life during that speech. . . .

FULBRIGHT: Agent Almeida, when the assassination attempt failed, Ira Gaines had no reason to keep Teri and Kimberly Bauer alive any longer. Isn't that right?

ALMEIDA: Yes, and according to Teri Bauer's debriefing statements, it was around that time that she and her daughter had guns put to their heads execution style. Gaines made contact via walkie-talkie and stopped the shooters at the last second.

FULBRIGHT: Do you know why?

REPORTER'S NOTE: According to a statement submitted by Secret Service Special Agent Aaron Pierce, after the alert from Tony Almeida he informed all his agents on duty at the Santa Clarita power plant breakfast to treat Jack Bauer as a threat.

One of Pierce's detail, Special Agent Alan Hayes, spotted Bauer and approached him. Bauer reached out, attempting to grab the agent's weapon. The agent yelled, "Gun!" and physically restrained Bauer.

Secret Service agents rushed Senator David Palmer out of the building to a waiting limousine, and Jack Bauer was taken into custody.

FROM THE DESK OF

MARC CERASINI

SUBJECT: JESSICA ABRAMS

At the end of this twenty-four-hour period, the news was finally leaked to the press that Jack Bauer had saved David Palmer's life.

With Bauer suddenly seen as a national hero, Jessica Abrams, an old high school classmate of Bauer's, came forward to give a number of television interviews. It seems Abrams was working as a press assistant on Senator Palmer's campaign staff. On the morning of Palmer's power plant speech, she had approached Bauer, whom she said she saw milling around, waiting for Palmer's speech to begin.

"I was really surprised to see Jack that morning at the power plant. I'd heard he joined the army, then went into some sort of government work, but I never knew what exactly. Anyway, I went over and said, 'Hi!' You know, like 'Remember me? Want to catch up?'

"He seemed really preoccupied, a little nervous even, and I was thinking, Hey, maybe the guy's nervous about seeing ME again. You know? Ha! But clearly he had bigger things on his mind!

"So Senator Palmer started his speech. Then it happened. It was all really intense. Someone at the back of the plant yelled, 'Gun!' Then this herd of Secret Service agents just rushed Palmer out of the room. I looked around for Jack again, but he was already gone."

In one local Los Angeles interview, Abrams was asked what she remembered about attending high school with Bauer. "He was a real hottie back then," said Abrams. "Still is, I think—and he was this real big daredevil, too. Jack raced motorcycles and surfed. He wasn't part of the crowd that counts, but all the girls were really into him."

In that same interview, when informed of Teri Bauer's death, Ms. Abrams expressed concern for Agent Bauer. "Poor Jack. I feel so bad for him, losing his wife and everything. . . . I wonder if he still lives in the area. . . ."

RIGHT: Jessica Abrams, former classmate of Jack and press assistant for the Committee to Elect David Palmer.

ALMEIDA: I have to assume it was because I convinced Jamey to call her employer and tell him that Division had gone to pick up Bauer at the power plant, since he'd been breaking protocol all night.

FULBRIGHT: And how did you convince Jamey Farrell to place that call?

ALMEIDA: Jamey watched the assassination attempt fail on TV right along with us. I reminded her that her boss was looking at the television, too, and that he was going to blame Jack for the screwup and kill his family.

I told Jamey that if she didn't place a call to get Jack off the hook, I would *personally* see her tried for accessory to murder. I assume she realized the only way to keep Jack's family alive was to place that call, so she did.

FULBRIGHT: I think I understand. Gaines needed to believe Jack Bauer wasn't in Secret Service custody, that Bauer was still free. Which meant he still needed Bauer's family alive to manipulate him. Is that about right?

ALMEIDA: It's exactly right.

8:00 A.M.–9:00 A.M.

REPORTER'S NOTE: The following testimony by federal agent Tony Almeida covers the events that occurred between 8:00 A.M. and 9:00 A.M. on the day of the California presidential primary.

CHAIRMAN FULBRIGHT: Agent Almeida, I'd like to get something on record here. According to Jack Bauer's testimony, the assassin called "Jonathan," who got close to Palmer by posing as Martin Belkin, was about to fire a sniper rifle at David Palmer when Bauer went for the Secret Service agent's gun. Do you believe Bauer?

AGENT TONY ALMEIDA: Yes, and it was a brilliant strategy. Jack Bauer knew his family was being held hostage and he couldn't openly interfere with the shooter without risking their lives. In reaching for the agent's gun, he caused enough of a commotion to set the Secret Service into motion, whisking the senator out of harm's way. In effect, he protected his family *and* saved David Palmer's life.

FULBRIGHT: So noted. Now tell us more about your interrogation of Jamey Farrell.

ALMEIDA: She gave up the name of her boss as Gaines and admitted to setting up the surveillance cameras for him inside CTU—

FULBRIGHT: (Interrupting) Wait a moment, Agent Almeida. Sam, where's that profile on Gaines? (Mumbling, papers shuffling) Yes, here it is. Go on, Agent Almeida.

IRA GAINES
AGE: 43

MERCENARY/CRIMINAL ACTIVITIES
- Alleged assassin, Jacques Chabon, Chief Investment Banker, Une Banque des Marseilles, 2001
- Alleged mastermind, San Diego Commuter Bank robbery, 2001
- Alleged assassin, Judge Carlos Novena, Cartagena, Colombia, 2000
- Suspected shooter, Old Town Massacre, Cartagena, Colombia, 1999
- Sniper, Civil War in Zimbabwe, 1997-98

EXPERIENCE
- Hostage Rescue Consultant, Cartagena, Colombia, 1998-99
- Security Consultant, International Business Telecom, Mexico City, 1996

EDUCATION
- Master of Science, Chemical Engineering/Ballistics, Massachusetts Institute of Technology
- U.S. Navy Basic Underwater Demolitions/SEAL (BUD/S)

MILITARY
- Dishonorable discharge, U.S. Navy SEALs, 1995
- SEAL Team Leader, Covert Operations, Colombia, 1994
- SEAL Team, Mexico, 1993
- SEAL Team, Persian Gulf War, 1991

PERSONAL
- Single

FROM THE DESK OF

MARC CERASINI

SUBJECT: IRA GAINES

On condition of anonymity, a retired U.S. Navy SEAL master sergeant and Gulf War veteran agreed to comment for this publication on his service with Ira Gaines.

"Ira was an arrogant prick, but no more than the rest of us," the master chief said with a chuckle. "When you get that Budweiser [slang for the brass eagle, trident, and anchor symbol of the Navy SEALs] pinned to your chest, you have a right to feel like a ten-inch hard-on, but Gaines took it to extremes.

"He was great on a special reconnaissance team, and a good SCUD hunter. For a SEAL, he took to the desert real well, too. The thing about Ira was that he liked to pop hostiles more than he liked finding SCUDs. He must've scored ten or twelve of them—all from four or five hundred yards—with that sniper rifle of his.

"One night Gaines took out a Republican Guard colonel. Blew his head off and knocked the body right off the turret of his armored command car. Trouble was, we were on a no-contact mission, and Gaines compromised us with that shot. Our SEAL team had to exfiltrate before we ever found our SCUD site. NAVCOM [Navy Command] was plenty pissed.

"After the Gulf War, Gaines got his own team. They were transferred to Mexico—drug interdiction duty. Something real bad must've gone down south of the border, 'cause Gaines was thrown out of his team. Do you know what that means? No one, and I mean NO ONE gets tossed out of a SEAL team. Teams are closer than family. That's like your mother divorcing you!"

After Ira Gaines was dishonorably discharged from the SEALs, he took up security work in the private sector. Bobby Laughlin, an ex-marine and hostage rescue specialist, accompanied Gaines on an earlier mission to Mexico. He agreed to go on the record with the following comments.

"Gaines and me, we were on this hostage rescue mission, trying to find some veep from a big multinational corporation. Turns out the guy was nabbed visiting the bad side of MC [Mexico City]. Some underage hooker lured him away from his bodyguards, and the kidnappers snatched him up.

"The multinational contacted us, and we located the guy for them. These Mex kidnappers weren't as smart as some others we'd been up against before. They left a lot of clues. We followed the trail and found their hideout.

"Gaines, me, and a couple of locals busted in, snatched our hostage

(continued)

FROM THE DESK OF

MARC CERASINI

back, and piled him into the backseat of our van for the twenty-minute ride back to Mexico City. Ira was in the backseat with the victim—I figured he was giving the victim the post-rescue talk. 'You're okay now, the ordeal's over, your family's waiting for you, blah-blah-blah.' All of which was true—the guy's wife and kids were waiting.

"But I actually started listening. It turns out that Gaines was shaking the guy down! He said to the guy, 'We know about the teenage prostitute. You don't want your wife to find out, do you? I can hush this up, but it's going to cost you. . . .' Two minutes later the victim's on a cell phone, transferring money to Gaines's personal account.

"What a bastard! He got paid a crapload of money by the multinational to get their veep back, but it wasn't enough for Gaines—he goes and blackmails the victim, too. I wouldn't do it. But you gotta admit, the guy has balls."

ALMEIDA: So we knew Gaines was watching from the active cameras. Because we wanted to kill his tap, but we didn't want him to know we'd caught Jamey, we got her to call Gaines for us. She told him that Milo Pressman, our computer consultant, was getting close to discovering the camera tap she'd set up within the network, and that's why she had to pull the plug. Gaines bought it.

FULBRIGHT: What else did Jamey Farrell confess in that hour?

ALMEIDA: She divulged that she accepted three hundred thousand dollars to provide Gaines with information, claiming that her low pay at CTU was not enough to raise her son as a single parent.

She said she didn't know anyone would get hurt and that I couldn't possibly know how much "pressure" she was under. "Pressure"—that was her excuse. At the time, that answer really ticked me off.

FULBRIGHT: Why? You didn't believe her?

ALMEIDA: I believed she was under pressure, sure. But so are a lot of single parents. *Pressure* . . . we were *all* under pressure at

FINAL ANATOMIC AND FORENSIC SUMMARY

CASE #: 01–180 CLASSIFIED

SUBJECT: Jamey Farrell

CTU FORENSIC PATHOLOGIST: George R. Capaldo, M.D.

CAUSE OF DEATH:
Cardiovascular collapse secondary to massive exsanguination caused by 4 cm. longitudinal laceration of the left radial artery. No evidence of hesitation marks.

MANNER OF DEATH:
Due to surveillance tape—homicide.

LAB TESTS:
Alcohol blood level is: 10 mg/dl.
Corresponding vitreous etoh [alcohol] samples confirm results.*
Further drug tests are negative.

NOTE:
No evidence of superficial electrical burns secondary to videotape evidence of administration of taser, consistent with the insulating effect of the protective overlying clothes.

ADDITIONAL COMMENT:
Although there was no evidence of hesitation cuts, which are often seen in suicide attempts, this is not 100 percent, and the autopsy alone cannot determine manner of death. However, in conjunction with the video evidence, homicide is our final determination.
[*The vitreous fluid of the eyes can have a level that corresponds as a certain multiple of the blood level and lasts longer.]

CTU. It was no excuse for becoming a traitor. Betraying your country, your coworkers, your friends.

FULBRIGHT: Go on, Agent Almeida. What more did she tell you?

ALMEIDA: At that point Jamey refused to say anything else until she got immunity in writing from our regional director, Ryan Chappelle. Well, there was *no way* I was going to contact Chappelle.

IA [Internal Affairs] would have been called in, and who knows who else. We just didn't have the time for a production like that. Palmer was exposed, and Jack's family was in danger. We needed Jamey to tell us everything she knew as soon as possible. It was Jack's idea to have us bring her young son in to CTU. He believed it would create the kind of pressure needed to crack her.

We told Jamey that Kyle was being brought in. We drove home the point that her boy was about to see his mother disgraced—and worse than that, Gaines would probably go after her son once he discovered she was in custody. Logically, he'd use threats against Kyle to prevent her from testifying.

This hit Jamey very hard. It appeared to me as if the full magnitude of what she'd done and the consequences of it were finally beginning to sink in. She asked to be given some time to think about her decision.

Nina and I left Jamey alone in the locked tech room, maybe about ten minutes. I remember that Nina went to the rest room during that period. At the time I thought nothing of it.

When I returned to the tech room with Nina, we found Jamey unconscious, a pool of blood at her feet. She'd been cuffed to a stationary table, but it appeared as if she'd broken a nearby coffee cup and used the sharp shards to vertically slash her left wrist.

Nina called for medics. Jamey was rushed to the hospital, but she died within the hour.

REPORTER'S NOTE: Jamey Farrell's mother, Erica Vasquez, was privately interviewed by CTU Intelligence Agent Tony Almeida after Jamey Farrell died. The transcript of this interview is included in the subcommittee's report: see testimony between the hours of 12:00 noon and 1:00 P.M.

POLITICAL CORRECTION

Pundits and insiders have a few things to say . . .

THREE LITTLE WORDS

By Stanford Shepard

Fox News Anchor

Photo ops with hard hats are about as predictable during campaign season as bitter coffee and stale doughnuts. Candidates like to be seen giving speeches to crowds of working people—because those are the folks who go to the polls. True to form, David Palmer's Santa Clarita power plant breakfast was vintage election-year stumping.

What wasn't so standard, however, was the shout of "Gun! Gun!" that echoed from the back of the room *just before* Palmer was about to *deviate* from a canned speech.

There I was, waiting in the press stable, knee deep in coaxial cable, portable audio tape machines, and reporter's notebooks. I was reading over the preprinted speech Palmer was *supposed* to be giving. I was ready for my live report. And I was genuinely excited.

Yes, it's true, your favorite jaded journalist was excited. Despite the fact that I'd seen it all before (the ubiquitous red-white-and-blue balloons, the prosaic party banners, the crowd of ebullient supporters and skeptical union rank-and-file) I sensed a different kind of charge in the air—and not just because the planners happened to put the press near the plant's massive power generators. We all knew that eleven other states were holding their primaries that day, but the truly righteous buzz was in California, because that's where David Palmer chose to spend his day.

Now, of course, the election year is over. It's the end of December as I write this, and we all know President-elect Palmer annihilated the competition. In January he will take the oath of office and become the first African-American commander in chief in U.S. history.

Last spring, however, on that sunny Super Tuesday, Palmer's big primary day got off to a supremely rocky start.

"Seven years ago . . ."

REPORTER'S NOTE: Fox News anchor Stanford Shepard was one of the many members of the press covering David Palmer's Santa Clarita power plant breakfast on Super Tuesday. In light of the publication of this House Special Subcommittee report, he agreed to provide some commentary and insight into what we now know really happened that day. . . .

POLITICAL CORRECTION

Pundits and insiders have a few things to say . . .

Those were the three little words he spoke just before the word "Gun!" ricocheted through the crowd. Within seconds, Palmer was blanketed with a shield of Secret Service suits and rushed from the building. We all watched as a then unidentified man was tackled and arrested at the back of the crowd.

What a day!

We now know, of course, that those three little words—"Seven years ago . . ."—were supposed to continue—"my son was involved in an accidental death." Palmer would come out with the end of that bombshell sentence later that evening. He would tell us that his son, Keith Palmer, had left the scene of an accident seven years ago. The accident involved a young man named Lyle Gibson.

Gibson had raped Keith's sister, Nicole Palmer, the night that Keith went to see him. According to Keith's testimony to the grand jury that convened that summer to review his case, he had gone to Gibson to convince him to turn himself in. Keith's sister was in a terrible psychological state, and Keith confronted Lyle to see if he could prevent a media circus. Lyle was white. Nicole was black. Lyle was rich. Nicole was the daughter of a prominent politician. Gibson's body was found on a concrete slab below his apartment balcony. His death was ruled a suicide. But Gibson had not committed suicide. He had gone over the balcony in a struggle with Keith.

The scandal that David Palmer was about to announce at the Santa Clarita power plant breakfast was that Keith had not reported the truth to the police seven years before. He had covered it up.

As we all now know, a grand jury cleared Keith. Because Gibson had pulled a knife. The grand jury saw the situation as one of self-defense, not manslaughter, and refused to hand down an indictment. So Keith was exonerated—and the news story about these events eventually ran its course.

But that spring *morning* on Super Tuesday, swilling our stale coffee, none of us knew anything about all that. We, the press, were left to wonder what the hell had happened "seven years ago." We had a hell of a field day with our speculations.

Just hours after the event, rumors spread like wildfire through the print and broadcast journalism community—rumors that continue in newsrooms and back rooms to this day—that a "government conspiracy" existed to have David Palmer killed, perhaps before he continued with whatever the heck happened seven years ago.

Staring at our preprinted speeches, we had no real leads. We were stuck wagging our tongues at the cameras with nothing to say, because no one close to Palmer or in the federal agencies would talk. And if there's one thing journalists hate—more than getting our stories cut from final broadcast—it's being left out of that all-important loop.

The publication of this subcommitee report pretty much opens up that loop to anyone willing to read it. We always knew that Special Agent Jack Bauer was a hero. He's been credited with saving David Palmer's life since the evening of Super Tuesday. What we now know because of this subcommittee's report is *how* he saved Palmer's life—at this breakfast, anyway. (He'd save it again later in the day.)

Busy boy, that Jack!

Bauer went for a Secret Service agent's gun because another assassin—the one that got away, as the saying goes—was waiting in the wings to gun down our next president. Thanks to Bauer, he never got the chance.

This finally clears up the ongoing rumors that a "government agent" was arrested for the attempted assassination of Palmer. A government agent *was* arrested, folks. But this subcommittee report proves he wasn't part of some inside-the-Beltway conspiracy to assassinate Palmer. It was a misunderstanding of supersize proportions.

This subcommittee report also makes some other things clear. Some not so wonderful things. We now know that David Palmer himself didn't mind ordering another fellow be placed in front of the business end of a gun barrel. That fellow was, of course, Victor Drazen. (If you doubt me, read over the testimony between the hours of 2:00 P.M. and 3:00 P.M.)

Drazen was admittedly a loathsome, genocidal nut job (to use the technical term), but it's worrisome that our next president cut so many legal corners to have him wacked. (The three little words in this case would clearly be: *Kill Victor Drazen.*) I mean, what are we, a nation of laws or an HBO mob family?

The other bone I've got to pick has to do with the scandal involving Palmer's son, Keith. Now, I know the public is supersick of the KP story. Once it broke that evening on Super Tuesday, it played on television, in newspapers, and on the Internet 24/7 through the rest of the spring, all summer, and part of the fall. I tell you, folks, even *we* got sick

POLITICAL CORRECTION

Pundits and insiders have a few things to say . . .

of reporting on it—I mean, there are only so many angles to a story. I admit, this one had about five or six hundred, but exhausting them was inevitable. We played it out; we moved along.

What is *not* known by the public, however, is how a respected cable news reporter got the stuffing scared out of her that Super Tuesday afternoon by some political thugs who didn't like the fact that she was *about* to break the Keith Palmer story—yes, the very one David Palmer broke himself in a speech at 6:30 P.M. that same day.

I'm talking about Maureen Kingsley. Forgive me, Maureen, but the First Amendment truth is that your life was threatened, and you quit your broadcast job because of it. I say this now because the assumption in the journalism community for months has been that Maureen pushed a false story and was fired by her network.

NOT TRUE.

Maureen had the Keith Palmer story cold in the wee hours of Super Tuesday morning. But then her one source (Dr. George Ferragamo, Keith's therapist) died mysteriously in a fire, which also destroyed all his files—and the piece of physical evidence that Maureen held mysteriously vanished.

From a source close to Maureen (that would be me—her longtime friend and colleague), I understand that David Palmer tried to talk to her that day, but Maureen wouldn't listen, believing that he was behind the thugs threatening her. When Palmer appeared on TV that evening, however, Maureen *did* listen, and she knew then that David Palmer had nothing to do with what had happened.

Palmer had confessed the not-so-pretty truth about Keith, Nicole, and his duplicitous financial backers to hundreds of millions of Americans, and for all he knew, he'd made himself textbook unelectable.

Maureen's faith was restored. Unfortunately, her boss's faith wasn't so easily recovered, and she has yet to find another broadcast job. Now that all this has come to light, I think Fox News should find a suitable position for her on one of its nightly reports. What do you think, Mr. O?

Three little words for you: *Hire Maureen Kinglsey.*

REPORTER'S NOTE: The following forensic summary was presented to the grand jury convened last summer to review the manslaughter charges against Keith Palmer. As the summary shows, Lyle Gibson, nineteen, the son of prominent Baltimore attorney Franklin Gibson, died from injuries sustained during a fall. Crime scene investigators confirmed that Gibson fell from the balcony of his fifteenth-floor Harbor Towers apartment. Additional injuries found on Gibson were consistent with Nicole Palmer's statement that she fought him off before he raped her. Physical evidence confirmed his rape of Nicole. According to sources who knew Gibson, he was known to be aggressive with young women and also known to flash a switchblade at parties. This is consistent with Keith Palmer's claim during the grand jury hearing that he had "pulled a knife."

12

AUTOPSY REPORT

MARYLAND DEPARTMENT OF HEALTH
VITAL STATISTICS

I performed an autopsy on the body of ➡

at the DEPARTMENT OF CORONER

CASE #:
J202-728

NAME:
Lyle Gibson

From the anatomic findings and pertinent history I ascribe the death to:

Complications of major head and body trauma sustained from a fall

MANNER OF DEATH: Indeterminate, Accidental vs. Homicide

FINAL ANATOMICAL DIAGNOSES:
1. Skull fracture (vertex) with associated basilar fracture.
2. Associated contrecoup contusions, without coup contusions.
3. Multiple fractures of bone and cartilage throughout body: bilateral extremities, significantly: upper and lower, sternum, ribs, cervical, thoracic and lumbosacral spine.
4. Marked traumatic damage to the associated visceral organs.
5. Very recent scratches of the arms and face.

LAB TESTS: Negative for etoh [alcohol] and drugs.

NOTE: The presence of contrecoup brain lesions without associated coup lesions is consistent with a fall rather than another type of blow (although not an absolute rule). The damage, overall, is very consistent with a fall. The more important question is whether the fall was accidental or not. The marks of an altercation, i.e., the scratches, were made very recently before death. The skin that was denuded in the scratching of the face and arms may be able to be DNA typed, if obtained from under a suspected assailant's fingernails.

9:00 A.M.–10:00 A.M.

REPORTER'S NOTE: The following testimony covers the events that occurred between 9:00 A.M. and 10:00 A.M. on the day of the California presidential primary.

CHAIRMAN FULBRIGHT: Agent Bauer, before continuing with your testimony for *this* hour, let's review a few of your actions between 8 A.M. and 9 A.M.

SPECIAL AGENT JACK BAUER: Yes, sir, what would you like to know?

FULBRIGHT: According to your written chronology, you were taken into custody by the Secret Service at about 8:00 A.M. And you *escaped* their custody at around 8:10 A.M. Is that correct?

BAUER: (Pause, papers shuffling) Yes, sir, that's the correct chronology.

REP. ROY SCHNEIDER, (R) TEX.: Good Lord, that's faster than Houdini!

FULBRIGHT: (After muffled laughter from other committee members) What happened next, Agent Bauer?

BAUER: I ran out of the power plant and onto the highway. I hijacked a car, demanding that the woman driving it, a waitress named Lauren Proctor, take me to a deserted construction site nearby, where from about 8:15 A.M. to almost 9:00 A.M. I took cover in a trailer and phoned—

REP. PAULINE P. DRISCOLL, (D) CONN.: (Interrupting) You took a woman *hostage*?

BAUER: Ma'am, I assure you, I never intended to harm Ms. Proctor, and I fully intended to turn myself in when my family was safe and I had found the people determined to assassinate Palmer.

FULBRIGHT: Just a moment, please. . . . (Mumbling) Sam, do we have a statement from Ms. Proctor? (Papers shuffling) . . . All right, let's see . . . Ms. Proctor says for the record that Jack Bauer did not harm her in any way, and he was, quote, "for the most part quite polite," end quote. She also says, quote, "Jack even spoke to the police to help clear up the reason for my absence in court that day, which I appreciated," end quote. Do you know what that means, Agent Bauer?

BAUER: (Soft laughter) Yes. It means the DA dropped the DUI charge against her.

FULBRIGHT: Oh, I see. Well . . . apparently, after Ms. Proctor learned of your part in saving David Palmer's life, she told the Los Angeles District Attorney's office that she was, quote, "happy and *proud* to help Jack Bauer in any way possible," end quote. Apparently Ms. Proctor saw no reason that you should be charged with anything criminal, Agent Bauer. All right, that's that. Go on with your testimony. What did you do while you were hiding at the construction site?

BAUER: I contacted Nina Myers. *At the time,* I was relieved to hear Nina's voice—to know she was all right after I'd shot her. Tony Almeida was nearby when I called, and he expressed concern for my situation. They both agreed to help me. Nina had a car with a briefcase of technical equipment sent over for me. While I waited for it to arrive, I worked myself free of my handcuffs.

I got into the car just before 9:00 A.M. and for most of the next hour did my best to elude the Secret Service and LAPD. I used the cell phone Nina sent over with the car and called CTU. I was even able to talk to my wife, who had stolen a cell phone from one of her guards.

Although Milo narrowed Teri's location down, it was still too expansive an area to pinpoint the exact spot, and the phone's battery died before we could find them. Before the signal vanished, though, I heard the guard brutalizing my wife and daughter. . . . I wanted to kill him.

FULBRIGHT: (After a pause) Agent Bauer, let's move on. Tell us about Ted Cofell.

BAUER: Ted Cofell . . . (Papers shuffling) . . . Ted Cofell was the only major lead I had after I'd escaped from Secret Service custody. Tony Almeida found an e-mail on Jamey's computer. The only thing not encrypted was the name Ted Cofell. Milo Pressman worked on decrypting the rest of it and eventually found information regarding a one-million-dollar wire transfer to Gaines from a Swiss bank account at 2:10 A.M.—

SCHNEIDER: (Interrupting) Any significance to that time that you know of?

BAUER: Yes. Let me just check my notes. (Papers shuffling) . . . Here it is. After Gaines received the one-million-dollar payment, he transferred it by wire out of his personal account and into another account. Then, within an hour, that exact same amount was transferred right back into his account. Our CTU analysts decoded and reviewed the encrypted log kept by Gaines—

DRISCOLL: Why would Gaines have kept a *log*?

BAUER: Gaines may have had petty criminals on his payroll, ma'am, but he ran the operation like a military mission. I'm sure the Drazens expected some sort of after-action report from him once the operation was complete.

DRISCOLL: And what possible purpose would *that* serve?

BAUER: An after-action report documents what worked and what didn't. Who on the team did a good job. Who would be used again. And who may have hampered or jeopardized the operation. Remember, this wasn't the first operation the Drazens had overseen, and it wasn't expected to be their last. I'm sure they wanted the intel for their files.

DRISCOLL: I see. Please go on. What was the reason Gaines made that million-dollar transfer?

BAUER: Our analysts believe one of Gaines's accomplices made a demand for more money. The woman he'd used to crash Flight 221—the assassin whose known aliases are "Miranda Stapleton" and "Mandy"—had an associate named "Bridgit" who apparently demanded the extra pay.

The CTU analysts write that they were unable to determine from the log notation exactly what transpired between Gaines, Mandy, and Bridgit during that time at the desert house, but they suspect that Gaines pretended to pay the extra million to Bridgit, then killed her.

FULBRIGHT: All right, so payoffs were being made, and Cofell was a part of that. He was essentially one of the Drazens' money-men, correct?

BAUER: Yes, that's correct. Cofell had a front as a legitimate investment banker in Burbank. When the Drazens needed to make a payoff, they would wire the money from the Balkans to Cofell so it couldn't be traced back to the Drazens. Nina Myers got me the background information on Cofell, as well as an office address, 21500 Riverside Drive.

From the car, I called the man's office and pretended to be an old college friend wanting to see him. His assistant told me that wasn't possible because Cofell was in a meeting and would be leaving the office for a business trip at 10:00 A.M.

I drove to Cofell's office and just missed him going down in an elevator. I pulled the fire alarm to delay his descent. Then I took the stairs to the parking garage in the basement. In the garage, I approached Cofell's driver, showed him my badge, and he backed off. I got behind the wheel of the limo, and when Cofell got into the back, he mistook me for his regular driver, Mark.

I pulled out of the garage and into traffic. . . .

THEODORE "TED" COFELL

AGE: 36

BIRTHPLACE: Philadelphia, Pennsylvania

EXPERIENCE

- Founder and CEO, Cofell Enterprises, Los Angeles, 1997
- Chief Investment Manager, Kurtis, Siebert, and Bates Financial, Boston and Los Angeles, 1990-96
- Investment and Acquisitions Officer, Roccelli and Stevens Banking Associates, New York, 1989-1990

EDUCATION

- Master of Business Administration, UCLA, 1988
- Bachelor of Science, Economics, Colgate University, 1986

PERSONAL

- Married — Krista Heldrun-Cofell
- Son — Theodore Cofell, Jr.
- Daughter — Courtney Cofell

The real Theodore Cofell, SS# XXX-XX-XXXX, was born at Philadelphia Children's Hospital in Philadelphia, Pennsylvania. The only child of Tabitha Cofell, a single mother, Theodore Cofell died before his second birthday, the victim of sudden infant death syndrome. Six months later, twenty-four-year-old Tabitha Cofell overdosed on Valium in her South Philadelphia apartment, an apparent suicide.

The identity of Theodore Cofell next appears in 1982 in Fair Lawn, New Jersey. Supposedly graduating from Fair Lawn Regional High School, he is accepted by Colgate on the strength of a 4.0 GPA and a score of 1572 on his SATs. Graduating from Colgate, he goes on to UCLA and a stellar career in investment banking.

REPORTER'S NOTE: CTU analyst and translator Darinka Brankovich, along with Raymond Gull, a banking regulator for the Securities and Exchange Commission, and Bruno Hecht, formerly an operative of the German intelligence service *Grenzschutzgruppe 9*, have pieced together what they believe to be the true history and identity of Ted Cofell. Though the full analysis is classified, this brief summary of their report was printed in the subcommittee report.

But the "Ted Cofell" who appeared on the Colgate campus for freshman year in 1982—according to secret KGB files recently obtained by Western intelligence services—was a young Serb named Borvo Sobrinna. Born in Vojvodina, he was recruited as a teenager by the League of Communist Yugoslavia after his parents were murdered by ethnic Albanians. He agreed to be trained by the First Directorate of the KGB to become a deep-cover mole within the U.S. financial community.

In the United States, he was placed with a family of Communist sympathizers willing to hide his true identity. After earning a B.S. at Colgate, he entered an M.B.A. program at UCLA. Graduating in time for the collapse of the Soviet Union, Sobrinna shifted his allegiance to the nationalistic Serbian 1389 Movement founded by Victor Drazen. Since then, Cofell has helped to fund the cause of Serb nationalism through his own personal wealth, his firm, and several dummy corporations that funnel money to pro-Serb groups.

10:00 A.M.–11:00 A.M.

REPORTER'S NOTE: The following testimony covers the events that occurred between 10:00 A.M. and 11:00 A.M. on the day of the California presidential primary.

SPECIAL AGENT JACK BAUER: At this point I was still wanted for the attempted assassination of then Senator Palmer. Alberta Green was appointed acting director and took over my office and my staff.

She began to turn up the heat on Tony Almeida as well as Nina Myers, a woman Green had once worked *under* but quickly surpassed in rank within the agency. Alberta presumed that Nina and Tony were in contact with me. She repeatedly asked them to give up my location. Of course, Nina had her own motivation for remaining silent. But I know Tony believed that compromising me would jeopardize the life of David Palmer, so he, too, remained silent.

CHAIRMAN FULBRIGHT: Are you aware, Agent Bauer, that Ms. Green submitted a written statement to the subcommittee?

BAUER: I'm not surprised.

FULBRIGHT: We didn't ask for it, actually, but she *insisted* after learning about this hearing. And I must say, her review of your actions is much, much harsher than that of any of your other colleagues, including even George Mason.

BAUER: Is that right?

FULBRIGHT: She claims she wanted to suspend Tony Almeida for helping you, but she could not find enough "actionable" evidence.

BAUER: Ms. Green does things very much by the book.

REP. ROY SCHNEIDER, (R) TEX.: (Chuckling) And you don't, Agent Bauer, that's pretty clear. You want to maybe give us some insight into that?

BAUER: In my experience, most by-the-book people haven't clocked a lot of hours out in the field. They've clocked a lot behind desks, though—in offices and classrooms. So books give them a nice warm, comfortable feeling inside, most especially rule books.

Don't get me wrong. I'm not saying rules and guidelines aren't

ALBERTA GREEN

AGE: 32

CTU MISSIONS

- None

EXPERIENCE

- CTU, Special Assistant to Regional Division Director
- CTU, Policy Analyst, Regional Division Office
- Senator Weldon Dexter Graham III, Staff Member
- Graham and Hastings, Attorneys at Law, Legal counsel specializing in international law

EDUCATION

- Juris Doctorate, American University Washington College of Law
- Master's in Public Policy, Harvard University, John F. Kennedy School of Government
- Bachelor of Arts, Government, Smith College
- Jean Picker Semester-in-Washington Program, Smith College

PAPERS PUBLISHED

Meridians Journal, "On the Formation of Racial, Social, and Political Consciousness"

American University Journal of Gender, Social Policy & the Law, "Transnationalism and U.S. Immigration Policy"

PERSONAL

- Divorced
- Ex-husband — Weldon Dexter Graham IV

important. They are. But the bad guys don't use them. In my business you measure your success at the end of the day by whether or not you got the job done. And rules don't always get the job done. My job was to make sure an important presidential candidate remained safe and alive. If the rule book can't help me do that, what the hell good is it?

SCHNEIDER: Green is a good bureaucrat and a bad hands-on intelligence director, is that your evaluation?

BAUER: It is, Congressman. But then that's just one man's opinion.

FULBRIGHT: More than one, Agent Bauer. You might be interested to know that Agent Tony Almeida agrees with you, and so does your regional director, Ryan Chappelle. In fact, when Mr. Chappelle approached Agent Tony Almeida and asked him for his criticisms of you at one point during this twenty-four-hour period, Almeida said . . . where is that . . . (Long pause. Papers shuffling) Here it is. And I quote: "I'm not the biggest fan of Jack Bauer . . . but since midnight tonight, you won't get me to disapprove of a single action he took," end quote. That's according to a formal statement Mr. Chappelle submitted to this committee.

BAUER: (After a pause) I appreciate your letting me know that, Mr. Chairman.

FULBRIGHT: You're entirely welcome. Now, let's get back to the events during this hour. You were driving around with Cofell during this time, correct?

BAUER: That's right. Ted Cofell was the only real lead I had. When he realized that his regular driver was not behind the wheel, he reached for his cell phone. I locked the doors, pulled over, and drew my weapon. Cofell feigned innocence for a time, claiming not to know about either Gaines or my family. So I asked Nina to put together an interrogation file on him—

REP. PAULINE P. DRISCOLL, (D) CONN.: (Interrupting) A *what*?

SCHNEIDER: It's personal background information, Pauline, meant to help the interrogator get the interogatee to divulge information. Am I right, Agent Bauer?

BAUER: You're right, Congressman. The trouble was that what Nina read to me over the phone was a profile of Cofell that Cofell himself had worked years to fabricate. He wanted the world to think of him as a high-achieving control freak on whom, as Nina put it, "the threat of pain could be more effective than pain itself."

Now that I look back on Nina's words, it seems to me she knew Cofell's true identity and was trying to keep me from really torturing him. Maybe she was afraid he'd talk if I did. Anyway, the truth about Cofell was that he'd been planted here in the United States as a teenager. He was KGB trained, the son of murdered parents who had a vendetta and political goals in line with Victor Drazen's.

SCHNEIDER: So your interrogation didn't work?

BAUER: No. The man made a good show of being an "ordinary businessman" whom I was terrorizing, but he wasn't the least bit threatened by me. First chance he got he pulled a knife—one he'd hidden in the backseat.

SCHNEIDER: And that proved something to you, Agent Bauer? It seems to me that lots of ordinary men carry knives.

BAUER: It was a Microtech HALO knife, sir.

SCHNEIDER: Oh! (Chuckling) Yes, I see what you mean!

DRISCOLL: Excuse me, but I don't.

FULBRIGHT: Neither do I.

BAUER: The Microtech HALO is a professional's weapon. It's not something an "ordinary guy" would carry. The general public is not even permitted to purchase one. By law, the HALO—like all automatic knives—can only be sold to authorized gun dealers, police officers, and military personnel.

FULBRIGHT: Thank you, Agent Bauer, please continue.

BAUER: He pulled the knife, and I fractured his wrist. The shock and pain of it finally broke his cover. Cofell began cursing at me in *Serbian*, calling me "scum" and "bastard" and telling me to "rot in hell."

Hearing the Serbian language alarmed me. I flashed back on my mission two years before in Kosovo. I continued to press him for information, and he said, "You deserve everything that's happening to you," and, "You will pay." I knew then that this wasn't just about Palmer. This was about me. I began connecting the dots between a

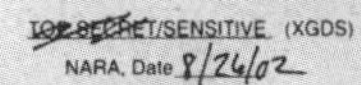

Serbian-speaking man and a plot to destroy my life and realized that only one thing made sense: *blowback.**

FULBRIGHT: (Interrupting) Agent Bauer, I've heard that term associated with covert operations, but I'd like you to define it for the record.

BAUER: Blowback is when some action set in motion during a previous covert mission comes back to haunt you . . . to hurt you. The sins of the fathers visited on the children—or in my case, my wife and daughter.

I knew now that something I had done on a mission in Belgrade or Kosovo had come back to blow up right in my face. And if all this mayhem was Serb related, I knew it had to be Operation Nightfall.

I tried to get more out of Cofell, but he refused to talk. He had a heart condition, and the physical struggle aggravated it. Although I tried to get medicine into him, he refused to swallow it, and he expired in the backseat of the limousine. I tried administering CPR, but he was gone.

I nearly went to pieces. My *only* lead to finding my family had just died, and I didn't know what to do next. I called Nina and told her about my blowback theory. I asked her to look for a link between my field assignment files and Cofell's background, specifically looking at Operation Nightfall, where I was in Belgrade and then Kosovo—

FULBRIGHT: Excuse me, Agent Bauer, but I thought we had your full dossier. (Papers shuffling, mumbling) Sam, I don't see anything in here about Agent Bauer's *field assignment* files—

BAUER: Sir, you must have my CTU dossier. My Delta files are classified.

FULBRIGHT: Oh, I see. Well, we'll want to review them before we make our final report. (Mumbling) Sam, make a note to call Tucker.

FULBRIGHT: Agent Bauer, go on with your testimony.

BAUER: By this time I was parked in an underground garage where Cofell had agreed to a last-minute meeting with a man he claimed was one of his clients, supposedly a machine tool salesman. I prayed the man who was about to show up would know something—*anything*—about the whereabouts of Teri and Kim.

CAPTAIN JACK BAUER,
U.S. ARMY, FIRST SPECIAL FORCES
OPERATIONAL DETACHMENT, DELTA

DELTA MISSIONS
- Operation Nightfall, Kosovo (date and details classified)
- Operation Collegiate, Belgrade (date and details classified) (Special Commendation)
- Operation Downtown, Pristina (date and details classified) (Special Commendation)
- Operation Lost Paradise, Chechnya (date and details classified)
- Operation Closed Coffin, Hac (date and details classified)

MILITARY EXPERIENCE
- Captain, U.S. Army First Special Forces Operational Detachment, Delta
- Instructor, U.S. Army "Q" Course Phase III Training
- Instructor, U.S. Army Special Forces Robin Sage Exercises
- First Lieutenant, U.S. Army Combat Applications Group
- Graduate, John F. Kennedy School of Special Warfare (course curriculum classified)

EXPERTISE
- HALO/HAHO [High Altitude, Low (High) Opening]
- SERE [Survival, Evasion, Resistance, Escape]
- PSYOPS [Psychological Operations]
- DA [Direct Action]
- CA [Civic Action]
- CP/N [Counterproliferation/Nuclear]

MEDALS/HONORS
- Purple Heart
- Silver Star (covert operations/record sealed)

CLASSIFIED

I propped up Cofell's corpse in the backseat, opened the passenger door, raised the bulletproof glass between the driver and passenger areas, and waited behind the wheel, watching through the car's mirrors.

When the man arrived, I felt as though I'd hit the lottery. It was the same scumbag who'd abducted Teri—Kevin Carroll—the man who claimed to be Janet York's father, Alan York.

Since I am under oath, I must *truthfully* admit to you that it got *personal* in those moments after Carroll shut the door and I locked it up tight. This man had abducted my wife and daughter, put them in harm's way, and put me through hell. For a few minutes I honestly remember thinking only one thing: *time for some payback.*

11:00 A.M.–12:00 NOON

SPECIAL AGENT JACK BAUER: The moment he saw me in the driver's seat of Cofell's limo, Kevin Carroll drew his gun and repeatedly fired at the bulletproof glass between us. As soon as Carroll had emptied his gun, I secured my seat belt and took off in the empty garage, driving recklessly to toss Carroll around in the backseat with Cofell's corpse until he was adequately softened up. Although I wanted to shoot the man where he sat, I knew Carroll was the only chance I had of getting to my wife and daughter. I couldn't kill him, but I had to break him—

REPORTER'S NOTE: The following testimony covers the events that occurred between 11:00 A.M. and 12:00 noon on the day of the California presidential primary.

REP. PAULINE P. DRISCOLL, (D) CONN.: Excuse me, Agent Bauer, but did you ever discover why Kevin Carroll showed up in that garage in the first place? You said Cofell claimed he was a "client," but what was his true connection to Cofell?

BAUER: As I've explained, Cofell handled money for the Drazens. He was the launderer, the middle man who made sure no one could trace a payoff directly to the Drazens. Kevin Carroll wasn't very smart. He was Gaines's *muscle,* and I believe Gaines sent Carroll to Cofell to coerce a final payment out of him before Cofell left town.

CHAIRMAN FULBRIGHT: So you think Gaines assumed he wouldn't be given his final payment otherwise?

BAUER: Yes. By 10:00 A.M., it was fairly obvious that Gaines had failed the Drazens. Senator Palmer was still alive. I was on the run, so Gaines no longer had direct control of me. He'd also lost touch with Jamey Farrell, his mole in CTU, so he was flying blind. Andre

Drazen never would have been patient with screwups like that. He'd already set up a Plan B with an international team, and it appears he *fired* Gaines at some point close to noon.

The pay was probably an issue. If Andre Drazen threatened to pay nothing more to Gaines, then Gaines most likely took matters into his own hands, sending Carroll to get the money he felt he was owed. If all else failed, Gaines was the sort to take the money—any way he could—before he ran. That's my best guess, anyway.

FULBRIGHT: Thank you, Agent Bauer. Please continue describing your interactions with Kevin Carroll.

BAUER: I drew my weapon, tied him up, and *convinced* him that he should help me get to my wife and daughter. Then I put Carroll into the backseat of his own car and drove to a compound in the North Valley, east of the 5 and between Tampa and Reseda, where he said I'd find my family.

As we neared the location, I called Nina Myers and asked for her help with satellite images of the area. Gaines had taken over an orange grove. He'd thrown up fencing with razor wire and hired guards to patrol the compound using automatic weapons. The satellite images showed about a dozen people on the ground and a number of outbuildings.

Before we reached the guarded front gate, I put Carroll behind the wheel and held a gun on him from under a blanket in the backseat. The guards recognized him, let him in, and I had him drive into the grove. I then tied him up, drew my weapon, and began to search the area for my family.

When I found Teri and Kim in one of the buildings, I discovered they'd shot the man who had been sent to kill them. One of the boys who'd kidnapped Kim—his name was Rick—had smuggled them the gun. This boy, Rick, then helped us escape. He told me that he had no idea Kim would end up in so much danger. His partner, Dan, was shot by Gaines, and Rick felt he was as much a prisoner as Kim and Teri. Rick did what he could to protect both Kim and Teri while they were being held by Gaines, and I've recommended the kidnapping charges against him be dropped in return for his full cooperation in the federal investigation of these events.

FULBRIGHT: I've reviewed your wife's and your daughter's statements about this boy's actions, and I do agree that he was very brave. However, he is clearly heading down the wrong path with his life. There are drug-related charges pending against him in Los Angeles, and I'm not sure that we want to be too hasty in freeing him from all responsibility for his other actions.

BAUER: I understand, sir.

FULBRIGHT: I'm sure your supportive statements will be taken into consideration in any judgment of his case.

BAUER: I hope so, sir.

FULBRIGHT: Now, I understand you contacted CTU around that time to finally admit your whereabouts?

BAUER: That's correct. I called Acting Director Alberta Green directly and let her know that I'd found the people behind the assassination attempt on David Palmer. I also let her know that they had kidnapped my wife and daughter, which was why I'd avoided custody. But now that I'd found them, I was ready to turn myself in. I just needed backup to be sent to my location.

Alberta Green obliged me, sending three field units by chopper. It took some time for them to get there, and I had to get my family to safety. Gaines and his crew were packing up by that time. They assumed Teri and Kim were dead, and that gave us an advantage.

Rick stole one of their vans and brought it to us. We piled into the van, and I drove through a fence. By then Gaines had found Carroll tied up in his car, and he and his guards saw us trying to escape. A firefight began. Gaines shot out our back tires, so we got out of the van, using it as a shield the best we could. I sent my wife and daughter into the woods with instructions to follow the creek bed to an old abandoned water tower near the service road where we would all meet up. Rick and I stayed behind as long as possible, using our weapons to hold off Gaines and his men. Then I punctured the van's gas tank, and we ran for the woods, too, firing behind us to send the van up in flames.

Unfortunately, Rick took a bullet in his shoulder as we fled, and I soon realized that Teri and Kim weren't at the designated meeting place. They were lost.

REPORTER'S NOTE: The fire-fight at Gaines's compound as captured by perimeter surveillance cameras and incoming CTU choppers.

12:00 Noon–1:00 P.M.

SPECIAL AGENT JACK BAUER: I called Alberta Green to let her know that my wife and daughter were missing and I intended to search the area for them. Green let me know that the CTU field teams were on their way by chopper with an ETA of fifteen minutes. I told her to have them use the water tower as the pickup point.

REPORTER'S NOTE: The following testimony covers the events that occurred between 12:00 noon and 1:00 P.M. on the day of the California presidential primary.

By this time I knew Gaines was searching the woods for me and my family. Andre Drazen would never let Gaines and his crew live if they allowed us to escape. It was kill or be killed—for all of us.

In the woods, Teri and Kim stumbled upon an abandoned cabin and hid inside. One of Gaines's men found them just about the time I did. I shot the man dead and grabbed his walkie-talkie. I could hear Gaines directing his men, so I took care to avoid the areas they were searching.

We came upon a reservoir across from the water tower. There was still no sign of CTU. Gaines fired on us. Knowing that I was the primary target, I headed toward Gaines alone. He pinned me with a constant barrage of rifle fire, but I found a way to distract him long enough to take the advantage. Using a piece of metal refuse I picked up in the woods, I shot a reflective sun glare toward Gaines as he looked through his rifle scope. It blinded him long enough for me to break cover and fire. I grazed him and he ran.

About that time I could hear the CTU choppers overhead. The rest of Gaines's crew had bugged out by then. I followed a trail of Gaines's blood. It was then that Gaines confirmed for me over the walkie-talkie what I had already guessed—he had no other option but to kill me. I asked him about the Belgrade connection and why my family had been brought into it. Gaines told me that the people involved wanted to "make it personal."

I spotted Gaines about then, and coming up behind him, I

demanded that he drop his weapon. I knew he was a very valuable link to the people who hired him. *They* were the people I wanted—and only Gaines could help me get to them. I offered him immunity in return for his help. Instead he said, "Good luck." Then he turned to me and leveled his weapon. He knew what I would do. I had no choice—I shot him dead.

I went back to the water tower to pick up my family. They were happy to see me . . . happy to see that *I* was okay. . . .

CHAIRMAN FULBRIGHT: (After a pause. Mumbling) Agent Bauer, we're aware of the loss of your wife at the end of this day. We know this examination is not easy for you. . . . But can you continue a little longer? We're almost ready for the midday break. Then it's Thanksgiving recess, and we can all get a good week's rest before we resume testimony. Just a few more minutes, shall we?

BAUER: Yes, sir . . . (Pause)

FULBRIGHT: Finish up with that hour then. You were all unharmed at that point?

BAUER: Yes. We—that is, Teri, Kim, and I—all boarded one of the CTU choppers and were flown back to Los Angeles. Some of Gaines's crew, including Kevin Carroll, had escaped, but others were arrested and flown back on other choppers. Alberta Green met us on the landing pad and took me into custody. My wife and daughter were taken to a clinic for medical treatment.

REP. PAULINE P. DRISCOLL, (D) CONN.: Excuse me, Agent Bauer, but you didn't mention that boy, Rick Allen. Was he in the chopper with your family?

BAUER: No. He had fled the scene by the time the choppers came, picking up a bus on the nearby highway.

DRISCOLL: Why did he run? Who was he afraid of?

BAUER: Not *who*. More like *what*.

DRISCOLL: Excuse me?

BAUER: Back when Kim and Teri had run for the woods, and I was alone with Rick at the water tower, he thanked me for helping him. I was glad he'd looked after Kim and Teri, but I reminded him that he was the one who had kidnapped my daughter and that he would have to live with that. I made it clear that some part of getting a second chance was taking responsibility for the mess he'd made in the first place. I know the world's a hard place, but I still can't understand how a kid could defy an armed camp of hired killers yet run like hell when I asked him to answer for his own actions.

REP. ROY SCHNEIDER, (R) TEX.: Oh, there's a one-word answer to that one, Agent Bauer. *Teenager.*

BAUER: Yes . . . I see that streak in my own daughter. (Pause) The thing is, Congressman, Rick was a brave kid. He had his own sense of honor. That's why I'm sorry he made the choice to run.

SCHNEIDER: That's where Gaines had something in common with Rick. Neither wanted to face the music.

BAUER: Yes, Congressman, but Gaines's choice was much more permanent.

FULBRIGHT: And I'd like to add for the record that Agent Bauer had no problem answering for his own actions. Your testimony confirms Regional Director Ryan Chappelle's written statements about that day. You chose to turn yourself over to Acting Director Alberta Green, who placed you under arrest. Correct?

BAUER: Essentially that's correct, sir. Alberta Green wanted the opportunity to question me before turning me over to the FBI.

FULBRIGHT: And you haven't taken the Fifth with this subcommittee, either, which will also be taken into consideration as we assess your part in this day's events.

All right, everyone, let's take a recess for lunch, after which we will hear once again from Intelligence Agent Tony Almeida.

REPORTER'S NOTE: The subcommittee turns again to Agent Tony Almeida. . . .

FULBRIGHT: Agent Almeida, you understand that you are still under oath?

AGENT TONY ALMEIDA: I do, sir.

FULBRIGHT: During this hour, you spoke with the mother of the confessed traitor, Jamey Farrell. Tell us more about that.

ALMEIDA: Yes, sir. If you recall from my earlier testimony, we had brought Jamey's young son, Kyle Farrell, into CTU. When Jamey was taken to the hospital, where she later died, we contacted Jamey's mother to pick up the boy.

FULBRIGHT: And the woman's name, for the record—

ALMEIDA: Erica Vasquez, a naturalized immigrant from Mexico.

DRISCOLL: Excuse me, Agent Almeida, but what is the relevance of her immigration status?

ALMEIDA: It's the reason she finally talked to me, Congresswoman. On the day we brought her in, she refused to say much to Nina Myers and me. She denied any knowledge of Jamey's actions and the source of the money—even though it was obvious, to me anyway, that she knew more. We were forced to arrest her, and Kyle was temporarily placed in a foster home because his father, who lives in Seattle, said he didn't want to "get involved."

Within a week, I approached Erica Vasquez again, this time as a fellow Hispanic. Speaking Spanish I was able to learn much more about how Jamey was turned.

DRISCOLL: You also secured immunity for Mrs. Vasquez after the interview, is that right?

ALMEIDA: It is. She is free now, cleared of all charges, and Jamey's son is back in her care.

FULBRIGHT: As I said, we have the transcript of that interview on record. [A transcript of that interview can be found at the end of this hour's testimony.] Now . . . can you tell us more about the money trail you followed during this hour?

ALMEIDA: Certainly. Before Mrs. Vasquez agreed to talk to me, I pressured her with CTU's revelations. The IRS confirmed she made less than forty-five thousand dollars a year working as a clerk for the MTA [Los Angeles County Metropolitan Transit Authority], yet a bank account in her name showed deposits that added up to more than three hundred thousand.

FULBRIGHT: And what did she say about that?

ALMEIDA: She admitted the money came from Jamey. But that's all she would admit that day at CTU. She claimed she "never asked" where the money came from, and that Jamey simply wanted there to be—quote, "enough money for Kyle if anything happened to her."

FULBRIGHT: I see.

ALMEIDA: At the time, I thought Jamey's words to her mother referred to someone killing her. But during my second interview with Mrs. Vasquez, I understood that Jamey was worried about more than that.

FULBRIGHT: You mean her father's illness?

ALMEIDA: Yes.

FULBRIGHT: It's still no excuse for turning traitor and causing the deaths of innocent people.

ALMEIDA: No, of course it isn't. I agree. I just meant that I get what Jamey was trying to say when she told me I didn't understand the "pressure" she was under. I don't doubt that Gaines leaned on her, and when the heat was turned up maybe the man even threatened her and her family—but there was clearly the added pressure of her father's condition.

FULBRIGHT: Go on, please. Describe what else you discovered.

ALMEIDA: I traced the background of the deposits to Mrs. Vasquez's account. They were made through a bank account in the Cayman Islands controlled by Ted Cofell. We already knew that Cofell was a front for someone else, so that was worthless. We continued to trace those funds. They led us to a holding company called Luca Univox based in Belgrade.

I contacted [NAME OMITTED FOR LEGAL REASONS]. He's a legitimate officer of the [NAME OMITTED] Bank, and also an informant for the CIA. He helped us run a check of account activity on Luca Univox.

As it turns out there was a major transfer of funds that morning to the account of a man in Belgrade who'd been twice charged but never convicted of murder. CTU classified him as a professional assassin—a "usual suspect," so to speak.

FULBRIGHT: Alexis Drazen?

ALMEIDA: Alexis Drazen, we later discovered, was one of the international assassins who had flown into Los Angeles from Yugoslavia—with a detour to Washington, D.C.—but there were two others involved with Drazen's "Plan B," as they called it in their records. Their names were uncovered later in the day.

REPORTER'S NOTE: CTU Intelligence Agent Tony Almeida conducted an extensive interview in Spanish with Mrs. Erica Vasquez four days after her daughter, Jamey Vasquez Farrell, died. A translation of the interview transcript was included in the subcommittee's final report. An excerpt of that transcript follows.

ALMEIDA: So, please, Mrs. Vasquez . . . will you talk to me?

VASQUEZ: (Crying) Yes . . . yes . . . what do you want to know?

ALMEIDA: I want to know whatever you know. What can you tell me about the man Jamey was working for, Ira Gaines?

VASQUEZ: Nothing. Just that he was a tall Anglo. I'm not sure why Jamey liked Anglo men so much, but she did. You think she would have learned better after how her husband treated her—

ALMEIDA: Kyle's father? Derek Patrick Farrell?

VASQUEZ: Yes.

ALMEIDA: I know Jamey's marriage went badly, but I was unaware of the details.

VASQUEZ: She met him right out of college, when she just started working with computers, at Microsoft, up in Seattle. I remember how she loved the mountains. She said it was very beautiful, but she felt very alone up there. She had no family nearby, and she began right away to sleep with Derek, who was her boss.

I told her not to do that, not to rush things, but she did. She got pregnant. Got married. So fast. She was worried for her new baby, Kyle. Didn't like to leave him in day care. She asked her husband if they could move down to Los Angeles, so me and my husband could help look

REPORTER'S NOTE: Among Jamey's personal effects at CTU was this picture of her and her son, Kyle.

after Kyle. Derek said no. And the next thing, he leaves her, that pig, for some redhead, some executive who was out of the country for two years but came back to Seattle to work again. Suddenly he tells Jamey that he does not love her anymore and that he is too young to be a father. Now he loves the redhead. Not even a look back. Just cleans out the bank account and leaves her.

ALMEIDA: Did Jamey try to sue Derek for child support and the money he took?

VASQUEZ: Have you ever tried to hire a lawyer when you are flat broke?

ALMEIDA: No, I can't say that I have.

VASQUEZ: I do not suggest you try. No, she went to her company higher-ups and complained about Derek to see if they would help convince him to pay the child support for Kyle. They did do this. But Derek was angry about it.

He got back at Jamey by getting her in trouble at work for something she created while she was at the company. Something that the company was angry she created. I do not understand enough about the computers. But you can ask her company.

ALMEIDA: She was fired by Microsoft, wasn't she? I remember seeing that in her dossier.

VASQUEZ: Yes, she was fired.

ALMEIDA: What did Jamey do next?

VASQUEZ: She wanted to move back to Los Angeles, but she needed a job here. So she called up her old friend Richard Walsh. He had helped her get into college, and he remembered her. He was the one who found a position for her at your CTU.

ALMEIDA: So Jamey moved back to L.A. with Kyle.

VASQUEZ: Yes. She moved in with me and my husband. She was still very angry. And she was put through a bad time by Derek. I wanted her to have a happy life, you know? Forget Derek. So when her old girlfriends called and said come out to clubs with us, I told her to go. And that was fine. I liked watching Kyle for her.

One day I noticed a big Cadillac bring her home from a nightclub. That was her new boyfriend, Ira Gaines. He told her that he had been a solider, a Navy . . . I can't remember . . . sea lion?

ALMEIDA: (Chuckling) SEAL?

VASQUEZ: Yes! Navy SEAL. He spent a lot of money on Jamey. He bought her jewelry and took her to fancy restaurants. He bought toys for Kyle . . . and . . . he even bought me and my husband some things. Just things for the house . . .

ALMEIDA: I see.

VASQUEZ: I know she liked him very much . . . and I think they were together a few times.

ALMEIDA: Sleeping together?

VASQUEZ: Yes . . . yes . . . she spent a few nights with him. . . .

ALMEIDA: And do you know when Ira Gaines began to ask Jamey for . . . favors?

VASQUEZ: No, I don't know anything about that. I'm sorry. What she did to help him . . . I don't know. I'd tell you if I knew, but I don't.

ALMEIDA: You told me at CTU that you never asked Jamey where the money came from. But I don't believe you. You *did* ask her, didn't you?

VASQUEZ: (Quietly) Yes. I asked her. I did ask her, but Jamey said, "Please don't ask. Just keep it."

ALMEIDA: So where did you think all that money came from, Mrs. Vasquez? Three hundred thousand dollars?

VASQUEZ: I trusted my daughter. I trusted her. And when she said not to ask, to just accept the money in case anything happened to her, I did as she asked. That's the *truth*!

ALMEIDA: All right. I just have a few more questions. . . . Before she died, Jamey confessed some of the things she did for that money. Think about your answer on this next question, Mrs. Vasquez: Can you tell me *why* you think your daughter decided to take a bribe and break the law?

VASQUEZ: (After a pause) Jamey sometimes said how she thought she was being taken advantage of at work. That she was doing more work than anyone else and that she was not being paid nearly enough.

ALMEIDA: And that was why? She was bitter because her bad marriage left her broke and she felt slighted at work?

VASQUEZ: Yes . . . and . . . (crying)

ALMEIDA: And what, Erica? What else?

VASQUEZ: Her father . . . my husband . . . (crying)

ALMEIDA: What about him? Did he need money—was there some kind of debt?

VASQUEZ: He was diagnosed with Alzheimer's—just before Christmas. We were all very upset. He is just at the beginning stages, but we know how bad it will get. We know it will mean long-term nursing care. Big expenses. I think Jamey . . . I think she was looking for a way to bring more money in . . . any way to make sure we'd all have whatever we needed. Her father, Kyle, me. I know my daughter, Tony, and she may have agreed to break some laws, as you say, but she never, *ever* would have done anything if she thought it would cause people harm. . . .

ALMEIDA: But she did cause people harm, Erica. She helped Ira Gaines murder people. She became a traitor for him.

VASQUEZ: (Crying) I know . . . I know . . . God forgive her . . . but she paid for it, she paid with her life.

ALMEIDA: (Long pause) I know, Mrs. Vasquez . . . and I'm sorry.

THANKSGIVING RECESS

REPORTER'S NOTE: At this point the House Special Subcommittee broke for a week-long Thanksgiving recess.

When Capitol Hill went dark, however, lights went on in other parts of Washington, D.C. Transition teams worked overtime at the White House to ensure a smooth succession of power in January, when former senator David Palmer would be sworn in as the first African-American president of the United States.

During this period, the supermarket tabloid *National Midnight Star* and the on-line news service AlternativeNews.com broke the story that President-elect David Palmer and Sherry Palmer, his wife of twenty-five years, had officially filed for divorce.

For almost seven months, speculation and rumor about the Palmers' marital troubles filled newspapers, magazines, and the airwaves-ever since David Palmer issued a terse statement shortly after winning the Super Tuesday primaries. Dubbed in media circles the "Splitsville" press release, Palmer's announcement made it clear to the voting public that he and his wife were separating. Nevertheless, public opinion polls showed that many people held on to the hope that the Palmer separation would not end in divorce.

Although sources close to the Palmer camp stated that the breakup was for good, and David Palmer himself publicly denied any plans for reconciliation, pundits often speculated that Sherry and David would get back together before Palmer took office. It's now clear those pundits were wrong.

1:00 P.M.–2:00 P.M.

REPORTER'S NOTE: The following testimony covers the events that occurred between 1:00 P.M. and 2:00 P.M. on the day of the California presidential primary.

CHAIRMAN FULBRIGHT: Special Agent Bauer. Your wife and daughter were now safe, and you were back in the hands of the CTU. Did you believe the ordeal was over at that time?

SPECIAL AGENT JACK BAUER: No, sir, I did not, and the moment I learned that a CTU security team was taking Teri and Kim to the clinic at Grace Memorial Hospital, I asked Nina to go with them . . . to watch over them. After finding out about Jamey, I didn't know who else to trust.

FULBRIGHT: What happened with you, after you were taken into custody?

BAUER: Frankly, sir, I was hung out to dry by my boss and an ambitious woman who wanted to move into my job.

FULBRIGHT: You're talking about Regional Director Ryan Chappelle and Acting CTU Director Alberta Green? You believe they were working against you?

BAUER: I thought Chappelle, at least, would help out a loyal agent. I had turned myself in, made them aware of how my family had been taken hostage. I honestly didn't expect to be thrown to the wolves.

REP. PAULINE P. DRISCOLL, (D) CONN.: Don't be naive, Agent Bauer. Alberta Green was simply doing her job. And Director Chappelle was simply going to turn you over to the FBI, not throw you to the wolves.

REP. ROY SCHNEIDER, (R) TEX.: Who's being naive now, Pauline?

FULBRIGHT: You should know, Agent Bauer, that Ryan Chappelle's recent statement to this subcommittee is supportive of you.

BAUER: (Dry laughter) *Now* he's supportive, because a month ago David Palmer was elected president, and Chappelle knows Palmer was the one who demanded I be reinstated.

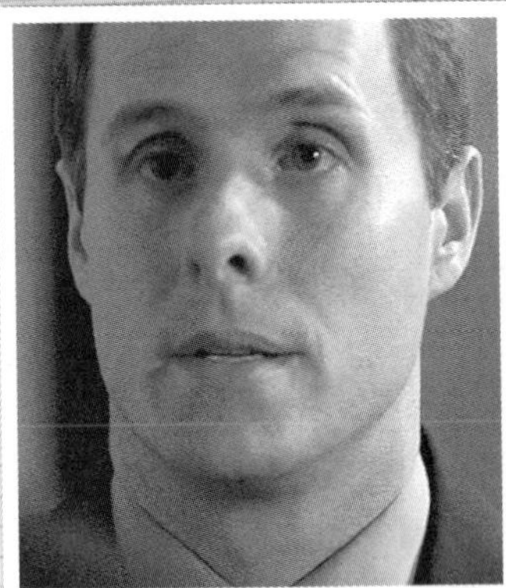

RYAN CHAPPELLE

AGE: 44

CTU MISSIONS

- Regional Administrator, Hotel Los Angeles attack, 1998
- Assistant Regional Administrator, Operation Farmhouse, 1997

EXPERIENCE

- Regional Director, Counter Terrorist Unit, Los Angeles
- Deputy Director of Administration, Central Intelligence Agency
- Assistant to the Deputy Director of Administration, Central Intelligence Agency

EDUCATION

- Master of Business Administration, Wharton
- Bachelor of Science, Government, New York University

PERSONAL

- Married — Victoria ("Vicky") Chappelle
- Son — Ryan Victor Chappelle, Jr.
- Daughters — Caitlin Keller Chappelle, Christine Temple Chappelle

FROM THE DESK OF

MARC CERASINI

SUBJECT: RYAN CHAPPELLE

Sources close to the CTU provided this reporter with the transcript of a private conversation between Richard Walsh and Jack Bauer, recorded by security cameras at the CTU regional office, Los Angeles, just six weeks before the California primary.

> WALSH: . . . he really burned me up in there. Thank God Chappelle's limited his exposure to field operations. As long as he stays nice and cozy in that bureaucratic seat of his, we'll be okay. But Lord help us if the shit ever hits the fan in this agency. The one thing more important to Chappelle than protecting his ass is selling someone else's to advance his career. So watch your back, Jack.
>
> BAUER: Richard, you don't need to warn me. Every field agent around here knows Chappelle is competent in performing administrative duties but worthless when it comes to doing real intelligence work. . . .

FULBRIGHT: I get the picture. Go on with how you were treated.

BAUER: I was isolated in an interrogation room. I was denied access to a phone, my family, my workstation. When Chappelle showed up, he made a big show of wheeling in a tape recorder. Before he let me speak, he turned the machine on—a not-so-subtle hint that my words would be used against me in a court of law, that he and Alberta were already building a case.

I explained the timeline of events, but Chappelle wasn't very sympathetic about my family's kidnapping. When he did refer to it, he was incredibly patronizing. It wasn't long before he was talking about "protocols" and "procedures"—code for "I'm covering my ass, so I've got to nail yours."

I argued that I should be reinstated, that I was a resource, the only one who knew about all the pieces of the still unfinished puzzle—Cofell and the money; Belgrade and Kosovo; blowback and some personal vendetta. But Chappelle was adamant—they were going to hand me over to the Justice Department as soon as possible.

But while Chappelle was planning my prosecution and Alberta was getting comfortable in my office, the Drazens were busy, too. Tony and Milo discovered that three international assassins hired by the Drazens had come into the L.A. area from the Balkans. They uncovered the names of two of them: Mishko Suba and Jovan Myovic.

BAUER: At about 2:14 P.M., the Los Angeles County Fire Department responded to reports of an explosion at a building in the North Valley where the rest of Gaines's thugs had fled. The structure had been blown up, using Semtex, a Czech-made plastic explosive. Several corpses were discovered inside, burned beyond recognition. Firemen also discovered another body—this one shot at point-blank range. CTU forensics positively identified this corpse as Kevin Carroll. It was fairly clear from the evidence that the Drazen family was tying up loose ends.

SCHNEIDER: And *your* family?

BAUER: At Grace Memorial's clinic, Teri and Kim were being examined by physicians when Nina raised an alarm. She said she'd confronted a man who claimed he was an FBI agent but was not.

The thing is, I know now that Nina was dirty. And this may have

REPORTER'S NOTE:
No clean surveillance photos available at this time.

MISHKO SUBA
AGE: 32
BIRTHPLACE: Smedervo, Serbia

EXPERIENCE
- International Sales Representative, Luca Univox Holding Company, Belgrade (According to Interpol, Luca Univox is "a shell company created to launder money earned by the Drazens through various criminal enterprises.")
- Activist, "Blue Rose"* (Quasi-political pro-Serb organization at the University of Belgrade)

CRIMINAL ACTIVITIES
- Zurich, Switzerland: Charged with one count of homicide for the murder of Rudolf Kaspar Schoss, 46, Chief Financial Officer, Berne Banc Suisse. (Charges dismissed for lack of evidence: Prosecution witness "vanished.")
- Rome, Italy: Tried in absentia for the murder of Hamat Gorunian, 64, an Albanian national who funded several anti-Serb organizations in Eastern Europe. (Acquitted.)
- Wanted for questioning in alleged arms-smuggling ring operating in Eastern Europe.

EDUCATION
- Bachelor of Science, Engineering, University of Belgrade

MILITARY
- Serbian Army Special Operations

PERSONAL
- Mother — Katrina Suba
- Father — Emil Suba (deceased)

been just an excuse to get my family to a place where the Drazens could reach them. No one else saw the fake agent, and when a CTU specialist tested the phone the man supposedly used for fingerprints, he found nothing.

DRISCOLL: Nothing?

BAUER: The prints had been wiped by a professional. Nina, as we know, is a professional and could have done that herself.

Whatever the truth, Nina used this revelation as an excuse to move Teri and Kimberly to a safe house at [INFORMATION WITHHELD FOR SECURITY REASONS]. It was one of several safe houses the Agency maintains in suburban Los Angeles County. The house had good security, including alarms monitored by CTU security personnel, motion detectors every ten yards to sense intruders, and a backup security team, disguised as telephone linemen, working outside.

FULBRIGHT: What happened next at CTU? Your interview with Ryan Chappelle did not go well, is that correct? He refused to reinstate you at that point?

BAUER: Yes, sir. Chappelle sent Acting Director Alberta Green in to finish debriefing me. Right off the bat, she tried to soften me up with a lot of talk about how "uncomfortable" she felt about conducting

JOVAN MYOVIC
AGE: 28
BIRTHPLACE: Sombor, Vojvodina
ALIASES: "Joe Ragey," "Tuvo"

EXPERIENCE
- International Sales Representative, Luca Univox Holding Company, Belgrade (According to Interpol, Luca Univox is "a shell company created to launder money earned by the Drazens through various criminal enterprises.")

CRIMINAL ACTIVITIES
- Wanted for questioning in the disappearance of Helmet Dantine, 24, Personal Assistant to the Chief Financial Officer, Berne Banc Suisse. (Dantine was the sole witness to the alleged murder of his boss, Rudolf Kaspar Schoss, by Drazen associate Mishko Suba.)
- Wanted for questioning in alleged arms-smuggling ring operating in Eastern Europe.

MILITARY
- Corporal, Serbian Army Special Forces
- Private, Serbian Army

PERSONAL
- Single
- Sister — Ivestia Myovic

ENSITIVE (XGDS)
8/24/02

such procedures on my turf. She was trying to *handle* me, of course, and I don't like to be handled, but—I cooperated, anyway. I told Alberta to convince CIA headquarters at Langley [Virginia] to open up their data files on the Balkans. I told her about Ted Cofell and the money trail that led to Belgrade. I began to fill her in on what I'd learned in the past twelve hours. . . .

REPORTER'S NOTE:
According to the separate testimony of Jack's daughter, Kimberly Bauer, during this same time period she and her mother, Teri, were brought to Grace Memorial Hospital's clinic.

KIMBERLY BAUER: . . . then me and my mom were taken to a clinic to be checked out. The doctor who took care of us, Dr. Kent, asked if there was anything more she should know about besides my mother's stomach pains.

Mom wasn't going to tell the doctor the truth, I could tell. But I looked at her like *you better tell the doctor or I will!* They had me go into the next room, and that's when she told the doctor she'd been raped. Mom told me later, at the safe house, that the doctor gave her an exam and tests and everything was okay.

It was that scum Eli who raped her, the one who beat up Rick when he tried to help us. Sometime between eight and nine in the morning, he came into the room where they were keeping us and pointed at me and said I should get up and come with him to the next room. He said he wouldn't hurt me.

Mom saw the look on his face, and so did I. It was sick. We both knew he was going to do something bad.

I screamed "No," but he came at me. I fought him off, kicked and scratched. I know I hurt him. He was really angry and pulled out his gun. I got a piece of wood and began to swing. That's when Mom got between us and calmed him down saying, "Hey, hey . . . *I* won't hurt you."

Before I knew what was happening, he took her into the other room and locked the door between us. I couldn't help her. She let him do that to her so she could (crying) . . . so she could protect me . . . (crying).

When she came back, I hugged her and she told me she was fine. She said, "What happened in the other room just now . . . there are some things in life that you have to let go of." She promised that we would escape and that we would be a family again. She said, "We're going to be with Dad and have our lives. This is not going to be part of that life. . . . Do you understand what I'm saying?"

I did. She never wanted Dad to know she'd been raped. She even told the doctor that my dad should never see her medical file.

INTERVIEWER: Kim, to set your mind at ease, you should know that the CTU files show that Eli is dead. His body was picked up at the Gaines compound and brought to the CTU morgue.

KIM BAUER: *Of course* I know he's dead! He was the one they sent to shoot us. But my mother shot *him* first. . . . I'm glad she did—I'm glad he's dead.

"ELI"
REAL NAME: ELIJAH TIMOTHY STRAM
OTHER ALIASES: "LIE," "E.T."
AGE: 25

CRIMINAL ACTIVITIES

- Three juvenile arrests in Los Angeles for assault, possession of an unlicensed firearm, and criminal sale of narcotics (crystal methamphetamine and Rohypnol), two years served in a juvenile detention facility.
- Two adult arrests in Los Angeles County for attempted sexual assault, charges dismissed. One arrest for homicide, acquitted.
- Two years before the California primary, charges against Elijah Stram were dropped in one pending federal narcotics case. Drug Enforcement Agency case officer responsible for prosecution was former agent Kevin Carroll.

NOTE: Subject deceased.

DECLASSIFIED

~~TOP SECRET~~/SENSITIVE (XGDS)
NARA, Date 8/26/02

REPORTER'S NOTE: Teri Bauer's attached medical file was unsealed for review by the House Special Subcommittee.

[...]MORIAL HOSPITAL

[...]Y PRACTICE CLINIC

PATIENT EXAMINATION FORM

Examining physician: Rose M. Kent, M.D.

A. Patient Name: Mrs. Teri Bauer
Address: Santa Monica, CA Age: 34 Sex: Female Height: 5′ 9′′ Weight: 130 lbs.
Next of kin: Jack Bauer Relationship: Husband

B. Condition on admission: stable Blood pressure 36.9C Respiratory rate 20
If female, date of last normal menstrual period: 24 days ago
Frequency of periods: every 28 days

C. Initial diagnostic impressions: Patient reported she was sexually assaulted. Complains of right lower quadrant abdominal pain.

D. Initial physical examination comments: Minor bruising in perineum and vaginal regions; rape kit used for exam. Additional bruising on upper arms, minor abrasions on legs.

E. Diagnostic studies: Bedside ultrasound revealed remnants of a ruptured follicular cyst on the right ovary. Small amount of free fluid noted in pelvis. Left ovary, uterus, and pelvis appeared otherwise grossly normal.

F. Laboratory Tests

a. Complete blood cell count normal
b. Urinalysis normal
c. Electrolytes normal
d. HIV test normal*
e. RPR [syphilis] negative*
f. Gonorrhea, chlamydia test negative*
g. Wet prep negative for trichomonas, +sperm found
h. HCG [pregnancy] positive*

*Patient forced to leave clinic before these lab results available to her.

Additional comments: Patient reported sexual assault occurred approximately 4 hours before this visit. Abdominal pain started shortly thereafter. Best evidence is that this is a ruptured follicular cyst possibly related to the sexual assault.

Patient under federal protection and left hospital prior to all lab tests being completed. Patient unaware of positive pregnancy test at time she left hospital; however, urine test given to patient to perform at home. Will need to contact patient in the next 24 hours to review lab results and to schedule a follow-up ultrasound. No need to offer postcoital contraception since patient already approximately 4 weeks pregnant. Biological father is husband. According to patient, no other sexual partners at that time.

Referral made to rape counseling service, however patient at this time refused referral. Patient requests this record be confidential. Does NOT want her husband to know this happened to her.

Follow-up: Will call patient within 24 hours with test results. —RMK, M.D.

24-hour follow-up: Patient called, message left on telephone machine to contact Dr. Kent for test results. —GAA, R.N.

48-hour follow-up: Patient deceased. —GAA, R.N.

2:00 P.M.–3:00 P.M.

REPORTER'S NOTE: The following testimony covers the events that occurred between 2:00 P.M. and 3:00 P.M. on the day of the California presidential primary.

CHAIRMAN FULBRIGHT: So, Agent Almeida, you received new intelligence at about 2:00 P.M., is that correct?

AGENT TONY ALMEIDA: Yes, Milo uncovered the name of the third assassin. Alexis Drazen. Former sniper. Serb Special Forces. He was Victor Drazen's son and Andre Drazen's younger brother.

Alexis flew into LAX [Los Angeles International Airport] on the Saturday before Super Tuesday. He came in from Belgrade after a few days' stopover in Washington, D.C.

Days later, we put together his movements in D.C. He had been sleeping with an aide to Senator David Palmer named Elizabeth Nash. Nash, along with others on Palmer's campaign staff, had been in D.C. right before traveling to Los Angeles for the Super Tuesday primary.

REP. PAULINE P. DRISCOLL, (D) CONN.: Excuse me, Mr. Chairman. I'd like to ask Agent Almeida about several details not covered in the previous hour's testimony.

FULBRIGHT: That's fine.

DRISCOLL: Agent Almeida, how would you describe the welcome Jack Bauer received when he returned to CTU on the afternoon of Super Tuesday?

ALMEIDA: I was glad to see him. I think we were all happy his family was safe. But the mood at CTU was tense. We'd had a terrorist bombing of an airliner, an assassination attempt, a lockdown, and a command turnover in a fourteen-hour period. And the presence of Alberta Green and Ryan Chappelle was a distraction.

FULBRIGHT: What about Green and Chappelle? Be honest, Agent Almeida. Your comments won't get further than this room, I assure you.

ALMEIDA: Truthfully, sir, I think they were both looking for a scapegoat, and I think they were eyeing Jack for the part.

DRISCOLL: They said this to you in so many words?

ALMEIDA: They got their message across. First Alberta Green asked me if I was happy being in third place at CTU. Then Chappelle insinuated that if I cooperated in the prosecution of Jack Bauer, good things would happen for me, career-wise.

REP. ROY SCHNEIDER, (R) TEX.: Why were you singled out, Agent Almeida?

ALMEIDA: To smear Jack, Green and Chappelle needed my help. I was the one who initially called for the lockdown, and Chappelle told me outright that the case against Jack might boil down to my testimony *because* I was the one who reported Bauer's erratic behavior—

SCHNEIDER: Before you knew what was going on?

ALMEIDA: Before I knew about Jack's family, about the kidnapping, yes.

DRISCOLL: We have a statement from Ryan Chappelle, but for the record, what do you recall saying to him?

ALMEIDA: I told him the truth. I told Chappelle that I didn't approve of Jack Bauer's methods, with the way he delegated authority or the way he ran his operations. I also told Chappelle that since

ALEXIS DRAZEN

AGE: 29

BIRTHPLACE: Kragujevac, Serbia

EXPERIENCE

- Member, Advisory Council, Serb International Coalition for Justice, Cayman Islands
- Member, Kosovo/1389 (Serbian nationalist paramilitary organization banned in 1986)
- Activist, "Blue Rose" (Quasi-political pro-Serb organization at the University of Belgrade)

CRIMINAL ACTIVITY

- Wanted for questioning in alleged arms-smuggling ring operating in Eastern Europe

EDUCATION

- Bachelor of Arts, Serbian History and Folklore, University of Belgrade

MILITARY

- Lieutenant, Serbian Army Special Operations

PERSONAL

- Single

midnight that night, I could not disapprove of a single thing Jack Bauer did.

DRISCOLL: You were loyal to your boss.

ALMEIDA: I told the truth. And I don't like to be handled.

FULBRIGHT: You don't like to be *handled,* you say? Interesting . . . Jack Bauer expressed the same view. Can you give us some insight into that, Agent Almeida?

ALMEIDA: (After a pause) We had a saying in my Marine Corps platoon, sir, "A good officer *commands* his troops, the other kind of officer *handles* them."

Ryan Chappelle and Alberta Green were handlers.

SCHNEIDER: I was a marine, too, son. And I'm sorry to point this out to you—but Jack Bauer and yourself *were* being handled all along . . . by Nina Myers. It's fairly clear she was so good at it, you simply hadn't caught on yet. . . .

REPORTER'S NOTE: The subcommitee turns again to Special Agent Jack Bauer. . . .

FULBRIGHT: Agent Bauer, about your debriefing with Alberta Green—

SPECIAL AGENT JACK BAUER: I *ended* it the moment she informed me that my family had been moved from the clinic to the safe house without my knowledge. I was furious and *done* cooperating at that point. I was willing to help them hang me, but not if it meant leaving my family vulnerable. And unless I knew what was happening with them, I felt helpless to protect them. So I made the only move left open to me on the board. I blocked Alberta.

She was angry, but as my wife often said, pissing people off is pretty much my unofficial hobby. It was about then that CTU had a collective heart attack because David Palmer walked right through their front door and demanded to see one person—*me.*

DRISCOLL: I'm surprised Ryan Chappelle allowed Senator Palmer access to you.

BAUER: Chappelle stalled. Then he sent Tony out to delay Palmer some more. I understand Palmer made a phone call to the Pentagon to finally end the charade. Within minutes Chappelle had me ushered into a new interrogation room where I found Palmer waiting for me.

SCHNEIDER: Palmer thought *you* were the assassin at that point, correct?

BAUER: Yes, he did. He thought I wanted revenge for what happened to my men in Kosovo. I was stunned. I had no idea Palmer was associated with that mission. I thought it was Robert Ellis's operation from start to finish.

DRISCOLL: Agent Bauer, what precisely did Senator Palmer reveal to you about his role in Operation Nightfall, and please remember you are under oath.

BAUER: David Palmer revealed that he had been following Drazen's various war crimes through reports by the CIA, but he couldn't get anything done through the usual channels. In his opinion, no one was dealing with the Drazen situation fast enough. So Palmer decided to cut through the red tape. He authorized the Operation Nightfall mission himself.

DRISCOLL: You mean he bypassed the proper channels?

BAUER: Yes, ma'am, but he had good reasons for what he did. He wanted to rid the world of a terrible monster.

DRISCOLL: Drazen's supporters don't view him that way. And now he'll never get his day in the world court to defend himself, will he?

SCHNEIDER: What about Robert Ellis, Agent Bauer? Would you mind describing his role for us again, please.

BAUER: Palmer gave NSA agent Ellis the order to kill Drazen and the money to do it through a discretionary fund. It was Ellis who gave me the job to execute the order. In that room with David, I concluded that if the assassins knew Palmer and I were connected to Nightfall, then they had to know about *Ellis,* too.

We tracked down Ellis in New Orleans, and Palmer got on the phone first with him. Initially he was very pissed that Palmer and I were in the same room. He had worked hard to see that we were never connected. Then he understood that there was major blowback coming our way—and his. Ellis set up a feed through Milo's computer, then he downloaded the Nightfall files to CTU's server. One file was missing—

FULBRIGHT: The one that turned up on Drazen's computer?

BAUER: That's correct, Mr. Chairman. Milo printed out the other files, and Senator Palmer and I reviewed them. Ellis's Nightfall files included a separate after-action report compiled by the Department of Defense and a copy of the original order to launch Operation Nightfall. I read through the pages and found lots of surprises—

FULBRIGHT: Such as?

BAUER: First of all, Ellis's report to the DOD stated that we'd hit a bunker and command center—not a farmhouse in the middle of nowhere, as I'd originally thought.

DRISCOLL: You're saying Ellis *lied* about the target in his report to the DOD?

BAUER: No. Victor Drazen had spent three million dollars to build a reinforced concrete bunker *under* that farmhouse. He spent another four million dollars for high-tech surveillance, radar, and communications equipment. The place was a command and control center. It was going to be the heart of his new headquarters, a center for power and a place to train more Black Dog assassins. And it was days from going on-line. Palmer knew all this when he authorized the mission. It was a valid target; he just didn't want to waste valuable time going through the proper channels to prove it.

SCHNEIDER: So what does that mean, Agent Bauer? Put it into bottom-line terms.

BAUER: By designating that the strike was on a command and control center—a perfectly legal and legitimate target in NATO's bombing campaign—Ellis had shielded Palmer from political fallout. The truth is, Palmer didn't care about the bunker—he just wanted Drazen dead. But Ellis knew that the assassination alone could create political problems for Palmer, so he fudged the orders *after* the event to make the *bunker* look like the target, not Drazen.

DRISCOLL: I'm still a bit confused. There was a bunker . . . *under* the house, you say?

BAUER: Yes, ma'am. And that bunker explained a lot of things. Why air defenses were protecting the farm. Why there were so many Serb militiamen in the region. And why my team never knew that two innocent women—Victor Drazen's wife and daughter—were in that bunker. I never knew until I reviewed those files that there was collateral damage. Neither did Palmer.

FULBRIGHT: So this was all about revenge?

BAUER: Yes, Mr. Chairman. Against me. Against Senator Palmer. Against Robert Ellis. And against my family. Palmer and I knew our families would never be safe until we flushed the assassins out into the open. To that end, Palmer went to Chappelle with me and backed up my provisional reinstatement as director of CTU's Los Angeles office. Until the end of the day, I would have my old job back. After that, Chappelle was free to hold me accountable for disciplinary action or turn me over to the Justice Department.

The clock was ticking, so I got back to work.

3:00 P.M.–4:00 P.M.

CHAIRMAN FULBRIGHT: Robert Ellis was murdered at approximately 3:00 P.M. Is that correct, Agent Bauer?

REPORTER'S NOTE: The following testimony covers the events that occurred between 3:00 P.M. and 4:00 P.M. on the day of the California presidential primary.

SPECIAL AGENT JACK BAUER: Yes. I was speaking to him on the phone at the time. He was in the men's room of a bar in New Orleans. I heard a scuffle, then the phone went dead. About that moment, I figured Bob was dead, too.

REP. PAULINE P. DRISCOLL, (D) CONN.: That's rather coldly matter-of-fact, Agent Bauer.

BAUER: (Sigh) Ma'am, if you knew Bob Ellis, you would understand. The autopsy report indicated he was more than legally intoxicated. He'd been drinking for years, and it impaired his judgment the day he was killed and on all too many occasions before then.

The truth is, Ellis was being edged out of covert operations. He could no longer be trusted because of his drinking and carelessness. That day in New Orleans when we called him, we warned him, yet he still failed to take precautions. He died because he let his guard down. I really liked the guy, but the sad fact is that Ellis had been letting his guard down for years.

FINAL ANATOMIC AND FORENSIC SUMMARY

SUBJECT: Robert Ellis
CASE #: 01–097
CTU FORENSIC PATHOLOGIST: George R. Capaldo, M.D.

CAUSE OF DEATH: Ligature Strangulation

MANNER OF DEATH: Homicide

EXTERNAL EXAMINATION:

The 5´ 11´´, 220-pound body is that of a normally developed and well-nourished white male consistent with the stated age of 46 years.

The scalp is unremarkable. The scalp hair is brown.

The ears are unremarkable.

The irides are brown. The pupils have a bilateral diameter of 0.4 cm. Scleral hemorrhage and conjunctival petechiae are present bilaterally.

The bones of the bridge of the nose are freely mobile and the external nares are unremarkable.

The face shows marked congestion and brown stubble is present.

The oral cavity is unremarkable. The upper and lower dental arches show fair dentition.

The neck is markedly edematous and shows an indenting ligature mark which extends circumferentially 21 cm.

The chest is symmetrical and the breasts are unremarkable.

The abdomen is flat.

The external genitalia are intact and atraumatic.

The right and left upper extremities are unremarkable.

The right and left lower extremities are unremarkable.

The back is atraumatic and unremarkable.

Evidence of Medical Therapy: None.

INTERNAL EXAMINATION:

The 380-gram heart has a smooth and shiny epicardial surface. The major coronary arteries depart from the base of the aorta and follow their anatomic course. The left main, left anterior descending, circumflex, and right coronary arteries are elastic, widely patent, and free of thrombosis or atheromatosis. The myocardium is homogeneously red-brown, firm, and free of focal mottling or fibrosis. The endocardium and trabeculae carneae are smooth and glistening. The valve leaflets and valve cusps are freely mobile and the chordae tendineae are delicate. The orifices of the coronary arteries are free of obstruction. The carotid arteries are elastic and free of atheromatosis. The aorta is elastic with minimal atheromatosis.

The trachea and major bronchi are pink-tan and free of obstruction.

The hyoid bone and thyroidal cartilage are fractured.

The 530-gram right lung and 340-gram left lung have smooth and shiny blue-gray visceral surfaces with mild to moderate anthracotic reticulation. The cut surface of both lungs is spongy gray with focal red mottling. The minor bronchial passages are patent and free of lesions. The pulmonary vasculature is free of atheromatosis and thromboemboli.

The 1400-gram liver has a smooth and shiny brown capsule. The parenchyma shows mild-moderate fatty changes and is otherwise without prominence of lymphoid follicles. The major lymph node groups of the body are not enlarged.

The 180-gram right kidney and 170-gram left kidney have smooth and shiny brown surfaces. The parenchyma is homogeneously brown, firm, and with distinct corticomedullary junctions. The calyces and pelves are unremarkable. The ureters are patent and not dilated. The bladder has a tan mucosa.

The testes have a light tan parenchyma and are free of nodularity. The prostate gland is gray-white, firm, and nonenlarged.

The 1490-gram brain has translucent arachnoid membranes. The sulci and gyri are flattened. The Circle of Willis remnants are free of atheromatosis or aneurysm. The skull, after stripping the dura, is free of anomaly.

The esophageal serosa is pink-tan, smooth, and unremarkable. The esophageal mucosa is light gray and free of ulceration or stricture. The stomach contains approximately 35 cubic cm. of a green-tan, pasty liquid. The underlying gastric mucosa is light gray and free of ulceration.

The surfaces of the small and large intestine are gray-tan, smooth, and glistening. The mucosal aspect varies from green-tan to pink-tan and is free of ulceration, neoplasia, or diverticula.

The pancreas is yellow-tan, firm, and well-lobulated. The adrenal glands are present bilaterally with distinct corticomedullary junctions. The thyroid gland is amber brown and free of nodularity. The pituitary gland is situated in the sella turcica and is not enlarged.

The surfaces of the pleural cavities are smooth and glistening. The peritoneal cavity has a shiny surface.

LAB RESULTS:

Alcohol blood level is: 0.3 g/100 ml. Further drug tests are negative.

AUTOPSY FINDINGS SUMMARY:

1. Ligature strangulation with attendant organic changes.
2. Positive alcohol blood level.
3. Hepatic fatty changes.

FULBRIGHT: Continue with your activities during that hour, Agent Bauer. You said you were provisionally reinstated.

BAUER: Yes, Ryan Chappelle and Alberta Green both went back to division headquarters. But my reinstatement wasn't what I'd call a *full* reinstatement.

FULBRIGHT: Explain.

BAUER: Chappelle pulled the plug on my security clearance. I was now on the same clearance level as Milo. Chappelle also sent George Mason to closely supervise me and my unit. So Mason was sitting in my office, I could barely download my own files without Milo's help, and Chappelle got busy behind the scenes, making sure we were out of the loop—

REPORTER'S NOTE: At the time of death, Robert Ellis's blood alcohol concentration (BAC) was quite high. At .30 it was well over the legal definition of intoxication in most states, which is .08. Measured in percentages, the BAC is the amount of alcohol in an individual's bloodstream. If you have a BAC of .10 percent, for example, that means you have 1 part alcohol per 1,000 parts blood in your body. Driving skills and especially judgment are impaired in most people long before they exhibit visible signs of drunkenness. Alcohol also depresses the central nervous system, which slows reactions.

DRISCOLL: (Interrupting) *We?*

BAUER: CTU, Los Angeles. The whole division was isolated by the rest of the Agency [CIA] out at Langley [Virginia, CIA headquarters]. The Company [slang for CIA] acted like they couldn't trust me, yet they believed me when I told them about Walsh's suspicions—that there was a mole in CTU. Until that mole was revealed, our entire division was being *contained*. We just didn't know it yet.

REP. ROY SCHNEIDER, (R) TEX.: What do you mean by "contained," Agent Bauer?

BAUER: I mean a blackout of information. Sometime between 3:00 and 4:00 P.M. two assassins struck the safe house in an attempt to kill my family. They killed the outside security team first, then entered the house and killed Agent Ron Breeher with a single dart to the carotid artery. Agent Derek Paulson was stabbed in the back and shot twice. My wife and daughter barely escaped the house. After a high-speed chase, there was an accident and my wife and daughter were separated.

DECLASSIFIED

I was not informed of this attack for hours, long after my daughter called Tony Almeida to alert him. Almeida and Mason were both told that my wife and daughter had escaped—which was true—and that there were no survivors at the safe house—which was false. I learned later that Agent Paulson had survived the attack—barely. . . .

REPORTER'S NOTE: This testimony was taken by Special Agent Vance Rickard, Central Intelligence Agency, in the emergency room of Grace Memorial Hospital, Los Angeles, at 9:18 P.M.

SPECIAL AGENT VANCE RICKARD: Can you hear me?

SPECIAL AGENT DEREK PAULSON: (Faintly) Yes . . .

RICKARD: Do you remember what happened, Agent Paulson?

PAULSON: They got into the safe house . . . I don't know how. The motion sensors should have warned us even if the guys outside were dead.

RICKARD: How many were there?

PAULSON: One . . . no, there were two. I got one . . . didn't I?

RICKARD: You did, Agent Paulson. He's dead.

PAULSON: And Ron [Ronald Breeher]?

RICKARD: I'm sorry. Stay with me, Agent Paulson. Do you remember what happened to Teri Bauer? To Kimberly Bauer?

PAULSON: They got out . . . drove away. I don't know where.

RICKARD: What happened to the men outside, Derek? What happened to your security team?

PAULSON: The motion sensors . . . they should have worked . . . they . . .

RICKARD: Paulson! Stay with me. . . . Derek?

VOICE OF PHYSICIAN: That's enough, Rickard. Out of the way! Let's go, people, we're losing him.

REPORTER'S NOTE: Special Agent Derek Paulson passed away at 9:29 P.M. He was awarded a Special Commendation posthumously.

CTU investigators later determined that the security monitors and motion sensors had been deactivated by Nina Myers using a laptop computer hacked into her own terminal at CTU from a remote location.

BAUER: One break finally came when Milo downloaded surveillance photos of the three suspected assassins—Mishko Suba, Jovan Myovic, and Alexis Drazen. I had the photos sent over to Palmer campaign headquarters, and the Secret Service showed the photos to the staff. A Palmer aide named Elizabeth Nash recognized one of the shooters. She had been drawn into a relationship with him and was due to meet him at his hotel room in one hour.

4:00 P.M.–5:00 P.M.

CHAIRMAN FULBRIGHT: Elizabeth Nash . . . (pause).

SPECIAL AGENT JACK BAUER: Yes, Mr. Chairman?

FULBRIGHT: What a mess.

BAUER: Yes, Mr. Chairman.

FULBRIGHT: You should know, Agent Bauer, that we requested Ms. Nash appear herself to testify about her actions during this hour. Unfortunately, we were informed by her attorney that she is not mentally fit to testify. A memo from her psychiatrist confirms that she is in a "fragile state."

REPORTER'S NOTE: The following testimony covers the events that occurred between 4:00 P.M. and 5:00 P.M. on the day of the California presidential primary.

REP. ROY SCHNEIDER, (R) TEX.: Ah, yes, the handy-dandy doctor's note.

FULBRIGHT: This is not the place for humor, Roy.

SCHNEIDER: It's not the place for political favors, either. FOP, Jayce . . . FOP.

FULBRIGHT: For the record, I have no hesitation in admitting that Ms. Nash's father is a close personal friend of President-elect Palmer. Burton Lee Nash, a highly respected Maryland attorney, and David Palmer were roommates at Georgetown University. And David Palmer is also Ms. Nash's godfather. Out of respect for that relationship, we would prefer not to pressure what could be a mentally unstable young woman—

REPORTER'S NOTE: FOP is Beltway slang for "Friend of Palmer," which means a person who seeks favors or perks by claiming a personal relationship with President-elect David Palmer.

SCHNEIDER: *Could* being the key word.

FULBRIGHT: I'm going to ignore that remark, Roy, and advise this subcommittee to give Ms. Nash the benefit of the doubt. If Agent Bauer cannot supply adequate answers to this subcommittee, we will certainly revisit the decision to subpoena Ms. Nash, who—I might point out to Representative Schneider—is very likely to take the Fifth for all the good it will do.

SCHNEIDER: True. You've got a point there, Jayce.

FULBRIGHT: Therefore, Agent Bauer, if you could explain to us the situation surrounding the *unfortunate* incident with Alexis Drazen and the . . . ah . . . what was it (papers shuffling) . . . the letter opener?

BAUER: Certainly, sir. Elizabeth Nash was, as you know, a member of David Palmer's campaign staff. She was very unhappy to learn that she'd been duped into having an intimate relationship with the assassin Alexis Drazen. He used Elizabeth to learn vital information about Palmer's schedule, including travel itineraries, hotel stays, and public appearances.

ELIZABETH NASH
AGE: 26

EXPERIENCE
- Senator David Palmer, Campaign, Staff Aide
- National Gallery, Washington, D.C., Curator's Assistant
- IFE Internship, Paris

EDUCATION
- Bachelor of Arts, (Dual Major) Art History and French Literature, Vassar
- Study Abroad Program, L'Université de Paris
- St. Ann's Preparatory School

HONORS
- Vassar Women's Lacrosse Team, Regional Division Champions
- Hunter Seat Equitation, USET National Finals, Bronze Medal

PERSONAL
- Single

We could have set up an arrest trap for Alexis, but we knew our best chance of stopping the Drazen plan was to tail him. So Elizabeth agreed to see Alexis one more time in his hotel room and plant a small tracking device in Alexis's wallet.

I made it very clear to her that her safety was the most important thing. If she felt uncomfortable in any way, all she had to do was utter the phrase "I hope I'm not getting a cold," and in seconds I would have a SWAT team of federal agents through the door and in the room to help her.

We had the hotel room hooked up with fiber-optic cameras and listening devices. I watched as she entered the room and gained Alexis's confidence through physical contact, and when he had left her alone for a moment, I watched as she took his wallet from his jacket and placed the tracking device inside.

The operation was over then—or it *should* have been, anyway. I called her cell phone so she could answer, make her excuses to leave, and get out of there. If she had done that, we would have tracked Alexis's every move, flushed out and set up his assassination team, and ended it on *our* terms.

But Elizabeth was . . . she was not as mentally *stable* as she appeared to be before entering that hotel room. It was a very high-pressure situation, and I remember she did express concern that she was somehow to blame for allowing Alexis to use her—even though I and my colleagues assured her she was not. I also remember her saying she appreciated the opportunity to "redeem herself."

The trigger appeared to come when Alexis Drazen said that he had "fallen in love" with her. It was about then I called her cell phone—*twice*. The first time she hung up. The second time, she shut the phone off completely. And very deliberately.

She seemed to be baiting Alexis after that. She told him to tell her again that he loved her. He did, and he then said (pause, paper shuffling) . . . he said, "If I am not very much mistaken, it seems that you are falling in love with me, too." She took her jacket off, and he called room service for a hamburger because she said she was hungry.

She paced the room, and when he hung up the phone and approached her again, asking if there was "anything else," she said,

"Yes," and plunged the sharp end of a letter opener into Alexis's stomach, shouting . . . uh (paper shuffling) . . . yes, shouting, "You son of a bitch, you son of a bitch."

Frankly, I couldn't believe she did it. You can view the tape for yourselves if you like. Alexis had not threatened her in any way. She'd just . . . just *snapped.* The SWAT team and I burst into the room, and I asked Nina to call for a medevac. Alexis was our only live suspect in this case, and he was in our hands. But he was quickly bleeding to death.

It was about then that Alexis's cell phone rang. I took a chance and answered, keeping my voice clipped. The man on the other end of the call instructed me to bring the money to a restaurant called Connie's. The man said he'd be wearing a red baseball cap. I knew then that we had our next lead.

FULBRIGHT: Agent Bauer, I understand that David Palmer was *unhappy* with the outcome of the Nash operation.

BAUER: Yes, *very.* Elizabeth was taken into custody at that point, of course, and he advised her to tell us nothing until she spoke to a lawyer. I was out the door minutes after that, following that next lead.

FULBRIGHT: (Pause) In light of Agent Bauer's very thorough testimony, I recommend that . . . rather than *forcing* Ms. Nash to testify through a subpoena, we ask her attorney that she submit a personal statement for our final report.

Agent Bauer, do you know anything more about the charges pending against Ms. Nash?

BAUER: I understand from my contacts that she is pleading not guilty by reason of temporary insanity to the homicide charge and that she has been released on bail. But the likeliest outcome of her case is a plea bargain. Considering the circumstances, I doubt it will ever go to trial.

FULBRIGHT: I'm sure you're right, Agent Bauer. And I'm sure she'll do little if any jail time.

SCHNEIDER: And *I'm* sure it's politics as usual.

FULBRIGHT: Roy! I'm going to move to have that last comment stricken from the record—

SCHNEIDER: Like hell you will.

FROM THE DESK OF
ELIZABETH NASH

SENATE SUBCOMITTEE
MARKED FOR EVIDENCE
EXHIBIT #24

TO: Rep. Jayce Fulbright, Chairman, House Special Subcommittee
FROM: Ms. Elizabeth Nash
RE: Requested statement on my relationship with Alexis Drazen

As I'm sure President-elect David Palmer will tell you, I am one of the hardest-working members of his staff. From the moment he kicked off his campaign, I wanted nothing more than to see Senator Palmer enter the White House—he is my godfather, after all—and as one of his most important staff aides, I fully expected to be going to the White House with him. That is why I was utterly horrified to hear that I had been used by a man who meant to hurt or kill Senator Palmer.

Alexis Drazen first approached me approximately one month before the day of the California primary. It was a Saturday night, and the Palmer campaign was back in Washington, D.C., for a few days, which meant I was, too. I took the opportunity to go out with a few of my girlfriends from the advance team. We'd been on the road with Senator Palmer for weeks, and on our best behavior. It felt good to have some downtime, to be able to blow off some steam, let down our hair, so to speak.

We hung out at Bar La Chat in Georgetown, which has always been a favorite spot of mine, I guess because a lot of the foreign embassy staff hangs out there. I've always liked foreign men—their accents, I suppose, seem sexy to me, and they often have exotic stories to tell. They also do things differently than American men. They possess more class. More style.

At the Georgetown bar that night, a blond man in a black leather jacket walked in and caught my eye right away. I thought he looked familiar and recognized him from earlier in the day. He had been at the Capitol Hill Starbucks. I remember he ordered a double espresso and smiled at me. Alexis had a killer smile—really hard to resist. At the bar, he kept looking over at me. Then he had sent over a sangria. That's my *favorite* drink, and I was impressed he'd guessed that. We started talking, and then kissing, and before we knew it we'd left together. He bought me dinner, and I took him back to my Dupont Circle apartment, and we slept together.

He told me he ran an importing company based in Berlin, but he did business in Madrid, Paris, Hamburg, Prague, and Belgrade. He said he had been born in Eastern Europe but now lived all over the world. I was impressed. He also said he was just beginning to build relationships with new clients in the United States, which meant it would be easy for him to see me, even though I was traveling so much with the campaign.

I thought he was the perfect man for me—we could rendezvous wherever the campaign took us. He really turned me on, and he was clearly very successful. By our third date, he had bought me a diamond bracelet—ten thousand dollars easily—and we saw each other whenever we could. It was a terrible shock to learn that he was an assassin and that he had used me to get to Senator Palmer. A terrible blow. I was so angry that he had embarrassed me like that, I wanted to do anything to help stop him. That's what I remember most—thinking I must *stop him.*

I honestly tried my best to go into that hotel room with Alexis and pretend everything was all right. It was very difficult. Special Agent Jack Bauer and his team tried to be nice, but their directions before I went into the room were a little hard to follow, maybe because I was so nervous. I don't think I really understood about the phone call—that I was supposed to answer and then leave.

I was feeling trapped. Trapped with a killer. The pressure really was difficult to withstand. Then, when he said that he loved me, I don't know what happened . . . I just felt a cold chill run through me. I saw that letter opener and I remembered the letters—all the love letters he said he was going to write to me but never did, probably because he didn't want to leave evidence of our relationship behind—proof of how he'd used me. And I remember thinking, I have to stop him!

As I said, I don't recall the details of what happened next. I remember that he came up to me at that point, and I didn't want him to touch me again. Then it felt like everything went black. The next thing I knew, I was on the floor screaming with blood all over me. I earnestly wish I could provide more insight into what happened in those moments when they say I turned and stabbed Alexis in the stomach, but that's all I can remember.

My psychiatrist has me on medication and advises rest for my nerves. She can provide you with details of my treatment if they are needed. I thank you, Chairman Fulbright, and the entire House Special Subcommittee, for accepting this statement in lieu of testimony in person, which I know would not be the best thing for my mental health at this juncture.

I sincerely hope—as I know my good friend and godfather, President-elect David Palmer, also hopes—that this statement will sufficiently answer any questions you may have about this matter.

Sincerely yours, Elizabeth Nash

SENATE SUBCOMITTEE
MARKED FOR EVIDENCE
EXHIBIT #24

POLITICAL CORRECTION

Pundits and insiders have a few things to say . . .

REPORTER'S NOTE: Assassins weren't the only thing David Palmer was worried about on Super Tuesday. As the public eventually learned, a political scandal was threatening him as well.

David Palmer and his son, Keith Palmer, were being blackmailed by David's campaign adviser, Carl Webb, and PacAmerica, a political coalition of wealthy Los Angeles businessmen who funded much of Palmer's presidential campaign.

At approximately 4:00 P.M. on Super Tuesday, Keith Palmer sought to derail Carl's blackmailing scheme by covertly recording his confession during a private conversation near Los Angeles' Griffith Park Observatory.

Filled with incriminating statements, this tape was given to David Palmer, who handed it over to the Justice Department for evaluation of wrongdoing. A few weeks after Super Tuesday, a copy of the tape was sent to Fox News anchor Tim O'Malley by an anonymous Justice Department source.

The tape was aired in its entirety on Tim O'Malley's nationally syndicated cable show on May 29. It detonated a political bombshell. Here is the transcript of that tape.

[Bracketed comments are reporter's notes.]

Unknown voice: Smile . . .

Unknown voice: Come on, kid, stay together . . .

Keith Palmer: He's dead! Ferragamo's dead.

[*Keith is referring to Dr. Ferragamo, his therapist seven years ago.*]

Carl Webb: I have no idea.

Palmer: Don't try to blow me off, Carl.

Webb: The authorities are looking into it. Let them do their jobs.

Palmer: We both know they won't find anything.

Webb: Look . . . Keith. I've already been through this with your father—

Palmer: My father's his own man, and so am I. So now you can go through it with me.

Webb: Okay . . . okay . . . let's go. What do you need? Tell me what you need.

Palmer: Ferragamo was there for me when nobody else was. I might not be alive today if it wasn't for him.

[*Keith is referring to the fact that Dr.*

Ferragamo counseled him through a period of depression as Keith wrestled with feelings of responsibility for the accidental death of Lyle Gibson, the boy who raped his sister, Nicole. He was also struggling with the fact that he covered up the truth and did not report the accident to the police.]

Webb: He also betrayed your confidence, Keith. He's the one who went to Maureen Kingsley.

[*Maureen Kingsley was a highly respected CNB news correspondent who was about to leak the story of Keith's cover-up.*]

Palmer: That still doesn't justify murder.

[*Keith is accusing Webb and PacAmerica of having Dr. Ferragamo murdered to silence the incriminating story against Keith for good, thereby clearing his father's way to the presidency.*]

Webb: Justice! Ah, justice is a tricky thing, Keith. Take Lyle Gibson, for example. You want justice for that?

Palmer: Gibson's death was an accident.

Webb: Maybe so. But let's be objective. He rapes your sister, you pay him a visit, he ends up dead. . . . "Accident" could be a tough sell.

Palmer: So if I go public with the truth about Ferragamo, you'll go public with a lie about Lyle Gibson. Is that what you're saying?

Webb: (Inaudible) Oh brother.

Palmer: There's just one catch, Carl. There are two cover-ups here—and you're involved in both of them. So however it plays out, it's bad for you.

Webb: I can take care of myself.

Palmer: No. The moneymen behind my father's campaign take care of you. But if things get ugly, they'll make sure you're the one who takes the fall, won't they, Carl? Or maybe they'll do to you what you did to Dr. Ferragamo.

Webb: You are in way over your head.

Palmer: And you're getting nervous. I can smell it.

Webb: Okay, you listen to me. Whatever you think you can do to me or anyone else, it'll be a hundred times worse for you—

Palmer: I'm not so sure.

POLITICAL CORRECTION

Pundits and insiders have a few things to say . . .

Webb: Well I am. Because if you push things too far, they'll do whatever they have to do.

Palmer: Killing David Palmer's son might get a little messy.

Webb: I think they'd be a little more subtle than that.

Palmer: I'm not following you.

Webb: There is some physical evidence in George Ferragamo's office that leads directly to you. Subtle enough so that the fire marshals didn't see it the first time around . . . but with a little help, they'll find it.

Palmer: So I'll be framed for Ferragamo's murder?

Webb: Like I said. Whatever it takes. That's why your father backed off. And that's why you'll back off.

TWO JURIES, TWO JUDGES

By Will Hertz, *Washington Gazette*

To understand the full ramifications of this tape, we must go back to the morning of Super Tuesday, when respected CNB journalist Maureen Kingsley alerted her producer, Jay Pierce, in an e-mail that she had "the biggest story of the day, and it isn't Palmer's lead in the polls."

Later that same morning, Kingsley pulled back from her original prediction, delaying Jay Pierce with the excuse that "she hadn't yet solidified all the details" so the story had to wait.

Twenty-four hours later, Maureen Kingsley's employer, CNB, issued a tersely written statement to the effect that Ms. Kingsley had left the network to "pursue other interests." It quickly became apparent that Kingsley either had abandoned her career or was fired.

What happened?

There was wide speculation in the journalism community that Maureen Kingsley had been caught manufacturing a story that would hurt David Palmer. Media watchers deduced that CNB producer Jay Pierce had caught her in the

REPORTER'S NOTE: Will Hertz of the *Washington Gazette* originally agreed to provide a news analysis of the Palmer scandal for this publication. As he worked on the piece, however, his interest in the story led him to do some original investigative work. Hertz reveals his discoveries in the following article, which will simultaneously appear in a *Washington Gazette* series during the same week this book is published.

lie shortly before the story was set to air on national television. This, we assumed, was why she'd gone into a very early and very hasty retirement.

The truth was revealed in this tape. We learned that Dr. George Ferragamo, a noted Los Angeles therapist who had treated Keith Palmer for depression several years before, leaked confidential doctor-patient information to Maureen Kingsley—information that seemed to prove Keith Palmer had a role in Gibson's death.

Keith Palmer insinuates that Carl Webb, his father's political adviser, and PacAmerica, the political coalition of wealthy Los Angeles businessmen who funded much of Palmer's presidential campaign, had a hand in Dr. Ferragamo's death.

The death of the esteemed therapist does seem freakish—a gas main under his office exploded on the morning of Super Tuesday—yet authorities ruled it an accidental death from the start. However, independent forensics experts and crime scene investigators consulted for this news analysis suggested that the entire investigation was botched in the extreme and an alarming amount of evidence was mishandled.

Considering the large amount of money and influence wielded by PacAmerica, one must wonder whether the blatant mishandling of evidence by officials was simply coincidental in this case.

A forensics specialist reviewed the autopsy report on Dr. Ferragamo [included in this publication] and raised many questions. For instance, there were indications of head trauma, which might suggest that Ferragamo suffered a blow before the blast and subsequent smoke and fire killed him.

The only way to deduce this was through a close evaluation of the crime scene—where and how the body was found, etc. However, as stated above, the crime scene investigation was botched. Evidence was mishandled, photographs were severely blurred, and written notes were sketchy at best.

Two grand juries were convened to study these cases.

The grand jury looking into the death of Lyle Gibson—and Keith Palmer's role in it—met in August and in less than a week returned a decision not to pursue charges against young Palmer. Keith was exonerated, and by fall's election season, the press had dropped the story.

The grand jury looking into the possible involvement of Carl Webb in the death of Dr. Ferragamo met in July and took considerably longer but ended in November with an identical outcome—no charges were ever pressed. But the public reaction to *Webb's* verdict was quite different from their reaction to *Keith's*.

POLITICAL CORRECTION

Pundits and insiders have a few things to say . . .

In both cases, the accused were judged in a court of law, but in the sometimes more explosive court of public opinion, Keith Palmer was vindicated and Carl Webb condemned.

Now Keith Palmer is one of the most in-demand speakers on the college circuit, while Carl Webb has retired from politics and is currently living in Cancun.

But this is not the end of the story. After a long investigation, I have uncovered another disturbing fact. Two weeks before Super Tuesday, three-quarters of a million dollars turned up in an offshore account in Dr. Ferragamo's name.

According to sources in the Beverly Hills community, where Ferragamo had many clients, the therapist was suffering from chronic money troubles. His two ex-wives had both won large alimony settlements, and in the last several years his practice—and his income—had fallen off sharply.

Tracing bank records, I was able to follow the money trail back to an account operated by the Committee to Elect Hodges, a California political action group supporting Palmer's opponent in this year's primary race.

The Committee to Elect Hodges was quite active in Los Angeles and paid for negative television ads against David Palmer after he took a commanding lead over Hodges in the polls.

It seems clear from these revelations that Dr. Ferragamo was willing to violate doctor-patient confidentiality in an effort to secure funds to pay off his creditors. He took money from David Palmer's political enemies to leak the story of Keith Palmer's involvement in Lyle Gibson's death.

Unfortunately, Ferragamo did not consider the ruthlessness of Carl Webb, or the lengths to which he would go to kill a story that would hurt David Palmer's chances of winning the primary.

If there is one happy note to this whole sordid affair, it is the fact that in late December, just before this book went to press, Maureen Kingsley accepted a job as a Washington reporter for Fox News.

SUNSHINE BANK OF THE CAYMAN ISLANDS

Checking	Account #879-5598-0032	Dr. George Ferragamo
Date	*Account activity*	*Amount*
04/01	Opening of account	$1,000
	Transfer from account #090-865972	$750,000
	#0001 check paid	$10,000
	#0002 check paid	$10,000
	#0003 check paid	$5,000

BBSC BAYSIDE BANK OF SOUTHERN CALIFORNIA

Checking	Account #090-865972	CEH
Date	Account activity	Amount
	#5433 check paid	$11,020
	Transfer to account #879-5598-0032	$750,000
	#5434 check paid	$100,000
	#5435 check paid	$55,038
	#5436 check paid	$17,500

COUNTY OF LOS ANGELES

CORONER'S OFFICE

CASE FILE: 01-0013

NAME: George Ferragamo

CAUSE OF DEATH: Severe Head Trauma

MANNER OF DEATH: Indeterminate: Accidental vs. Homicide

EXTERNAL EXAMINATION: The 5'9'', 160-lb. body is that of a normally developed, well-nourished white male consistent with the stated age of 47 years. Uniform flash burns of partial thickness cover 70% of the exposed body surface.

The scalp shows an irregular laceration, 5 cm. in length, in the superior midparietal skull, immediately lateral to the sagittal suture. Male pattern baldness is present with the remaining hair uniformly singed. Both eyes have burn damage and are otherwise indeterminate.

The ears show flash burns and no internal pathology.

The face shows total involvement by flash burns. Singed, well-trimmed mustache and beard are present. Good dentition is seen.

The chest shows flash and flame burns of varying thickness, altered from above burns by the presence of clothing.

The abdomen shows flash and flame burns of varying thickness, altered also by the presence of clothes.

The external genitalia are only remarkable for irregular flash and flame burns.

The extremities also show varying thickness flash and flame burns.

The back shows less than 20% involvement by flash and flame burns of varying thickness.

INTERNAL EXAM: The area of the calvarium underneath the above-mentioned skull laceration shows a circular fracture with the fracture lines radiating to the frontal, parietal, temporal, and occipital bones. The 1510-gram brain shows coup contusions underneath

Page 1

the area of skull fracture with contrecoup contusions on the ventral brain surface. Minimal intracranial hemorrhage is noted. Laceration of the corpus callosum is also observed.

The 400-gram heart has a smooth epicardial surface. The coronary arteries follow a normal anatomic course. The left main, left anterior descending, circumflex, and right coronary arteries are elastic, widely patent, and show occlusion with 25-30% atheromatosis. The myocardium is homogeneously red-brown, firm, and free of focal mottling or fibrosis. The endocardium and trabeculae carneae are smooth and glistening.

The valve leaflets and valve cusps are freely mobile and the chordae tendineae are delicate. The orifices of the coronary arteries are free of obstruction. The carotid arteries are elastic and free of atheromatosis. The aorta is elastic with minimal atheromatosis.

The trachea and major bronchi show no evidence of soot or other obstruction.

The 600-gram right lung and 400-gram left lung have smooth and shiny blue-gray visceral surfaces with mild anthracotic reticulation. The cut surfaces of both lungs are spongy gray with focal red mottling. The smaller bronchi are pink-tan and free of obstruction. The pulmonary vasculature is free of atheromatosis or thromboemboli.

The 1400-gram liver has a smooth and shiny brown capsule. The parenchyma is firm and homogeneously brown. The gallbladder contains approximately 20 cc. of dark green bile without calculi.

The 120-gram spleen has a light blue-gray wrinkled capsule. The parenchyma is homogeneously red-brown, firm, and without lymphoid follicles. The major lymph node groups of the body are not enlarged.

The 160-gram right kidney and 150-gram left kidney have smooth and shiny brown surfaces. The parenchyma is homogeneously brown, firm, and with distinct coricomedullary junctions. The calyces and pelves are unremarkable. The ureters are patent and not dilated. The bladder has unremarkable mucosa.

The testes have a light tan parenchyma and are free of nodularity.

(Continued) Page 2

The prostate gland is gray-white, firm, and nonenlarged. No lesions or calculi are present.

The esophageal serosa is pink-tan, smooth, and without lesions. The esophageal mucosa is light gray and free of ulceration or stricture. The stomach contains 35 cc. of a viscous green liquid. The gastric mucosa is tan and free of ulcers or other lesions.

The surfaces of the small and large intestine are gray-tan, smooth, and glistening. The mucosa is pink to green-tan and free of ulcerations, diverticulae, or other lesions.

The pancreas is yellow-tan, firm, and well-lobulated. The adrenal glands show distinct corticomedullary junctions. The thyroid gland is free of nodularity. The pituitary gland is present in the sella turcica and is not enlarged.

The surfaces of the pleural cavities are smooth and glistening. The peritoneal cavity has a shiny surface.

LAB RESULTS: Drug and etoh [alcohol] screen: negative.

MAJOR AUTOPSY FINDINGS:

1. Major skull fracture with resultant brain damage.
2. Extensive flash and flame burns consistent with gas explosion.

REMARKS: While there was no presence of soot in the trachea and bronchial passages, this does not absolutely mean that the subject was dead before the fire occurred. Obviously, the amount of head and brain damage was enough to have caused his demise on its own. The more significant question is what caused the head trauma? Usually in falls, one has only contrecoup contusions, whereas in deliberate blows to the head, one has coup contusions but not contrecoup lesions. The present case has both types of lesions and is consistent with either a fall of great velocity or a strong blow from an object with a broad surface. Of course, a possible fall in itself may have been accidental or deliberate. The absence of a significant amount of hemorrhage intracranially is often seen in head trauma, since vasospasm occurs posttraumatically and prevents massive blood loss initially.

Page 3

5:00 P.M.–6:00 P.M.

SPECIAL AGENT JACK BAUER: I had forty-five minutes to get to a meeting with my next lead—a man in a red baseball cap—at a restaurant in California Plaza, which was a twenty-minute drive from the hotel. And I was supposed to "bring the money," which I didn't have. Elizabeth Nash was still hysterical and taken into another room. I ordered all my CTU agents to search Alexis's room for the payoff money. They tore it apart and found fifty thousand dollars in bearer bonds.

REPORTER'S NOTE: The following testimony covers the events that occurred between 5:00 P.M. and 6:00 P.M. on the day of the California presidential primary.

I still had blood on my shirt from trying to save Alexis's life, so I switched with another agent and took off for the Plaza with Nina Myers, who volunteered to help. Unfortunately, as we arrived at the Plaza to set up security for the meeting, I found out that a CTU agent named Teddy Hanlin was assigned to be my armed backup. This was very bad news. Hanlin had a grudge against me because his ex-partner, Seth Campbell, was one of the men I helped bust for taking bribes. I remember he made a pointed remark to me about target confusion, words to the effect of "I'd hate to take down one of the good guys by mistake." I warned him not to jeopardize the mission and hoped he'd back off.

Teddy took his position across the Plaza, targeting his rifle to my area. He began making remarks through the radio receiver about his ex-partner and some tragic events that befell Campbell's family. He was openly hostile.

WIFE AND MOTHER HANGS HERSELF

Judy Rawson Campbell, 44, wife of former Intelligence Agent Seth Campbell, 45, and mother of four was found dead in Griffith Park. The Glendale woman had hung herself from a tree, using jumper cables from the trunk of her car. Seth Campbell, who was convicted of accepting bribes, is presently serving a ten-year sentence in a federal penitentiary.

Ms. Lynn Rawson, 42, of San Diego said her late sister, Judy, a full-time homemaker for the past ten years, had been depressed ever since her husband's conviction and incarceration. Mrs. Campbell's body was discovered near Griffith Observatory, where her husband had proposed to her eighteen years before.

"The family had been in terrible debt even before Seth's legal troubles," said Ms. Rawson. "Seth had a gambling problem, and that was part of the reason he took the bribe in the first place. I tried to help them, but the debts were so massive they were about to lose their house. Judy was distraught. I came up to L.A. to help with the kids, and I urged her to get treatment, but she refused."

The four Campbell children: Jeremy, 12, Brenda, 10, Bobby, 7, and Samuel, 5, have been placed in the San Diego home of Ms. Rawson, who will assume guardianship until Mr. Campbell is released from prison.

I knew why Teddy was angry and I just let him vent. It was Nina who called George Mason back at the command center and asked him to conference into our radio to warn Hanlin to bury whatever problem he had with me. That did the trick. Hanlin shut up after that, but I was still uneasy.

It was days later that I discovered *who* had assigned Hanlin as my armed backup. Alberta Green had insisted on the assignment through district level managers, and when Mason called to complain, they refused to give him a new backup man.

REP. ROY SCHNEIDER, (R) TEX.: Are you saying that your superiors purposely assigned you a backup man with a personal grudge against you? A man who would be holding a rifle pointed at your head?

BAUER: You can confirm it with George Mason, but *yes,* that appears to be what happened.

CHAIRMAN FULBRIGHT: Can you give us some insight into that?

BAUER: Chappelle and Green were furious with me for my actions at the Palmer breakfast earlier in the day, and even though Palmer himself had me provisionally reinstated, I was on their shit list—(pause) sorry, sir. Excuse my language.

FULBRIGHT: It's all right, Agent Bauer. Continue, please.

BAUER: Alberta Green had already told me she held me personally responsible for compromising the integrity of CTU. And since the credibility of the agency was what mattered most to her, I'm sure she meant to royally—uh—(short pause) royally obstruct and impede me. At that point with Chappelle's blessing.

FULBRIGHT: So she purposely assigned Hanlin?

BAUER: Yes. Hanlin would either take out his anger at me by shooting me—or by fouling up the mission. He threatened me, but didn't harm me. In the end, he fouled up the mission.

SCHNEIDER: Lord, talk about politics as usual—

FULBRIGHT: Go on, Agent Bauer.

BAUER: The man in the red baseball cap finally appeared. I later learned that his name was Alan Morgan. I approached Morgan and indicated that the briefcase I was carrying contained his payoff. He called me "Alexis," so I knew I wasn't made. I got him to spell out the reason he was being paid off.

Photo courtesy of California Plaza Security.

Apparently Morgan worked for Pacific Electric in Saugus, California. The Drazens were paying him to turn off the electricity in one section of the city's power grid—sector 26GG—for five minutes at 7:20 P.M.

At that point Morgan became suspicious of my questions and figured out I wasn't Alexis. He bolted, so I quickly took off after him, warning everyone on the backup team to hold their fire.

Hanlin said he had a clear shot to clip the fleeing man. I ordered him *not to shoot*—warning him at least five times—but he ignored me and fired anyway. Alan Morgan's body crashed through a glass railing and fell to the ground. He died instantly. My lead was gone. I couldn't even question him.

I was furious with Hanlin and dressed him down for disobeying a direct order. I understand that since this incident, Division has promoted him.

6:00 P.M.–7:00 P.M.

SPECIAL AGENT JACK BAUER: How the hell was a Saugus power outage going to help the Drazens? That's what I asked myself. But it's all I had to go on until I received a call from David Palmer. By that time David had twisted some arms at the Pentagon and had them retrieve Ellis's Operation Nightfall folder from their records. Ellis's missing file was there. It listed dates and locations of Victor Drazen's movements in the months before Nightfall. Its final entry was an address unrelated to anything else—21911 Kipling in Saugus.

REPORTER'S NOTE: The following testimony covers the events that occurred between 6:00 P.M. and 7:00 P.M. on the day of the California presidential primary.

I called Agent Almeida at CTU who confirmed that the address fell within the grid coordinates that were going to be blacked out at 7:20 P.M. Nina returned to CTU, and George Mason accompanied me on the drive to Saugus.

CHAIRMAN FULBRIGHT: You say the Saugus address was in Robert Ellis's missing file?

BAUER: That's correct.

FULBRIGHT: And you eventually discovered a Level 3 detention facility there—part of an underground prison system operated by the Department of Defense, correct?

BAUER: Yes, sir.

FULBRIGHT: What do you make of that, Agent Bauer?

BAUER: Clearly, Ellis knew that Drazen had been captured and imprisoned, that he wasn't dead. At *what point* he knew is unclear. The notation in the files is obscure and not dated. It's possible Bob learned the truth about Drazen *after* the outcome of Operation Nightfall. It's also possible he set me and my team up to fail, then destroyed any evidence of his contact with General Henderson or DIA's Special Unit for Counterintelligence Initiatives—the team that ultimately captured Drazen.

I liked Bob, but he was a dark horse. It could have gone down either way. . . . In any event, it's not something I can enlighten you on.

FULBRIGHT: Very well. I'll turn this matter over to the Joint Congressional Intelligence Oversight Committee to pursue, along with their investigation into the DOD's underground prison system. Continue, please, Agent Bauer. Tell us about Saugus.

BAUER: Saugus is an industrial area outside of Los Angeles, yet the area where we were headed was sanctioned as a wildlife preserve. It made no sense. And when we arrived, I saw no sign of animals.

I used my handheld GPS to find the correct address—it was the middle of a field. Mason and I noticed a brand-new power transformer nearby. It was about then that I heard a chopper approach. I was convinced that someone had followed us. I just didn't know who.

It was around 7:00 P.M. at that point, and all afternoon I had been wondering about my family. I hadn't talked to them for hours, but George Mason had assured me earlier that they were all right and simply sleeping at the safe house. I found out later, of course, that George Mason had instructed Tony Almeida and others at CTU to keep me in the dark about the shootout at the safe house. He may have had his reasons, but I don't know if I'll ever forgive him for that. I never had the chance to help my daughter and my wife during those hours when they needed me. During those hours when they were both missing . . .

REPORTER'S NOTE: In separate testimony, Philip Parslow, M.D., a Los Angeles surgeon, recounted events involving Teri Bauer. . . .

CHAIRMAN FULBRIGHT: Thank you for agreeing to testify, Dr. Parslow.

DR. PHILIP PARSLOW: I'm happy to help you in any way I can. I cared deeply for Teri Bauer. She was a very lovely human being, and I know what an extreme loss this is to her husband and daughter.

FULBRIGHT: Yes, we all share your condolences. . . . You can help us today by filling in some of the blanks about Mrs. Bauer's movements between the hours of 4:00 P.M. and 7:00 P.M. on the day she died.

PARSLOW: About four-thirty I received a call at my office from a nearby restaurant owner, who said Teri Bauer had wandered in off the street very confused. He thought she needed some help and asked if I wouldn't mind coming over to talk to her—

REP. PAULINE P. DRISCOLL, (D) CONN.: (Interrupting) Excuse me, Doctor, but could you tell us a little more about how you knew Mrs. Bauer? Give us some background so we know how she regarded you.

PARSLOW: We had met six months before at the Getty Museum. There was a cocktail party in honor of a new exhibit, and I was there with some colleagues. Teri had an abiding passion for art and knew a great deal about it. It was a treat going through any gallery with her. I remember how much she admired the Titian that evening— it's this lush painting of the goddess Venus trying to restrain her lover Adonis from going off to the hunt. She clings to him, appears to be pleading with him not to go, but Adonis is depicted as aloof, unaffected.

At the time, I thought Teri's preoccupation with that painting was superficial—the brush strokes, the use of color. But looking back, I think it had more to do with the problems between her and her husband, from whom she'd just separated.

Anyway, as I said, she was a lovely human being and she appeared to be free, so I began to see her. We became close, but to be perfectly frank, we never slept together. She was afraid, she told me, of losing her family. I never even met her teenage daughter, Kim. But then she hadn't met my two children either—I'm divorced. We figured it would be less complicated if we kept the kids out of it for a while, at least until we knew where we were going.

Well, we weren't going anywhere, as it turned out. I was a shoulder for Teri to lean on for a few months. When her husband asked to move back in, she decided to give it another try. At that point she asked me not to call her anymore, so I didn't.

DRISCOLL: Thank you for your honesty, Doctor.

FULBRIGHT: Please continue with the events of the day in question. What happened after you arrived at the restaurant?

PARSLOW: I found Teri in a peculiar state. She couldn't remember her name or anything about her family or where she'd come from. I wanted her to come with me to the hospital, but she was very frightened by that idea. She was convinced it would be "dangerous." Her panic alarmed me, so I decided to try to examine her there.

I saw that she had been roughed up by someone—frankly, at the time, I thought it might have been her husband who had done it. Otherwise, she seemed stable. Most importantly, she seemed to show no sign of an injury to the head. I'm a surgeon, not a neurologist, but given her mental state, I guessed she was suffering from some form of dissociative amnesia—

FULBRIGHT: (Interrupting) Doctor, please define that term for the record.

PARSLOW: Certainly. While some amnesias can be a result of a blow to the head or other medical traumas, dissociative amnesia is a type caused by a traumatic event of some sort. The dissociative aspect is thought to be a coping mechanism—the person literally dissociates himself from a situation or experience too traumatic to integrate within the conscious self.

DRISCOLL: And which was the traumatic event Teri Bauer was trying to block out or cope with at *that* point in the day? The poor woman had many—as you must know by now.

PARSLOW: I do, ma'am. The event that I believe triggered her condition was witnessing her daughter's death.

DRISCOLL: Kimberly Bauer? But the girl's alive—

PARSLOW: At that point in the afternoon, Teri didn't know that. She had witnessed a car going down an embankment and bursting into flames. Her daughter had been inside that car.

From what I understand, a killer was after Teri and her daughter. Teri tried to escape the man by turning her car sharply off the road and into some bushes, but she didn't realize that the front end of the car was extended precariously over a steep embankment. When she briefly left the car to check the road and see if they had lost the man, the car slid over the edge and burst into flames.

At the time, Teri thought she had just caused her daughter's death. The truth is, Kim opened the door halfway down the hill and was thrown from the car. Seeing the explosion, after the other traumas of the day, sent Teri over the edge, too, so to speak.

FULBRIGHT: How did she get to the restaurant?

PARSLOW: A young woman driving by picked her up. Teri couldn't remember anything about her life at that point, including her name. But when the woman drove past a restaurant that Teri and I had frequented, some memory stirred deep inside her. She asked to be let off there. She seemed terribly disoriented, so the owner, who knew us both, called me.

FULBRIGHT: What happened after you examined her? Did you manage to convince her to go to a hospital?

PARSLOW: She absolutely refused—she began to panic and plead. I didn't want to push her because she was in such a fragile state, so I took her to her home, hoping it would trigger other memories of her life.

DRISCOLL: And that's where the assassin was waiting, correct?

PARSLOW: That's right. That's how I was shot. A CTU agent had been murdered before we even arrived, and another agent, a man named Tony Almeida, arrived in time to save our lives. I'm sorry to say that my friend Chris, a private security guard who worked in my office building, was killed, too. I had asked him to come over to help protect Teri. I had no idea how much danger she was really in—if it had been her husband who roughed her up, I thought Chris and his gun would be enough to scare away any further threat.

DRISCOLL: When did Mrs. Bauer finally recover her memory?

PARSLOW: She was still mentally struggling when we walked around the house. Right before the assassin appeared, she seemed to be making a breakthrough. Then the assassin began gunning us all down. Although Agent Almeida arrived in time to stop him from killing us, it seems that this latest trauma is what restored her memory.

REPORTER'S NOTE: In separate testimony, Agent Tony Almeida confirmed the identity of the shooter at the Bauer house. He was Drazen's associate Jovan Myovic.

Teri was hysterical when the memories flooded back to her. She thought her daughter was dead. She finally calmed down when Agent Almeida assured her that Kim was alive. After surviving the car's fall, Kim had phoned CTU looking for her father. Unfortunately, Kim didn't trust anyone, not even the other agents at CTU. So she hung up before Agent Almeida could confirm her whereabouts.

That's all I know. After I was shot, Agent Almeida drove me to the hospital, and I never saw Teri again. . . .

FULBRIGHT: (After a pause) Doctor Parslow? Are you all right?

PARSLOW: The story ends tragically, you know?

FULBRIGHT: Excuse me?

PARSLOW: The story behind that Titian painting. Venus cannot prevent Adonis from going on the hunt. Ultimately, he's killed. . . . I think deep down Teri feared that the same thing would happen between her and Jack—that their story would end tragically, too.

FULBRIGHT: Thank you, Doctor Parslow, you are excused. Let's take a short recess.

POLITICAL CORRECTION

Pundits and insiders have a few things to say . . .

TEXTBOOK UNELECTABLE

By Rick Norris

"A senator's duty, a president's duty, an elected representative's duty is not only to his country, but also to his family. If he can't manage the personal interactions of the people closest to him, then he can't expect the electorate to believe in his abilities to lead a nation."

—SENATOR DAVID PALMER, SUPER TUESDAY PRESS CONFERENCE

How did he do it? The moment David Palmer uttered those words, every hardened political mind in the nation was thinking the same thing: the man has just rendered himself textbook unelectable. According to sources close to the campaign, Palmer's own wife referred to this as his "concession speech." Mike Hodges, Palmer's opponent in the primary, said Palmer was "toast."

Things were looking pretty bleak for candidate Palmer. As the sun rose on Super Tuesday, he found himself neck-deep in a personal and political scandal. Yet by 9:00 P.M. Pacific time, Palmer was the decisive winner of all eleven primaries. The most surprising thing about this scandal was that the electorate had heard all about Palmer's dirty laundry—from him! And they not only gave him a pass, they also handed the senator from Maryland an approval rating of 86 percent.

REPORTER'S NOTE:
Rick Norris, a trusted Washington insider, is a man who's commanded troops in many a political war room, serving as a campaign adviser for two presidents and five senators. Norris agreed to provide some insight into David Palmer's now famous "Super Tuesday Address," which he gave between 6:30 P.M. and 7:00 P.M. on the day of the California primary.

What caused this turnaround? What was Palmer's strategy? How was this modern political miracle achieved?

As it turns out, David Palmer relied on a controversial and previously untested political formula called honesty. He stepped up to the microphone, smiled for the camera, and told the American people the truth.

It was refreshing. It was unheard of. And by God it worked!

What David Palmer did on that historic Tuesday was more than expose his own mistakes—he bared his soul and revealed his basic humanity for everyone to see. Palmer admitted the mistakes of the past, and unlike previous seekers of high office, he took responsibility for them, too.

Overwhelmingly, the American people loved him for it. That was because the average citizen could relate to a bumbling and sometimes clueless father out of touch with his family. A man whose daughter was the victim of an unspeakable crime. A man who put the needs of his children before his own ambitions, even if it meant an end to a lifelong career.

The voters know how to forgive. What David Palmer discovered on Super Tuesday was how to ask for that forgiveness. He asked for forgiveness the way we all should do—with a frank confession, honest contrition, a willingness to accept full responsibility and the consequences of his actions, and the promise to do better in the future.

What more can we ask of a man—or a president?

IT'S A CIRCUS! IT'S A FIREWORKS DISPLAY! NO . . . IT'S A PRESIDENTIAL CANDIDATE

By Noreen Stroud, *Washington Gazette*

Wow, what a show! I don't know whether to applaud or weep. Perhaps I'll indulge in a little of both, for I am hunched over my spare Ikea desk, typing away on my tiny iMac keyboard in my spartan little room, and I realize how downright unexciting my life really is. Especially when compared with the latest and greatest of our presidential candidates, David Palmer.

Things sure are exciting over at the Palmer Ranch. Not at all like my house. Why? Not one of my children has gone near a ledge—let alone plunged off!

And our moneyman—we call him Dad—doesn't have time to conspire against the family, let alone knock off a therapist.

And there hasn't been an explosion in our house in weeks!

My goodness me. And I used to think a glimpse of thong was shocking!

I do remember that a little thong could sell newspapers, but I fear there are not enough trees left in America to keep readers abreast of the soap opera that is the life of our esteemed senator from Maryland—a state I once thought of as staid and sober and certainly no California.

Gee, I may have to reconsider.

Rumor even has it that the Super Tuesday Address caused a severe rift between the previously happy couple. David flew one way, Sherry the other after Tuesday's very eventful night.

REPORTER'S NOTE: From the personal and political scandals revealed by David Palmer's speech to the rumors that the Palmer marriage was showing signs of strain, print and broadcast journalists had a field day reporting on the events of Super Tuesday. Here are just two examples. . . .

POLITICAL CORRECTION

Pundits and insiders have a few things to say . . .

Should the three-ring circus we call Senator Palmer be sworn in as president? Will we witness press conferences with divorce lawyers instead of international heads of state? And interviews on Court TV instead of *Face the Nation*? Time will tell.

But perhaps I'm being too harsh. Well . . . times is tough, folks. We've got to sell papers, and may I remind you, you're the ones buying.

America loves its suds—whether it's J. R. Ewing, Princess Di, Luke and Laura, or that Man from Arkansas—fiction or fact makes no matter, it's a story to be chewed, swallowed, and sometimes, sometimes choked on.

Then there's that other little item to consider—what we like to call free elections—even though, just between you and me, those elections seem to cost an awful lot of money for something billed as "free."

I guess that's why we end up with all those nasty, evil moneymen who corrupt and manipulate helpless senators and maybe presidents, too.

Funny how presidents can't control the moneymen. Dad was so easy to tame.

Transcript from Fox News' Sunday Morning with Brett Hughes. *This segment aired five days after the events of Super Tuesday.*

HOST BRETT HUGHES: What are we to make of the events of Super Tuesday? Has the election cycle gotten a little rougher, or is it just me?

POLITICAL COMMENTATOR FRANK FARNES: (Laughing) It's you, Brett. Politics has always been rough. Ask Gary Hart. Seriously, though, I haven't seen anyone trash a hotel room like that since The Who.

COLUMNIST ART CONACKIE: (Laughing) If Palmer wins the election, maybe he should smash the podium after he's sworn in.

POLITICAL COMMENTATOR TONY RAINES: (Laughing) Meet the new boss. . . .

FRANK FARNES, ART CONACKIE: (Singing) Same as the old boss!

BRETT HUGHES: We're showing our age here. We shouldn't ignore our younger viewers. Our motto is "Objective and Honest."

ART CONACKIE: Do any of these kids today wreck hotel rooms? Eminem, maybe?

BRETT HUGHES: (Chuckling) Plain or peanut?

7:00 P.M.–8:00 P.M.

REPORTER'S NOTE:
The following testimony covers the events that occurred between 7:00 P.M. and 8:00 P.M. on the day of the California presidential primary.

SPECIAL AGENT JACK BAUER: After the sun went down, George Mason started to get second thoughts. I was determined to stick it out at the wildlife sanctuary until seven-twenty when the power grid was supposed to be shut down, but George was getting antsy. A call came in to him about then from the hospital—Alexis Drazen was conscious. Mason left to question him, and I remained behind.

CHAIRMAN FULBRIGHT: But there was nothing in that Saugus field, according to George Mason.

BAUER: George isn't the best observer in the world. The sanctuary had wooden fences, paths, and property markers. It was also well tended. There were markers citing buried power lines, and that new transformer, too. After George left, I moved deeper into the area and spotted the old silo complex—

FULBRIGHT: Farm silo?

BAUER: Missile silo, sir, the underground facility. The sanctuary was obviously an old antiaircraft site left over from the dawn of the Cold War. Back in the nineteen fifties and sixties, antiaircraft sites were established outside of most American cities. I traced the origin of the site in Saugus to 1959.

REP. PAULINE P. DRISCOLL, (D) CONN.: And this was the (papers shuffling) . . . the "Level 3" facility operated by the Department of Defense?

REP. ROY SCHNEIDER, (R) TEX.: Ah, yes, the secret prison system.

BAUER: That's correct. And the guards there had quite a welcome waiting for me as I entered their underground facility—there was an ultrasonic alarm to disorient and confuse me and a taser to take me down. I woke up on a cot in a cold concrete cell and promptly threw up.

Mark DeSalvo came in shortly after. He was a DOD operative serving as warden of this facility. I identified myself, but he'd already checked me out. He wanted to know what I was doing at his prison, so I told him.

When I mentioned the time of the power grid shutdown, seven-twenty, I knew I'd touched a nerve. He admitted that a prisoner transfer helicopter was due at that time. I wanted to know the identity of the prisoner, but DeSalvo said it was classified—even he didn't know.

I warned him that something heavy was about to go down. He chose to trust me. From my own military experience, I knew DeSalvo had to be army or ex-army. I'm sure that's why we got along. . . .

DeSalvo called for backup, but his request was going to take time

CAPTAIN MARK DeSALVO, U.S. ARMY

AGE: 36

MILITARY EXPERIENCE

- Department of Defense, Mobile Underground Detention and Detainment System, 2002
- Department of Defense, Special Unit for Counterintelligence Initiatives, 2000
- U.S. Army Capture Management Program, Albania, 1999
- First Lieutenant, U.S. Army Command, Seoul, South Korea
- Master Sergeant, 10th Mountain Division, Somalia, 1993

EDUCATION

- U.S. Army Prison Management Systems and Theories
- U.S. Army Interrogation and Intelligence Gathering
- Ranger Training School

PERSONAL

- Married – Teresa Su-Ji Chiang DeSalvo

Note: Teresa Su-Ji Chiang DeSalvo passed away of complications from pancreatic cancer on June 11, 2000.

to move up the chain of command. So I convinced him to arm and outfit everyone at the facility, down to the maintenance and technical staff, to make it appear the prison was more secure than it was.

When that helicopter arrived, I figured the Drazens would have some sort of strike team watching, waiting for the grid to fail so they could make their hit. But their power grid mole was dead, and the power would *not* go down. I just hoped that would be enough to deter the strike team until reinforcements arrived.

The chopper—a civilian model—landed without a hitch. The prisoner was bound, shackled, and hooded, so I never got a good look at him as the guards hustled him out of the chopper and down into the prison.

DRISCOLL: What about your family, Agent Bauer? Were you still worried about them?

BAUER: Yes, *of course.* They were *always* on my mind, but I had no idea, during all those hours, that they were in any acute danger. George Mason continued to lie to me, making me believe that my wife and daughter were secure in a CTU safe house. So I continued to put my energies into ending the threat against them—into stopping the Drazens.

REPORTER'S NOTE:
At this time Teri Bauer was transported back to CTU, but Kimberly Bauer was still missing. The following testimony by Kim Bauer covers those missing hours. . . .

KIMBERLY BAUER: After I climbed up that hill, I called for my mom. She had gotten out of the car before it rolled, so I knew she would be okay, but she wasn't there, and I figured she got kidnapped again.

I was scared for her more than for myself. I found a pay phone and dialed CTU, looking for my dad. A man's voice answered, said his name was Tony Almeida, but I didn't know him. He said my dad wasn't there. My mom had gotten tricked by a dirty CTU agent named Jamey Farrell, and I didn't want the same thing to happen to me, so I hung up.

Right away I thought of Rick, because I wanted to find my mom, and his dead friend, Dan, knew the people who took us in the first place. I thought maybe he could help me find out more. He gave me his address in Echo Park, so I got a taxi and drove there.

When I arrived, I was in for a big shock—Rick had a girlfriend already, named Melanie. I sort of liked Rick, but I didn't know he was seeing anyone, you know? Anyway, I told them both that I just wanted to search Dan's room. Rick helped me look for any information that could help me find my mom.

Then Dan's brother, Frank, showed up at the house. What a psycho. He had arranged for a drug deal to go down at the house, and he wouldn't let me leave. I guess he suspected I might tell someone about it.

Dan was dead, but Frank didn't know it—Rick had been too scared to tell him. And Frank was *still* expecting Dan to show up with the twenty-thousand-dollar payoff for kidnapping me and Janet.

I let it slip that Dan was dead, and Frank went ballistic. He was so angry—and then he got worried. He said that the drug dealers were going to want their money, but it was too late to stop the deal from going down.

When Frank stepped out of earshot, I really let Rick have it. I told him he should turn his life around. He was a good guy—smart, kind, brave, handsome—he had so much going for him, but he was surrounding himself with these low-life criminals.

Rick said he did want to turn his life around, but at that moment Frank was making it difficult. I decided to make a run for it. But just as I got to the door, Frank's friends barreled in with a duffel bag full of guns. Since he had no money to make the buy, Frank said he was going to *rob* the drug dealers.

When they came to the house, Frank acted like a real badass. He demanded the twenty thousand dollars' worth of Ecstasy from them. The dealers spotted Frank's gun and pulled out their own. Suddenly there was this standoff. Frank's crew came in with *their* weapons drawn. The dealers dropped their guns, and as Frank went to disarm them, he smashed Rick in his injured shoulder, saying, "All this because you couldn't keep my brother alive."

Then Frank shattered the nose of one of the drug dealers with the butt of his gun. That's when the dealer told us all we had the right to remain silent. He was a cop! Suddenly a SWAT team burst through the doors and arrested Frank and his crew. I tried to explain that I wasn't a part of their stupid drug deal, but they didn't believe me—of course, right? Who would? So they carted me off to jail.

REPORTER'S NOTE:
Agent Bauer's testimony regarding his actions at the DOD's Level 3 underground prison continues. . . .

FULBRIGHT: What did you do next at the detention facility?

BAUER: While DeSalvo and the guards processed their prisoner, I checked the place out. It was run-down, with a bad electrical system and no backup—my house was more secure than this place. The DOD relied on the prison's remote location and its secretiveness for security—but that wasn't enough when the enemies you were facing had reliable intelligence.

And I knew the Drazens had come too far to quit—I knew that Andre would still attack that night. The strike team had just been delayed from accomplishing their mission, they had not been stopped.

I needed to know the identity of the prisoner—that was the key to solving this whole mystery. I reached out to Senator Palmer, who promised to make a few calls. But time was running out. I had to act. I crept into the security command center of the prison facility and saw the interior of the cell on the monitor. The prisoner was sitting at a table, his back turned to me. As he rose, DeSalvo came in and caught me observing. Then I saw the prisoner's face—

I thought there could be no more surprises that day. But I was wrong. When I looked into that monitor, I thought I was seeing a ghost. . . .

DRISCOLL: It was Victor Drazen?

BAUER: Yes, ma'am—the Butcher of Belgrade—the man I thought I'd assassinated during Operation Nightfall, exactly two years before.

I knew in that moment that Operation Nightfall had been set up to fail from the start. The world was supposed to think Victor Drazen was dead—and me and my team were supposed to die, too, just to make the story of Drazen's assassination more plausible.

In my estimation, there was a *traitor* at work here—someone *beyond* Nina Myers, someone who had a higher position in the intelligence community.

FULBRIGHT: Where do you think we should look for this traitor?

BAUER: Sir, I wish I could tell you. This person could be operating out of any number of intelligence agencies—CIA, CTU, DIA, DOD.

All I know is that a traitor set me up, killed my team, authorized the capture and secret imprisonment of Victor Drazen, and aided Drazen's sons in breaking their father out of prison. This traitor is also responsible for every single death that occurred on the day of the California presidential primary.

One thing is clear—Robert Ellis may have been in on this deception, but he was definitely not the mastermind. Someone *else* was responsible, and he or she remains at large today.

FULBRIGHT: These are troubling revelations, Agent Bauer. If true, then our national security may still be compromised.

BAUER: Yes, sir.

FULBRIGHT: (After conferring with his colleagues) Please continue with your testimony.

BAUER: I pleaded with DeSalvo to move the prisoner before the strike team lurking outside hit the facility. DeSalvo put me off, but agreed to give me five minutes with Victor Drazen inside his cell.

SCHNEIDER: You interrogated him?

BAUER: I . . . tried. But it was like talking to a wall. When I introduced myself, it was apparent that he already knew who I was. He said next to nothing. Then I met his gaze and I knew . . .

FULBRIGHT: (After a pause) Agent Bauer? What did you know?

BAUER: How do I put this? Ever hear that saying "Be careful when you stare into the abyss. You might find the abyss staring back at you"? That's what it felt like, staring into the eyes of Victor Drazen. You could see that he'd checked out of the human race a long time ago.

DRISCOLL: That's a rather extreme evaluation.

BAUER: Ma'am, if you had seen what I saw in those eyes, you'd agree. Mark DeSalvo saw it, too. It's something you learn in this business. With men like Drazen, all the signs are right there in the eyes—a kind of insane warning that something very bad is about to go down and you're going to be on the receiving end of it.

So when DeSalvo burst into that cell and took a hard look into Drazen's eyes, he agreed to move his prisoner right away. We didn't know it then, but it was already too late.

8:00 P.M.–9:00 P.M.

REPORTER'S NOTE:
The following testimony covers the events that occurred between 8:00 P.M. and 9:00 P.M. on the day of the California presidential primary.

CHAIRMAN FULBRIGHT: You said it was too late, Agent Bauer. What did you mean?

SPECIAL AGENT JACK BAUER: DeSalvo, his guards, and I began to move Victor Drazen. We were in a corridor when the lights went out. That meant the strike team had cut the power—probably by blowing up the transformer. It was an act of desperation—taking out part of the electrical system would send all kinds of ripples through emergency services. In such events the power company immediately dispatches investigation and repair teams. Police and local fire departments are notified because there's a danger of forest fire. That was why the Drazens tried to bribe a power company worker—it was more expensive, but less likely to attract attention. As it was, lots of people were going to be showing up at the detention center real soon, maybe even before the CTU team I'd requested arrived—*if* it ever arrived.

REP. ROY SCHNEIDER, (R) TEX.: You'd contacted CTU?

BAUER: I spoke to George Mason directly. I told him everything—about the prison system, about Victor Drazen, and about the Serb strike team knocking at our door. I begged for a CTU tactical squad, but Mason sounded like he wasn't going to do anything more than pass my request up the chain of command.

I figured I was doomed, but it didn't matter anymore. I couldn't fight this battle alone. If Mason couldn't help, then it was over.

I didn't know it then, but Mason had tried his best to secure help. He stuck his own neck out and sent in a tactical team without

Chappelle's authorization. Then he tried to smooth things over by contacting the DOD to help unify command at the scene. But Mason's efforts were stalled by someone in General Henderson's office.

Ryan Chappelle was ducking Mason, too. No doubt part of Langley's efforts to isolate the Los Angeles Division of CTU and contain the damage—or maybe Chappelle was just covering his ass.

REP. PAULINE P. DRISCOLL, (D) CONN.: What happened after the lights went out?

BAUER: We were in the hallway, totally exposed, when the door to the detention center was blown open. The Serbs used Semtex to take the steel door off its hinges. The strike team was inside.

De Salvo ordered a retreat, but we didn't get far. As Drazen's men surrounded me, I held a gun to Victor's throat—threatening to kill him.

Andre emerged from the darkness, DeSalvo his prisoner. He

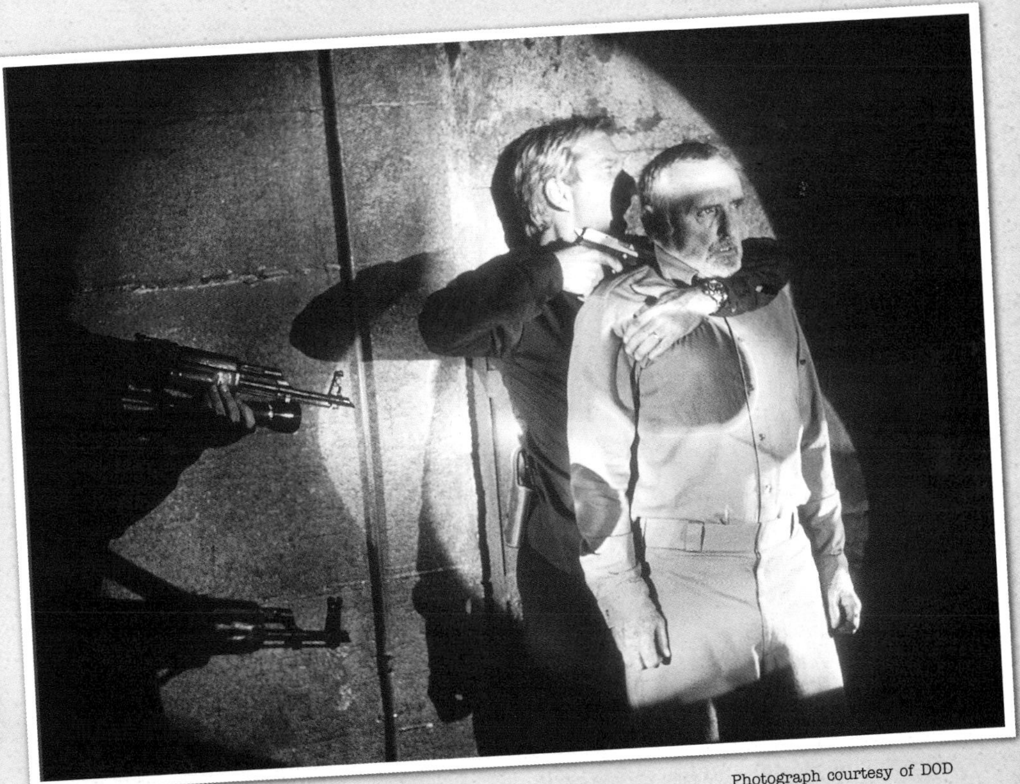

Photograph courtesy of DOD

threatened to kill DeSalvo if I didn't lay down my weapon. Andre gave me three seconds to make up my mind. (Pause) I couldn't live with more blood on my hands. . . . I surrendered.

As soon as Victor was safe, Andre killed DeSalvo. Father and son had their little reunion. Then Andre began to beat on me. (Pause) He was very . . . professional . . . very well trained. Andre knew how to inflict pain without mortal injury. (Pause)

FULBRIGHT: Agent Bauer, where was the CTU action team at that point?

BAUER: (Pause) They were there. They were moving in on the detention center when Victor contacted George Mason to negotiate. Mason handled it just right—no negotiations.

By that time the CTU tactical team had found DeSalvo and the others. They were dead. When they pursued the Serbs deep into the prison corridors, the Serbs brought the roof down, cutting the CTU team off.

ANDRE DRAZEN
AGE: 36
BIRTHPLACE: Požarevac, Serbia

EXPERIENCE
- Chairman, Serb International Coalition for Justice, Cayman Islands
- Chief of Special Operations, Black Dogs (Slobodan Milosevic's ultrasecret police organization)
- Founder, Kosovo/1389 (Serb nationalist paramilitary organization banned in 1986)

EDUCATION
- Master of Science, Engineering, University of Belgrade
- Bachelor of Political Science, London School of Economics

MILITARY
- Captain, Serbian Army Special Operations
- Instructor, Serbian Army Special Operations

PERSONAL
- Single

FROM THE DESK OF

MARC CERASINI

SUBJECT: ANDRE DRAZEN

One begins to understand the scope of the Drazen clan's increasing power from the informative passage found here and on page 324 of Valery Illyushin's recently published memoir, *Fifty Years Inside the Kremlin: A Survivor's Story*.

Illyushin is one of the Kremlin's great survivors, having served under Soviet premiers from Khrushchev to Gorbachev. After the fall of the Soviet Union, Illyushin made the successful transition to public service under the flag of the Russian Federation, serving as an adviser to Boris Yeltsin and then briefly to Vladimir Putin before retiring.

I recall one January morning, rather too early for an old man in winter. It was the end of an old century and the beginning of a new one. Boris Yeltsin had just resigned, having appointed Vladimir Putin as acting president.

Putin summoned me to his office inside the Kremlin. Over a samovar of steaming tea we talked of many things—the snows, the situation in the Balkans, America. Finally we spoke of Chechnya.

"Valery, my friend, tell me, what would you do to stop the rebellions?" Putin asked.

"There are certainly measures that can be taken to quash dissent," I told him. "Look at what Victor Drazen and his son Andre have accomplished. Their Black Dog secret police have cowed all who challenge Milosevic's power. Political enemies—even whole villages—simply disappear."

Putin considered me for long moments. "The Russian Army deserves our support. But what you speak of are the old days. Like the days of Stalin. Those days of blood are over."

I smiled at him and shook my head. "Not so long as Victor Drazen remains alive. . . ."

—Valery Illyushin, with Leo Kerne, *Fifty Years Inside the Kremlin: A Survivor's Story*

324

I thought we were going to be trapped inside the detention center, but I was wrong. Andre had the schematics, as well as an exit strategy—a concrete wall in one of the halls ran parallel to a drainage tunnel. The Serbs blasted through that wall, moved into the drainage system, and emerged several miles away.

At that point Victor Drazen ordered his son to kill me. To buy time, I did what George Mason refused to do—I negotiated. I told Victor that CTU had Alexis. To prove I was telling the truth, I told Andre I knew about Elizabeth Nash and about the scheduled meeting at Andre's hotel room.

SCHNEIDER: You did this to buy time?

BAUER: I did it to regain control of the situation. To stop the Drazens. To save my family and the life of David Palmer. I also knew I had to finish the job I'd started in Kosovo—I was going to do everything in my power to wipe the Drazen family off the face of the earth.

REPORTER'S NOTE:
The following testimony covers the events that occurred between 9:00 P.M. and 10:00 P.M. on the day of the California presidential primary.

9:00 P.M.–10:00 P.M.

SPECIAL AGENT JACK BAUER: We had escaped the detention center. A vehicle was waiting for us on a rural road. I was bound and hooded, then tossed into the back of a van.

As we raced down the freeway, Andre called CTU and demanded to speak with his brother. Tony patched him through to the hospital.

Victor and Alexis spoke briefly. Then Victor made his intentions clear to Mason. He was willing to trade me for Alexis. Mason told him no deal. I figured I was finished, but at least my family was safe—or so I thought.

Back at CTU, Tony had located Kimberly, only to lose her again when some of Drazen's special-ops boys slammed into the police car delivering her to CTU. A Los Angeles policeman—a uniformed officer—was murdered, and a narcotics detective was seriously wounded. Now they had my daughter, and I still wasn't even being told she was in danger. That son of a bitch Mason—

CHAIRMAN FULBRIGHT: Calm down, Agent Bauer—

BAUER: Mason wasn't the only problem. I didn't know it at the time, but it was Nina Myers who alerted Victor Drazen to Kimberly's whereabouts. Nina set my daughter up to be recaptured.

REP. ROY SCHNEIDER (R) TEX.: Where did the Drazens take you, Agent Bauer?

BAUER: As I said before, I had a hood covering my head, so I couldn't see—I had to rely on my other senses and my special operations training. I knew when the van stopped that we were still close to the freeway . . . I could hear the cars rushing by. Then the Serbs dragged me into a restaurant, through the kitchen. I knew that because I heard the clanging of pots and pans and could smell food cooking—cabbage and bacon. Garlic. Paprika. Serbian food.

I was dragged down two flights of steps and tossed into a chair. The hood was removed. I was in the finished basement of an ethnic restaurant. It was run-down, real shabby. I caught a glimpse of a man sitting at a computer in the next room.

An elderly man rushed in and embraced Victor Drazen. It appeared that they were old friends—Drazen called him Nikola. His daughter's name was Mila. She was young and very pretty. Nikola told her to serve their guests.

REPORTER'S NOTE: Jack Bauer had been taken to Nikola's Delights, a restaurant specializing in Eastern European cuisine located on Grand Avenue, quite close to the auto repair center where the Drazens waited for Alexis to be delivered to them by George Mason and the CTU.

The restaurant was owned and operated by restaurateur Nikola Luminovic and his daughter, Mila. In Yugoslavia, Nikola's two brothers, his wife, and several in-laws were murdered by a terrorist bomb planted by ethnic Albanian activists. Nikola and his daughter came to America in 1997, seeking political asylum, which was granted in 1998.

Nikola's friendship with Victor Drazen began in Belgrade in the 1970s, when the Luminovic family restaurant was a haven for pro-Serb political activists, including Victor Drazen and his associates.

Victor ate with Nikola. He offered me food but I turned it down. I was ravenous, but I knew that a full stomach would make me sleepy—and I needed to remain alert. As it was, the pain from my beating was dulling my senses. I tried to focus and used my SERE training to shut out the pain. I had to be ready to exploit any opportunity to escape.

SCHNEIDER: How did David Palmer become involved in CTU's hostage negotiations?

BAUER: (Shuffling papers) According to Palmer, Nina Myers contacted him directly. Nina's secret objective with that call was to get Alexis Drazen released from federal custody. She told Palmer that Victor Drazen was alive and that I was their hostage and that they would only release me in exchange for Alexis. She told Palmer that Mason, Chappelle, and Langley were stalling the negotiations.

CIA command clearly had no interest in saving my life. They were obviously hoping Drazen would flee the country so that they could hide the truth from the media.

Palmer was on my side, however, and phoned Mason to cut through the red tape. Mason finally agreed to release Alexis in exchange for my life.

SCHNEIDER: And what did our new president-elect promise to do for George Mason's career in return for his help? I've heard rumors of a secret arrangement between Palmer and Mason. Any truth to those rumors?

BAUER: I wasn't there, sir. I wouldn't know.

SCHNEIDER: (Pause) Fair enough.

FULBRIGHT: Please continue, Agent Bauer.

BAUER: I watched Mila cater to Victor. He seemed gentle with her. Fatherly. Almost human. I knew I could use that to my advantage at some point.

Victor and two of the guards had finished their meal. They had been drinking and were comfortable now. They had let their defenses down. As Mila cleared the table, she came close to me. She was holding a tray with a large carving knife on it. I quickly reached for her, twisted her arm behind her back, grabbed the knife, and held the blade to her neck. Then I bluffed: "Put down your weapons or I'll cut her throat."

Victor told the others to lay down their arms, but he didn't lower his weapon—he shot Mila in the forehead. The force of the shot knocked both her and me to the floor. The girl was dead.

I called Victor a son of a bitch. He responded by saying Mila was one more death I had to atone for. But Drazen was wrong. I was through blaming myself for the crimes Victor Drazen and his sons had committed. The Drazens were accountable for a thousand murders, and I would make them pay for every single one of them.

After he killed Mila, Victor went ballistic. He had run out of patience and commanded Andre to call George Mason, giving him thirty minutes to bring Alexis to a garage at 2127 Grand Avenue.

Whatever David Palmer had said or done on my behalf, it worked. Mason agreed to the exchange and made it happen.

Then Nikola came downstairs and found his daughter. I got a sick feeling in the pit of my stomach watching this sad old man cradling his child in his arms. Drazen spoke to Nikola, blaming me for the girl's death.

Nikola didn't buy it. He began screaming about how Victor had murdered his daughter. He stumbled toward Drazen, and Victor shot *him*, too. . . .

REP. PAULINE P. DRISCOLL, (D) CONN.: (Softly) Terrible . . . terrible . . .

BAUER: Like I said, ma'am, Drazen's eyes didn't lie. He had checked out of the human race a long time ago. . . . Nikola fell across the table where Victor had enjoyed his meal, then hit the floor. At that moment, two Serbs came through the door dragging my daughter.

Kim was bound and gagged with duct tape. Victor and Andre made sure I saw her—alive. And I'm certain they also wanted her to see what Victor had done to Mila and Nikola. The Drazens well knew that terror was a weapon.

I called out to Kim, but the guards put a hood over my head again and dragged me away. I realized at that point that there was more to the Drazens' plan than getting Alexis back. They were still after Palmer. Before I could actually speak to Kim, they beat me some more and dragged me to a van. I was taken to a remote oil field—we drove for approximately fifteen minutes, maybe less.

There I was dragged from the van and handcuffed to an oil pump. Andre shoved a scrambled phone in my pocket. He told me it was impossible to trace.

I asked, "What do you want me to do?"

He punched me and said, "Not yet."

Then he explained that there was a sniper watching me. If the exchange was made, they would release me. If the Drazens didn't get Alexis back, the sniper would kill me.

I was helpless. The next few minutes were the longest of my life.

FULBRIGHT: What was happening back at CTU?

BAUER: Mason arranged the exchange. It went off without a hitch. They placed a tracer in the band on Alexis's arm, but the Drazens located and destroyed it. I knew the trade had been made when a single shot from a sniper rifle broke my cuffs and I was free.

The cell phone in my pocket rang. It was Andre. He told me that there was a car waiting nearby. He explained that if I wanted to see Kimberly again, I should drive toward Century City. He told me to talk to no one.

I followed Andre's instructions to the letter.

REPORTER'S NOTE: Many sources have confirmed that Super Tuesday was the defining moment for the Palmer marriage. Showing signs of strain all day, the relationship between David and Sherry Palmer finally broke down during the evening hours. David Palmer himself announced the separation from his wife in a terse official statement released shortly after Super Tuesday. A flurry of media coverage and commentary followed. Here are just a few examples. . . .

Liz Smart

Nationally Syndicated Columnist

Where's Patty?

What's the latest buzz out of the Palmer camp a week after Super Tuesday's crazy ride? Every reporter's got about, oh, three thousand or so questions for The Dave, and this columnist is no different. But the first one I've got for **Senator Palmer** isn't about personal scandals, blackmail, or even political action committees, it's about a missing campaign manager named **Patty Brooks**.

So where is she? Where's Patty?

Gone. Without a trace. That's what's happened to Patty Brooks, one of the most efficient and brightest young campaign managers to come along in ages.

Patty Brooks with former boss Sherry Palmer.

Now don't go calling **Carl Webb** just yet. Or the Maryland District Attorney. As far as we know, no one has seen her fall off a balcony. The word is Dave fired her. And on his big winning Super Tuesday night, to boot.

"A pleasure to work with," "She makes it look easy," "Polite and considerate," "Tirelessly devoted to Palmer's objectives" are just a few of the hosannas I've heard about this young woman inside the Washington circle.

So why would she get sacked, you ask? Well, the official word is she "resigned." But what I heard from sources close to the Palmer camp was a curious rumor about shoulder massages and hotel room keys.

Let's face it, infidelity in a politician is not exactly a "dog bites man" sort of story these days, but Palmer isn't your typical politician. Even his opponents consider him a man of honor.

No, I don't think he threw himself at Patty.

Sadly, rumor has it, Patty did the throwing. And Dave was not about to compromise his campaign, his integrity, or his honor.

So, where's Patty? Gone, baby, gone for good.

And sadly, maybe that's for the good of everyone involved.

PRESS RELEASE . . . PRESS RELEASE . . . PRESS

FOR IMMEDIATE RELEASE

CONTACT: Mike Novick, Chief of Staff

DAVID PALMER: OFFICIAL STATEMENT TO THE PRESS DELIVERED DURING NOON PRESS CONFERENCE

My statement to you today is short and simple. It is with regret that I must inform you that my marriage to Sherry Palmer is over.

Sherry and I have been together twenty-five years. We have raised two wonderful children of whom I am very proud. My son, Keith, is with me here today as a sign of his support, and as I've said before, I love my son dearly, as I do my daughter, Nicole.

Unfortunately, as sometimes happens in marriages, Sherry and I have grown apart. We are officially separated and plan to finalize our divorce before the year's end. I felt it was vitally important for me to be honest with you, my supporters, the press, and the voting public. I will answer no questions at this time. Thank you.

<<end statement>>

SPINNING SHERRY BY SUZIE QUINTZ

By now you know.

No first lady for David Palmer. He's going to the White House sans Sherry. The first single president since—I don't honestly know.

Now I could have my research assistant look it up, but the fact is, you don't care anyway. You just know there hasn't been a bachelor president in your lifetime, or your *grandparents'*.

The closest thing you've even seen is actor Michael Douglas playing one in *The American President*.

"So will that be what it's like?" you ask. Will some Annette Bening cutie of a reporter be asked to step out of the press room and stay after school for an exclusive?

Can you imagine a President Palmer personal ad? *Tall, sexy ex-basketball player and leader of the free world looking for intelligent, sultry policy analyst. I'm just a regular guy who likes state dinners, congressional breakfasts, and sleeps next to the red button that sets off my big thermonuclear device.*

Or how about featuring David on a new dating game show—"White House Mates" or "Meet the Cabinet." Maybe we should have a hundred bachelorettes show up at a TV network, and with one marathon 800-number call-in vote the American public can elect him a new first lady in one evening—reality-show-style!

Okay, maybe not.

How about we forget about David Palmer for a moment and consider Sherry. What's a girl to do after twenty-five years of marriage? Twenty-five years of dirty socks on the floor and beard hair in the sink, of fund-raising dinners and charity photo ops? What's a girl to do so close to being the first and ending up dead last?

We know what Princess Diana did when her marriage to Prince Charles began to crack. She spun, folks, she spun. Leaks to the press and gossip from friends close to her made sure the world heard her side.

Well, Sherry Palmer isn't talking—yet.

No first lady for David Palmer. He's going to the White House sans Sherry. The first single president since—I don't honestly know.

Are Sherry's friends spinning facts in her favor?

Perhaps taking a page from the late princess, however, her friends around Washington are. Get a few strong drinks into these ladies who lunch, and the rumors churn faster than the restaurant's gin mill.

Rumor #1: David banished Sherry from his camp on the night of the Super Tuesday primaries. Sherry's friends claim David's young and pretty campaign manager came onto him big time. Sherry caught them together, and Dave didn't like the ultimatum she gave him. Afraid that Sherry would spill the beans to the press, he dumped the campaign manager and his wife in one night.

Rumor #2: Dave banished Sherry from his camp because she severely criticized his Super Tuesday Address. "You just lost the election," Sherry supposedly told him. Dubbing the speech one rung above a bad TV evangelist confessing his sins, she allegedly told him, "The voters don't want a president who sounds like a guest on a sleazy afternoon talk show." Dave was so angry that he threw her out then and there—the last straw in what had become an unbearably stressful campaign for them both.

Rumor #3: Dave banished Sherry from his camp because, say her friends, Dave resented Sherry running everything with his chief of staff Mike Novick—and Dave wrongly accused the two of colluding about more than just platform positions.

Rumor #4: Dave banished Sherry from his camp because she leaked to the press that he had survived the second attempt on his life—that terrible bomb that went off in his hotel suite. Remember how we all held our breath waiting for word that Palmer was alive? According to Sherry's friends, Dave wanted the press to believe he was dead so he could milk the national publicity. Also according to Sherry's friends, this was the last straw in Sherry "defying him," as he put it, and he ended it.

So there it is, the current D.C. cocktail circuit scuttlebutt—all the dirt that's fit to print.

"Are the rumors true?" you ask. Or are they spin?

In my experience, folks, all rumors have some truth to them, but most rumors have some lies in them, too. Time may sort out the true story for us all, or it may not. One day Sherry Palmer and David Palmer will, no doubt, write their own memoirs—and you'll probably find two different stories there, too.

You know, maybe it doesn't much matter how it happened or who said what to whom and when. Because, folks, when a marriage ends, it ends. The reasons can be debated till doomsday, but it won't change the outcome. Doom is doom when a marriage is done.

Late Night Laughs with Ray Bettelman

BETTELMAN: You know, Pat, our president's marriage is breaking up? It's really sad . . . don't you think? [**CROWD:** Awwws.]

PAT SINGER: Yes, it is.

BETTELMAN: I think he might be lonely. I think he needs a love life.

PAT SINGER: Really? You know, some presidents have no trouble getting a love life . . . even when they've got a wife.

[**CROWD:** Laughter. Catcalls and whistles, some boos.]

PAT SINGER: Hey, c'mon! I wasn't thinking of anyone in particular!

[**CROWD:** Laughter.]

BETTELMAN: To avoid just the kind of trouble you're talking about, Pat, we've come up with BETTELMAN'S BEST PICKS for the post as David Palmer's first lady! [**CROWD:** Applause.]

Best Pick Number Five. Britney Spears, because she's sure to liven up those dull fund-raisers with her leather outfits and that c-r-a-z-y snake dance. [**CROWD:** Laughter.]

Best Pick Number Four. Senator Hillary Rodham Clinton, because we hear she already has a lot of the White House furniture. [**CROWD:** Laughter/applause.]

Best Pick Number Three. Oprah Winfrey, because the next time David Palmer wants to give a confessional speech about his family scandals, he can do it on her show! [**CROWD:** Laughter/applause.]

Best Pick Number Two. Martha Stewart, because after she redecorates the White House, she can give Palmer pointers on defying Congress! [**CROWD:** OOOHs and scattered laughter/applause.]

And Best Pick Number One, the favored candidate to be David Palmer's first lady is . . . [**Drum roll**] The very sexy Kim Cattrall from *Sex and the City*, because, well, if Palmer doesn't have to heat the executive bedroom anymore, we may get a tax break! [**CROWD:** Screaming laughter/applause]

Stick around, because we have one of our very favorite actors, Golden Globe winner Kiefer Sutherland! [**CROWD:** Loud applause, shouts of excitement.] . . . and we have the rock group Turgid and our Animal Channel man, Craig Weedie. . . .

10:00 P.M.–11:00 P.M.

REPORTER'S NOTE: The following testimony covers the events that occurred between 10:00 P.M. and 11:00 P.M. on the day of the California presidential primary.

CHAIRMAN FULBRIGHT: At 10:00 P.M., you were on-station at CTU. What was the situation at the time?

AGENT TONY ALMEIDA: Jack Bauer called. But he couldn't come in yet. We all knew Jack wanted his daughter back and that he wasn't returning until he found her. When Jack ended the call, Mason got suspicious. He figured Drazen was controlling Jack by threatening Kimberly. We all agreed that the thing Drazen wanted most was Palmer dead. Mason put two and two together and deduced that Jack was on his way to see Senator Palmer. Mason alerted the Secret Service. He told them Jack was coming and that he might pose a danger to the senator.

All of us at CTU were still trying to trace the Drazens' movements that day. Nina ordered me to work on the detention center strike. She thought I might be able to retrace the steps of the strike team and maybe even find Drazen's headquarters. So far we were stumped. We had yet to figure out how the Drazens got out of the detention center after bringing down the ceiling and cutting off what we believed was their only means of escape.

I needed detailed schematics of the Saugus detention center, so I accessed CTU's division and district data banks and downloaded them. I also downloaded the same map from the DOD system as a backup.

When I compared the two schematics, I discovered that the Department of Defense map was different—and more accurate. An entire section of the facility had been erased from the CTU schematics. The Drazens used that area of the prison to escape. I concluded that someone with access to these files was helping the Drazens.

I called up the names of everyone who had downloaded that particular file in the last six months. The names of five people turned up. Four of them were computer technicians, people who backed up

GEORGE MASON

AGE: 53

CTU MISSIONS

- Special Agent in Charge, Los Angeles Domestic Unit
- Assistant Administrative Director, CTU, Los Angeles Domestic Unit
- District Commander, Operation Pinstripe, 2001
- Section Captain, Operation Proteus, 2000
- Section Captain, Operation Jump Rope, 1999
- Operative, Hotel Los Angeles attack, 1998 (Special Commendation)
- Operative, Operation Farmhouse, 1997
- Operative, Operation Caveat Emptor, 1996
- Operative, Operation Chickadee, 1994

EXPERIENCE

- District Director, Counter Terrorist Unit, Tacoma Domestic Unit
- Deputy Director of Administration, Central Intelligence Agency
- Coordinator, Special Drug Interdiction Task Force, U.S. Coast Guard

EDUCATION

- Master of Business Administration, Washington State University
- Bachelor of Arts, Government, Washington State University

MILITARY

- U.S. Coast Guard
- Ensign, U.S. Navy

PERSONAL

- Divorced
- Ex-wife — Carol Mason
- Son — John Mason

our systems. The other person was George Mason. According to the logs, he had accessed the prison schematics only four days before Super Tuesday.

REP. PAULINE P. DRISCOLL, (D) CONN.: What did Nina Myers say when you gave her this information?

ALMEIDA: She agreed with me. This evidence fingered Mason as CTU's mole. Nina wanted to call in Chappelle, but I'd already called for one lockdown in the last twelve hours—I didn't want to call another. Not without better proof than what we had. So Nina ordered me to shut George Mason out. Deny him access to the data banks, the servers—everything. Mason would catch on sooner or later, but we had to at least contain the damage until we could prove conclusively that George was dirty.

DRISCOLL: You didn't suspect anyone else? Jamey Farrell? Perhaps she'd altered the files before you caught her.

ALMEIDA: Jamey didn't have the codes or the security clearance to go into division or district files. Full access to intelligence data is limited.

DRISCOLL: To whom?

ALMEIDA: Chappelle. George Mason. Jack Bauer. Nina Myers. Me.

DRISCOLL: (Pause) You were intimate with Ms. Myers, is that correct?

ALMEIDA: Yes, ma'am. (Pause) It was a mistake—

DRISCOLL: A mistake! Then we have a consensus. That's what Agent Bauer called his dalliance with Ms. Myers. I sometimes wonder what *she* thinks.

ALMEIDA: I'm sure Nina Myers has regrets. She got caught.

DRISCOLL: But not by you, Agent Almeida. You never once suspected that it was Nina Myers who altered those schematics. You thought you'd found a clue, but you were really playing right into her hands—Nina Myers was moving to divide the CTU. She wanted suspicion to fall on George Mason, and you were helping her.

ALMEIDA: We didn't know she could alter data. That took special skills none of us were aware Nina possessed—

DRISCOLL: You didn't know she was a mole, either.

ALMEIDA: No, ma'am.

DRISCOLL: So I must agree with you for the record—that's what I'd call a helluva mistake.

FULBRIGHT: What happened next, Agent Almeida?

ALMEIDA: When Mason did finally catch on, he made a scene about being shut out and demanded that I get his terminal working again. That's when we heard the news on television—Palmer had been killed by a bomb blast at his hotel. . . .

REPORTER'S NOTE: During this time, Kimberly Bauer was still a hostage of the Drazens. The following is her separate testimony. . . .

KIMBERLY BAUER: . . . and then Alexis—the younger Drazen brother—died. They left me alone with his body. When the older one, Andre, came back, he took the duct tape off my mouth and gave me some water to drink.

He told me he once had a sister. But he said she was dead and that my father had murdered her. I told him he was a liar and that my father would never kill an innocent person. Then he asked me if I knew about my father's work, where he went when he was out of town.

I didn't.

I always wondered what my dad did. Sometimes, when he was away—I guess on one of his missions—I would hear my mom crying softly at night. You know, after she thought I'd gone to sleep.

I know that Andre Drazen was a bad guy and everything, but I sort of knew he was telling me the truth. I thought maybe my dad does do bad stuff—stuff I'll never know about. But he's my dad, you know? . . . He's my dad. . . .

INTERVIEWER: What happened next? How did you escape?

KIMBERLY: Well . . . my mind started racing for some way to fight back and get out. I saw that these guys were pretty sure of themselves, you know? Here I was this kid, and they were all big guys with guns, so they didn't watch me very closely. I guess they figured they could hurt me or shoot me if I gave them any trouble—no problem. So I decided to use that against them.

I saw a pot of hot coffee and pretended to want some. I asked a guard if I could pour a cup. He's the typical gruff type, you know,

he's not about to serve a girl, so he lets me do it myself. I took the pot and threw the hot coffee right into his face. He screamed, and I ran.

The Drazens chased me to the end of a pier at the Port of Los Angeles. I was cornered, so I took a deep breath and dived into the water. I'd been on my high school swim team and was really good, too. I tore the ropes away from my hands and swam away. It was dark, and the water was cold. So I figured, with any luck, Andre and his thugs would think I drowned. . . .

REPORTER'S NOTE:
Special Agent Bauer provides testimony about his actions during this period. . . .

FULBRIGHT: Agent Bauer, you say you suspected that the scrambled phone Andre gave you had a bomb inside of it?

SPECIAL AGENT JACK BAUER: I would have been a fool not to.

FULBRIGHT: But you went to Palmer's hotel suite anyway. You followed Drazen's orders to the letter.

BAUER: I knew the bomb wouldn't go off right away. I knew that Victor Drazen would speak to Palmer first, even if it was only to gloat. And that's exactly what he did. He said, "It must be nice to be reunited with your friend Jack Bauer."

I snatched the phone away from Senator Palmer then and threw it out the window. I was surprised at the intensity of the blast. It was not Semtex but something more powerful. A new plastique, maybe—certainly military grade.

DRISCOLL: After the explosion, Senator Palmer agreed to pretend he had been killed, just to buy you time to find your daughter?

BAUER: Yes. He gave me his word. But when his wife, Sherry, confronted me, I knew she would be a problem. She seemed to be the type to put her ambitions first. She knew that what her husband was doing—playing hide-and-seek with the national press—was politically risky.

REP. ROY SCHNEIDER, (R) TEX.: What happened next?

BAUER: Andre Drazen called me at Palmer's hotel, to verify my death. I told him I would trade my own life for that of my daughter. He agreed, believing that Senator Palmer had indeed been assassinated.

Andre gave me thirty minutes to reach Pier 11-A at the Port of Los Angeles, or Kim would die. Before I left the hotel to keep the rendezvous, I called my wife, and we spoke for the last time.

Teri told me . . . (pause) she told me I was going to be a father again.

I felt reborn.

I had been so afraid she was going to say something else. I knew she'd recently learned about my affair with Nina Myers. And I was afraid that news and the stress of the day had convinced her to end our marriage. That my job had ruined our lives together—that she would finally want out.

But Teri didn't want out. She loved me and she was going to have another baby. My baby. I was so pleased. I promised her that everything would be okay . . . that she would soon be reunited with Kim . . . and I told her that I . . . that I loved her very much. . . .

FULBRIGHT: (Mumbling. Softly after a long pause) Let's take a recess.

11:00 P.M.–12:00 MIDNIGHT

CHAIRMAN FULBRIGHT: So you drove to Pier 11-A, Port of Los Angeles, correct?

SPECIAL AGENT JACK BAUER: Yes, to save my daughter. CTU had delivered a car to Palmer's hotel, an operations vehicle that contained lots of extras, like a weapons kit with two pistols and extra ammo, a wireless communications system, a scanner, and an LED screen slaved to a computer and mounted on the dashboard.

REPORTER'S NOTE: The following testimony covers the events that occurred between 11:00 P.M. and 12:00 midnight on the day of the California presidential primary.

As I reconnoitered the boathouse and the surrounding docks, my cell phone rang—it was Andre. I told him I wasn't going to show myself until I talked to my daughter. Andre refused, and I sensed desperation in his voice.

I told him that I didn't trust him. He told me that I'd lied to him about Palmer being dead, so I shouldn't talk to him about trust. I was stunned. The Drazens *knew* Palmer was alive—which meant they were getting their information from an inside source . . . another mole in CTU.

Again I demanded to speak to Kim. Again Andre refused, so I hung up on him. Something was wrong. I could sense it. Maybe Kim had gotten away, or maybe the Drazens had already killed her. I began to fear the worst. . . .

REPORTER'S NOTE: By this time, Kimberly had escaped the Drazens and had hitched a ride with Carlos Valeros, twenty-seven, a truck driver bound for San Clemente. Valeros took Kim to the California Highway Patrol, where Kim told the troopers who she was. They called CTU and told George Mason they had found her near Pier 11-A. Mason ordered two CTU tactical teams dispatched to raid the boathouse.

I had to warn CTU that there was a traitor in their midst before more damage could be done, so I called the only person I trusted—Nina Myers. Nina told me that only three people in CTU besides herself knew that Palmer was still alive: Ryan Chappelle, Tony Almeida, and George

Mason. I told her that either Tony, George, or Ryan was a traitor and warned her not to trust anyone—

REP. ROY SCHNEIDER, (R) TEX.: (Interrupting) Excuse me, Agent Bauer, I was following the primaries at my ranch in Texas, and I recall CNB News broke the story that Palmer was alive just after midnight—that's a little after 11:00 P.M. California time.

BAUER: Yes, I learned later that Sherry Palmer leaked the truth to protect her husband's candidacy. At that point, thank God, Kim was safe—although I didn't know it yet. Andre, of course, found out about Palmer before then through the mole at CTU.

FULBRIGHT: What happened next, Agent Bauer?

BAUER: I was watching the boathouse when my phone rang. It was Nina calling. She told me to return to CTU. She said that the Coast Guard had fished Kim's body out of the ocean—that my daughter was dead. I'm sure they knew exactly how I'd react.

I lost it.

Nothing I'd done in the last twenty-four hours had been enough to save my little girl's life. I thought of Teri and broke down. I didn't know how I would be able to face her. . . .

Then something went cold inside me. I walked back to my car and loaded a second weapon. I saw a commercial van—a big yellow one. I broke the window and hot-wired the engine. Then I drove it right through the middle of the boathouse.

SCHNEIDER: Damn, son, that was practically suicide! How many mercs were in there?

BAUER: Six or seven. I didn't count. I just gunned them all down, one by one. Victor and Andre ran. I chased them out to the pier. A boat was in the water, coming to take the Drazens to a cargo ship waiting offshore.

I couldn't let that happen.

I reloaded, and with a weapon in each hand, I rushed Victor and Andre. I hit Andre with two or three slugs, and watched him go down with satisfaction.

Then Victor caught me above the kidney. It was a grazing wound, but it took me down anyway. Victor stood over me, aimed and pulled the trigger. The hammer clicked on an empty chamber.

I leveled my weapon at Drazen's chest. He raised his hands to surrender. I stared into his eyes and the abyss stared back. I shot him. Two, three, four times. With each shot, a .45-caliber slug tore through him. I kept pulling the trigger, shooting until there was no ammunition left in the cartridge. He fell into the water and just floated there.

The CTU tactical team arrived a few minutes later. They found me on the pier, still staring at Drazen's lifeless body, thinking, *This is how they found my little girl. . . .*

The tactical team called in to CTU immediately, reporting that I was alive and that the Drazens were dead. It's clear, based on the evidence, that Nina Myers panicked. She knew she'd been exposed, so she went to the main computer and began to download sensitive information—the names of covert operatives overseas, state secrets, anything she could grab. She also took my wife prisoner.

SCHNEIDER: When did you know for certain that Nina Myers was a traitor?

BAUER: After I'd killed the Drazens the wind went out of me. I still thought my little girl was dead. I grabbed a Coast Guard and told him I wanted to claim Kim's body. He told me they hadn't retrieved a body that night. And that's when I knew—*Nina* had lied to me about Kim's death. *She* was the mole.

I called George Mason and told him everything. He didn't believe me, of course. So I swore I'd get proof. My mind raced back over the events of the day. I followed a hunch and called Dale Wilson in Archives. I asked him for the security camera footage in the room where Jamey Farrell had committed suicide earlier that morning. Wilson said the tape had been erased, so I gave him my access code and told him to download the footage from the digital backup file and send it to my LED screen.

The tape shows it all. Jamey didn't kill herself, she was *murdered* by Nina Myers. I sent the footage to George Mason, for his eyes only. He locked down the CTU complex—interrupting Nina's download of sensitive intelligence data.

FULBRIGHT: Agent Bauer, tell us what happened when you finally got back to CTU.

REPORTER'S NOTE:
The following CTU memo regarding Nina Myers was included among the subcommitee's documents.

Page 16

. . . and as the body of the female maintenance worker found inside the transformer room. Please see attachment 23.6 for final anatomic and forensic summaries of these individuals as well as full autopsies.

Myers's laptop, which was left in the transformer room, had been plugged into the mainframe through a makeshift wall jack found behind the removed wall panel. Please see attachment 23.7 for a review of laptop contents and 23.8 for a review of CD contents, recovered from Myers's jacket pocket.

[Document 21 provides full analysis of transformer room forensics.]

Regarding restored digital footage from security camera archives: full analysis of Myers's physical movements, including the two recorded shootings, can be found in attachment 23.8.

No recovery of audio possible.

CTU lip-reading analyst #4379-G studied the digital footage and transcribed all conversations in the transformer room involving Nina Myers between 11:00 P.M. and 12:00 midnight. See attachment 23.9 for full and complete transcription.

Myers placed and received three (3) phone calls while in the transformer room. Phone calls took place on a cellular unit with a scramble device, recovered from Myers's jacket pocket. *Again, no audio available.*

The following excerpt of the lipreader's transcription primarily recounts Nina Myers's end of the phone conversations she conducted in the transformer room. Analyst #9351-J provided translations, where applicable, from German to English. See attachment 23.10 for analysis of speech pattern and accent.

TRANSCRIPTION OF MYERS PHONE CALL #1

11:33:21 P.M.

MYERS (into phone): Meine Duckung ist aufgeflogen. Du musst mich hier rausholen. (English: My cover is broken. You must get me out of here.)

RESPONSE: Unknown.

MYERS (into phone): Unreadable.

RESPONSE: Unknown.

MYERS (into phone): Ich kenn' das Protokol und bin schon dabei. (English: I know the protocol. I'm ready to go.)

CLASSIFIED

file: 342–56C document: 23 Page 17

[Teri Bauer physically enters room]

RESPONSE: Unknown.

MYERS (into phone): Just call me when it's time.

RESPONSE: Unknown.

MYERS: Yes.

RESPONSE: Unknown.

CLASSIFIED

[Myers terminates phone connection]

TERI BAUER (to Myers): You speak German?

MYERS (to Teri Bauer): Frankfurt Division. Something wrong?

[See attachment 4.4 for Myers-Bauer transcription]

Duration of call: 25 seconds

TRANSCRIPTION OF MYERS PHONE CALL #2

11:35:00 P.M.

MYERS (into phone): This is Myers.

RESPONSE: Unknown.

MYERS (into phone): That's right.

RESPONSE: Unknown.

MYERS (into phone): Where?

[Myers terminates phone connection]

Duration of call: 16 seconds

TRANSCRIPTION OF PHONE CALL #3

11:53:52 P.M.

MYERS (into phone): I'm leaving now.

RESPONSE: Unknown.

MYERS (into phone): Why Germany? Why can't I come to you directly?

RESPONSE: Unknown.

MYERS (into phone): Yeah. All right.

[Myers terminates phone connection]

[To Teri Bauer] I'm leaving now, Teri. I'm going to lock you in from the outside. Someone will find you soon. Everything will be fine.

Duration of call: 24 seconds

BAUER: As I drove in through the CTU garage, I saw that Nina was already driving away. She shot at me through her windshield. I returned fire. Nina crashed and I dragged her out of the car. I wrapped my hands around her throat and held a gun to her head.

She said, "If you kill me, you won't know who I work for. You think I work for Drazen, but I don't."

Mason and Tony arrived and talked me out of pulling the trigger. I wish they hadn't. I wish I hadn't put a flak jacket on her that morning, or slept with her months ago, or trusted her—*ever*. That's what my life is now, useless wishes. . . .

FULBRIGHT: (After a pause) Agent Bauer? Can you continue?

BAUER: Yes . . . (Pause) While I held the gun to Nina's head, Mason assured me that my family was waiting for me, that Kim had just arrived and Teri was inside.

That's what made me sane again—the thought of Kim and Teri.

I rushed into the command center and found my daughter. I hugged her with relief and joy. *It's all over.* That's what I told her. And that's what I thought. *The nightmare's over.*

I told her I loved her. Then I looked up for Teri. I could feel her close by. Right there. Right next to us. I was surprised to see that she wasn't.

I walked through the corridors, calling for her. Then I began to see the bodies—the wake of dead guards that Nina left in her path. I felt the dread rising in me as I began to run, checking every room. Finally I reached the transformer room. . . .

I almost didn't see her at first. But now it's an image I can't get out of my head. Teri was slumped down in a chair. . . . I had found my wife. I found her . . .

<< transcript ends>>

REPORTER'S NOTE: Special Agent Bauer was excused at this point in his testimony, which concluded his participation in the House Special Subcommittee hearings. Teri Bauer's autopsy was included among the subcommittee's documents along with these photos secured from CTU surveillance cameras.

FINAL ANATOMIC AND FORENSIC SUMMARY

CASE #: 01-109
SUBJECT: Teri Bauer
CTU FORENSIC PATHOLOGIST: George R. Capaldo, M.D.

CAUSE OF DEATH:

Cardiovascular collapse due to massive exsanguination and hemopericardium due to bullet wound of left ventricle and aorta.

Lodging of ____ caliber bullet in thoracic spine.

MANNER OF DEATH:

Homicide

OTHER FINDINGS:

Endometrial decidual changes and positive clinical history of pregnancy test, together with LMP: consistent with pregnancy of less than 4 weeks' duration.

Ruptured left ovarian follicular cyst, original diameter of approximately 4 cm.

Ligature marks on both wrists.

Negative drug and alcohol screens.

REPORTER'S NOTE:
In separate testimony, Kimberly Bauer offered these concluding remarks.

KIMBERLY BAUER: I thought it would go away. That I would cry and cry and just get it all out, you know? But you can never get it all out because it stays with you—this terrible emptiness. Nothing is the same anymore. Not anything. Not to me.

I can't be with my dad now. It's just too hard. I try not to blame him, but I can't help it, I do. . . .

When I think of my mother—and I think of her every single day—I try to remember what she said to me that morning when we were being held hostage, locked in that room.

We were scared, but we were together. And there were these rays of sunlight streaming in through the window, intense golden rays, and my mother looked so beautiful standing there. . . . She told me not to be afraid. She said, "We're in this awful place, but I want you to know you're not alone." She told me that no matter how bad things get or how good they get, I should remember what a simple and powerful thing her love for me was . . . that it would never change . . . that it would never end.

And you know, when I think about it now, I know it's true, because I close my eyes and I can feel her love. It's still with me. So I guess if my mom's love is still with me, then she is, too.

"HEROIC" CTU AGENT SAVES PALMER

Although details are still sketchy, Mike Novick, Senator David Palmer's chief of staff, confirms that two attempts were made on the candidate's life in one twenty-four-hour period.

Sources close to the CIA have credited Special Agent Jack Bauer of the Los Angeles Counter Terrorist Unit as the man responsible for saving Palmer on both occasions. Novick confirmed Palmer's appreciation of Bauer, echoing the senator's sentiments by calling his actions "heroic."

"I am indebted to Special Agent Bauer," Palmer said in a brief written statement released to the press. "His heroic actions twice saved my life."

Other details concerning the assassination attempts, including the perpetrators and their motivations, are being withheld.

Citing "national security," officials in federal government agencies including the Secret Service and FBI refuse to answer press questions about the identity of the assassin or assassins. Neither will they provide official comment on Bauer's role in the day's turbulent events.

Sweeping the eleven Super Tuesday primaries, Palmer last night became the first African-American candidate to win the nomination of a major political party. Yet this historic event was eclipsed by the late-breaking bulletin out of Los Angeles, California.

Speculation continues that a "government conspiracy" exists to assassinate Palmer. An anonymous source claims international criminals were involved in an elaborate scheme that included the bribing of personnel in federal agencies.

Talk has already begun of a congressional investigation.

by Special Subcommittee Chairman
Representative **Jayce Fulbright**, (D) California

Every day thousands of dedicated men and women arrive at their posts in the intelligence and defense communities and diligently strive to safeguard the citizens of our nation. We owe our thanks to the unflagging dedication of these agents, officers, administrators, and staff workers in the Department of Defense, Federal Bureau of Investigation, Central Intelligence and National Security Agencies, and Secret Service.

When any intelligence failure occurs, especially those that result in death, emotions run high. Regrets and recriminations lead to inevitable questions: Could this have been prevented? Who is to blame?

This nation's forefathers designed a government of checks and balances, creating mechanisms such as this special subcommittee to conduct fair hearings and investigations into such questions, including alleged wrongdoings in the powerful and separate executive and judiciary branches.

As we conclude these hearings, we are acutely aware of the security challenges facing this nation. In light of the serious threats on our horizon, we need to rise above pettiness and finger-pointing, and move ahead to aid the aforementioned agencies in focusing on the task at hand—protecting this nation's people and ensuring the security of the ideals on which it stands.

In that spirit, this subcommittee would like to commend Special Agent Jack Bauer. His tireless efforts saved the life of our president-elect, David Palmer, and exposed a dangerous spy in the intelligence community. It is this subcommittee's conclusion that Agent Bauer restored the security and *integrity* of the CIA's Counter Terrorist Unit.

Agent Bauer's alleged violations of procedure, protocol, and even laws were here fully examined and explained. His honesty and openness about his actions and his motivations are appreciated by this subcommittee, and we thank him for his thorough testimony, some of which was clearly painful for him personally to relive.

We would also like to commend CTU Agent Tony Almeida, whose dedication, loyalty, and bravery are more than apparent. We regret to find that one of his most admirable virtues, his *loyalty,* was used against him by a highly skilled double agent named Nina Myers, working against this country.

Agent Almeida's honest testimony in these hearings is evidence of his willingness to redeem himself in working toward uncovering the further objectives of Nina Myers and her associates and tracking down any other willing parties who may have been involved in her espionage.

Both of these men, Jack Bauer and Tony Almeida, were compromised by Myers. However, this subcommittee does not find them guilty of any criminal violations. We recommend that they be released from any further charges in these matters.

This subcommittee *cannot* in good conscience offer similar commendations to the regional office of CTU, whose management at times obstructed this subcommittee's investigation and whose actions clearly hampered the efforts of Special Agent Jack Bauer as he attempted to stop an assassination conspiracy.

In addition to the above findings, a number of troubling revelations have come to light during these hearings, among them:

- That a spy is still actively operating in the upper levels of the intelligence or defense community
- That a traitor or conspiracy of traitors intentionally compromised Jack Bauer's entire Delta unit, which led to the deaths of six Special Forces operatives on foreign soil
- That the Department of Defense is operating a covert underground prison system on American soil to detain international fugitives

This subcommittee has turned these matters over to the Joint Congressional Intelligence Oversight Committee for further investigation.

This concludes the findings of this House Special Subcommittee. These hearings are hereby closed.

REPORTER'S NOTE:
A number of sources were consulted to provide concluding summaries for the following key players featured in this report.

JACK BAUER

Special Agent Jack Bauer's provisional reinstatement as acting director of the Counter Terrorist Unit, Los Angeles, was revoked at midnight on Super Tuesday. The next day's national press credited Bauer with saving David Palmer's life, and the subsequent publicity discouraged Bauer's superiors from filing disciplinary or criminal charges of any kind against him. The Justice Department investigated the CTU, including Bauer's actions, and exonerated him. However, Congress insisted on holding its own separate hearing as a check on the executive branch. After the death of his wife, Bauer needed some time away. CTU listed his status during that time as inactive. He has since returned to CTU on assignment. Details of his current mission remain unspecified by the division.

KIMBERLY BAUER

Devastated by the loss of her mother, Kimberly moved out of the Bauer home, taking a live-in job as an au pair with a young family.

NINA MYERS

Special Agent Nina Myers is in federal custody. Myers is being held without bail, charged with espionage, conspiracy to assassinate Senator David Palmer, and multiple counts of murder in the deaths of Jamey Farrell, Teri Bauer, and additional CTU personnel whom she shot in her attempt to escape. Myers is considered a valuable source of information by our intelligence community. At the time of this publication, she has refused to offer anything more than a reiteration of her statement to Special Agent Jack Bauer the night she was arrested:

"If you kill me, you won't know who I work for. You think I work for Drazen, but I don't." Because of the level of Myers's skill and knowledge as a double agent, CTU analysts believe she was trained by an intelligence service hostile to our nation—one that shares common interests with Victor Drazen. CTU analysts have uncovered evidence of a contact in Germany named [INFORMATION WITHHELD FOR NATIONAL SECURITY REASONS], however, further evidence suggests she is not a German agent. The list of her possible employers includes [INFORMATION WITHHELD FOR NATIONAL SECURITY REASONS].

DAVID PALMER

After winning the nomination for president, Senator David Palmer ran a dedicated campaign throughout the summer and fall, winning the presidency. As president-elect he is working with a transition team to ensure a smooth transfer of power in the White House after he takes the oath of office in January. Although the press continues to report and comment on the scandals in Palmer's personal and political life, Palmer has maintained close to a 70 percent approval rating since Super Tuesday.

SHERRY PALMER

Sherry and David Palmer have been estranged since midnight on Super Tuesday. After twenty-five years of marriage, they officially separated shortly after Super Tuesday and jointly filed for divorce before the year's end.

TONY ALMEIDA

Since the events of Super Tuesday, Agent Tony Almeida has been promoted to the position of assistant special agent in charge (chief of staff), CTU, Los Angeles Domestic Unit—Nina Myers's old job.

GEORGE MASON

George Mason continues to work for CTU. He currently holds the position of special agent in charge, CTU, Los Angeles Domestic Unit.

RYAN CHAPPELLE

Ryan Chappelle continues to work in his position as director of the regional division office of CTU. Sources inside the CIA say he was short-listed for a major promotion within the Agency but, in light of the special subcommittee's conclusions, has been passed over.

ALBERTA GREEN

At her own request, Alberta Green has been transferred to the CTU office in Washington, D.C.

01:25 01:27 01:29 01:30 01:31 01:33 01:35
01:41 01:43 01:44 01:45 01:47 01:49 01:50
01:57 01:58 01:59 03:01 03:04 03:06 03:09
03:15 03:17 03:20 03:21 03:22 03:25 03:27
03:33 03:35 03:37 03:38 03:39 03:41
03:49 03:50 03:52 03:53 03:54 03:56 03:57
04:03 04:04 04:06 04:09 04:11 04:13 04:14
04:21 04:22 04:25 04:27 04:29 04:30 04:31
04:38 04:39 04:41 04:43 04:44 04:45
04:52 04:53 04:54 04:56 04:57 04:58 04:59
06:06 06:09 06:11 06:13 06:14 06:15 06:17
06:25 06:27 06:29 06:30 06:31 06:33
06:41 06:43 06:44 06:45 06:47 06:49 06:50
06:56 06:57 06:58 06:59 07:01 07:03
07:13 07:14 07:15 07:17 07:20 07:21 07:22
07:31 07:33 07:35 07:37 07:38 07:39 07:41
07:47 07:49 07:50 07:52 07:53 07:54 07:56
10:01 10:03 10:04 10:06 10:09 10:11 10:13
10:20 10:21 10:22 10:25 10:27 10:29 10:30
10:37 10:38 10:39 10:41 10:43 10:44 10:45
10:52 10:53 10:54 10:56 10:57 10:58 10:59
14:09 14:11 14:13 14:14 14:15 14:17 14:20
14:27 14:29 14:30 14:31 14:33 14:35 14:37
14:43 14:44 14:45 14:47 14:49 14:50 14:52
14:57 14:58 14:59 15:01 15:03 15:04 15:06
15:15 15:17 15:20 15:21 15:22 15:25 15:27
15:33 15:35 15:37 15:38 15:39 15:41 15:43
15:50 15:52 15:53 15:54 15:56 15:57 15:58
18:04 18:06 18:09 18:11 18:13 18:14 18:15
18:25 18:27 18:29 18:30 18:31 18:33 18:35
18:41 18:43 18:44 18:45 18:47 18:49 18:50
18:56 18:57 18:58 18:59 20:01 20:03 20:04
20:13 20:14 20:15 20:17 20:20 20:21 20:22
20:30 20:31 20:33 20:35 20:37 20:38 20:39
20:45 20:47 20:49 20:50 20:52 20:53
20:59 23:01 23:03 23:04 23:06 23:09
23:17 23:20 23:21 23:22 23:25 23:27
23:35 23:37 23:38 23:39 23:41 23:43

After-Action Review (AAR)—Group assessment and evaluation of a special operation after the mission is complete.

Air Force Special Operations (AFSO)—Based at Eglin Air Force Base, Florida, AFSO is composed of helicopter and aircraft units. Its primary mission is to transport special operations units to their area of operation and to provide resupply, support, and recovery.

ASTRO SABER Digital Radios—A wireless system that enables the transport of voice and data information over the same channel to portable radios and data terminals in the field, eliminating the need for separate data networks. With the addition of encryption modules, data is encoded before it is transmitted over the air, ensuring that confidential information is not intercepted by unauthorized parties.

Black Dogs—Serbian paramilitary secret police force established by Victor Drazen to "control dissent" and "quell foreign interlopers" in the former Yugoslavia. The Black Dogs were instrumental in preserving Serbian hegemony through a campaign of terror aimed at various ethnic and religious groups. At its peak, the Black Dogs fielded perhaps two hundred operatives, but their reach was long. Members were thoroughly trained by the Serbian Special Forces using Soviet tactics and weapons, and their skills were further honed under the tutelage of Victor Drazen. Their motto: "Black Dogs run at night."

Blowback—Intelligence term to describe when actions, groups, or individuals from past covert mission return to harm or compromise the intelligence operatives or nation that originated the mission.

"The Blue Rose"—Secretive group of dissident Serbs enrolled at Belgrade University. The origin and membership of this group are shrouded in mystery, but the organization's philosophy and goals were closely aligned with those of Andre Drazen.

Central Intelligence Agency (CIA)—Intelligence-gathering agency of the Executive Office of the President of the United States, the CIA is America's primary intelligence agency, responsible for keeping the government informed of foreign threats to national security or national interests. Charged with coordinating all U.S. intelligence activities by the National Security Council, the director and deputy director of the CIA are appointed by the president with the consent of the Senate.

Counter Terrorist Unit (CTU)—Elite branch of the Central Intelligence Agency. The Counter Terrorist Unit operates domestic counterterrorism divisional headquarters in major U.S. metropolitan areas. The purview of the CTU is to investigate the activities of domestic or foreign terrorists inside America's borders and to prevent terrorist attacks. CTU divisions are made up of investigative agents, intelligence agents, undercover operatives, crack tactical squads for major raids, and special agents to oversee unit activities. CTU is specifically set up to coordinate activities with the Federal Bureau of Investigation, the Justice Department, and the Secret Service as well as local authorities. As a branch of the CIA, CTU operations are overseen by both Congress and the Executive Branch of the federal government.

Defense Intelligence Agency (DIA)—Department of Defense combat support agency. The DIA is headquartered at the Pentagon and has seven thousand military and civilian employees worldwide. It is a major producer and manager of foreign military intelligence. The DIA provides military intelligence to the military, defense policymakers, and strategic planners in the Department of Defense and the intelligence community, in support of U.S. military planning, operations, and weapons systems acquisition.

Ethnic cleansing—Generally entails the systematic and forced removal of members of an ethnic group from their communities to change the ethnic composition of a region.

F/A-18 Hornet—A single-seat twin-engine jet aircraft used by both the U.S. Navy and Marine Corps, the F-18 is the most advanced carrier-based attack plane in the arsenal of the United States. Capable of carrying both conventional and nuclear bombs, the Hornet more commonly delivers precision-guided missiles like the AGM-65 Maverick air-to-ground missile. The F-18 provides all-weather, night and day fighter and attack capabilities.

Federal Bureau of Investigation (FBI)—Agency of the United States Justice Department and the principal federal criminal investigative agency. The function of the Federal Bureau of Investigation is to prosecute cases of espionage, sabotage, subversive activities, and other actions related to national security, organized crime, white-collar crime, drug interdiction, and terrorism.

First Special Forces Operational Detachment—Delta—Elite U.S. Army counterterrorist unit modeled after the British Special Air Service. One of the newest and most secretive components of America's Special Forces. Little is known of this special unit's size or deployment, but Delta teams have participated in firefights in Panama, Somalia, and Afghanistan.

FSB—Federal Security Bureau. Post-Communist Russia's equivalent of the Federal Bureau of Investigation. Once an arm of the KGB, the FSB now investigates crimes against the state committed by citizens of the former Soviet Union, including terrorism, treason, and the activities of organized crime.

Global Positioning System (GPS)—Worldwide navigational tool formed by twenty-four orbiting satellites and their corresponding receivers on Earth. GPS satellites transmit digital radio signals that allow pinpoint accuracy in the calculation of longitude, latitude, and altitude. This system is used to monitor weather, wildlife habitation, and the movement of people and objects.

GSG9—German intelligence. Unified Germany's equivalent of the Central Intelligence Agency.

HALO—High Altitude, Low Opening. One of the most dangerous types of parachute jumping, in which the parachutist is deployed from an aircraft flying at between 1,500 and 25,000 feet—approximately the altitude of a normal commercial aircraft. HALO operations involve the use of special breathing apparatus, insulated suits, and a wide array of special equipment, from altimeters to geopositioning equipment to especially durable parachutes—all in an effort to avoid enemy detection. Most members of America's Special Operations forces are trained in this covert insertion technique.

Interpol (International Criminal Police Organizations)—A nonpolitical, international intergovernmental body established in Vienna in 1923 to promote law enforcement cooperation among police authorities around the world and develop means of effectively preventing crime.

Joint Special Operations Command (JSOC)—Based at Fort Bragg, North Carolina, JSOC is responsible for counterterrorism training and operations of the U.S. Army's Delta Force, Navy SEAL Team Six, and elements of the Federal Bureau of Investigation's Hostage Rescue Team.

Kosovo/1389—Underground Serb nationalist organization established in the 1980s by Andre Drazen while he was an undergraduate at Belgrade University. The name was meant as a celebration and a warning—to celebrate the heroism at the Battle of Kosovo in 1389 and to warn contemporary Serbs that they will someday be summoned to fight for Kosovo. Though the organization began innocently enough, printing pro-Serb pamphlets and staging street demonstrations, in time members of Kosovo/1389 were connected to more violent acts. In 1986 the government staged a crackdown, arresting several members of Kosovo/1389 and banning the organization. Andre Drazen was never arrested or connected to any crimes.

M4A1 Carbine—Built by the Colt Manufacturing Company, the M4A1 is a smaller, more compact version of the M16 rifle used by U.S. troops in Vietnam. The M4A1 is a very capable and deadly weapon suitable to any Delta mission. The weapon has a rail that can be used to mount a wide variety of special scopes, an AN/PEQ-2 infrared illuminator/aiming laser, a sound suppressor, M203 grenade launcher, and more. The carbine weighs 6.65 pounds fully loaded with 30 rounds, and can fire with an effective range of over 400 yards.

MC-130 Combat Talon—Special Operations version of the Lockheed C-130 four-engine transport airplane flown by the Air Force Special Operations squadrons. The Combat Talon is designed for day and night infiltration, exfiltration, resupply, and psychological operations. Talon missions are usually flown at night using a very high or low altitude profile. Combat Talons are also equipped with night targeting sensors and a mix of heavy weapons, including Gatling-style machine guns, and are ideal to penetrate deep into enemy territory.

Mobile Underground Detention and Detainment (MUDD)—This secret network of prisons is not officially recognized by the U.S. government. Its existence has only been recognized within the pages of this report. MUDD holds foreign nationals wanted for international crimes. Victor Drazen was held here.

Mole—A traitor or foreign espionage agent who has secretly infiltrated another intelligence agency and seeks to undermine or compromise that agency's personnel or activities.

Operational Detachment Alpha (ODA)—Twelve-man U.S. Army Special Forces team combining combat, language, engineering, medical, and communications skills. Formerly known as an "A-Team."

PacAmerica—Political action committee of Los Angeles businessmen who provided major funding for the Palmer campaign. Formerly headed by Carl Webb. The activities of PacAmerica have come under scrutiny by the Justice Department and other state and federal agencies.

Pave Hawk—Sikorsky MH-60 K/L helicopter modified for use by the Special Forces. Includes an in-flight refueling boom and special terrain-following radar.

Secret Service—Agency responsible for investigating cases of counterfeiting and forgery or violations of federal laws relating to securities of the United States or foreign governments. The Secret Service also provides personal security protection to high government officials, including the president and vice president and their immediate families; the president and vice president elect and their families; the wives, widows, and children of former presidents; and candidates for the office of president and vice president and their immediate families.

Serbian Liberation Front—Secretive organization whose origins are shadowy. The SLF is not subordinated to a political party or civil authority but functions as a guerrilla movement consisting of lightly armed street and guerrilla fighters. Its members carry a visible insignia—a blue rose on a field of red—and execute the assignments of their command in a disciplined manner. The SLF's strength has swelled from about five hundred active members at the beginning of 1988 to a force of at least a few thousand armed guerrillas by 1999. The SLF is organized into small compartmentalized cells and typically performs actions in smaller groups, at times as few as three to five men. Many members of the SLF are professionally trained and include former special operations soldiers. The group functions very professionally underground, due in part to the fact that some of its leaders are former members of UDBA (the Yugoslav Internal State Security Service), the Serbian army, and even the local police.

SERE—Survival, Evasion, Resistance, and Escape. A rigorous training course undergone by members of America's elite Special Forces groups, including Delta. The exercise is conducted in inhospitable climates and conditions. Soldiers are abandoned in the wilderness, tracked by armed men, captured, imprisoned, and mistreated in order to teach them the basic skills necessary to survive enemy internment.

Special Unit for Counterintelligence Initiatives—This organization is not officially recognized by the DIA or DOD. Its existence has only been recognized within the pages of this report. This agency oversees security-related policy and focuses primarily on countering the threat from foreign intelligence activities. Additionally, the unit assists FBI and military investigative agencies in DIA related to criminal and counterintelligence investigations and provides full-service forensic support to worldwide DIA missions.

Super Tuesday—The presidential election season begins with the New Hampshire primary in late February or early March. By the end of March or in early April, Super Tuesday takes place. On this day up to twelve states—including some of the largest—conduct their primaries. The winner of Super Tuesday's primaries becomes the front-runner or—depending on how many states he has won—has secured his party's nomination.

SVR—Foreign Intelligence Service. Once an arm of the KGB, the SVR now investigates espionage, terrorism, and other crimes perpetrated against the Russian state by foreign nationals or foreign intelligence services.

DEPARTMENT OF STATE
UNITED STATES OF AMERICA

A

B

DECLASSIFIED

TOP SECRET/SENSITIVE (XGDS)
NARA, Date 8/26/02

G

H

M

N

P

Q

R

S

DECLASSIFIED

01:25 01:27 01:29 01:30 01:31 01:33 01:35
01:41 01:43 01:44 01:45 01:47 01:49 01:50 01:52
56 01:57 01:58 01:59 03:01 03:04 03:06 03:09 03
03:15 03:17 03:20 03:21 03:22 03:25 03:27
03:33 03:35 03:37 03:38 03:39 03:41 03:43
03:49 03:50 03:52 03:53 03:54 03:56 03:57
04:03 04:04 04:06 04:09 04:11 04:13 04:14
04:22 04:25 04:27 04:29 04:30 04:31
04:38 04:39 04:41 04:43 04:44 04:45
04:52 04:53 04:54 04:56 04:57 04:58 04:59 06:0
06:06 06:09 06:11 06:13 06:14 06:15 06:17
22 06:25 06:27 06:29 06:30 06:31 06:33 06:35
:39 06:41 06:43 06:44 06:45 06:47 06:49 06:50
06:56 06:57 06:58 06:59 07:01 07:03 07:04
07:13 07:14 07:15 07:17 07:20 07:22 07:25
30 07:31 07:33 07:35 07:37 07:38 07:39 07:41
07:47 07:49 07:50 07:52 07:53 07:54 07:56
9 10:01 10:03 10:04 10:06 10:09 10:11 10:13
17 10:20 10:21 10:22 10:25 10:27 10:29 10:30
10:37 10:38 10:39 10:41 10:43 10:44 10:45
10:52 10:53 10:54 10:56 10:57 10:58 10:59 14:0
06 14:09 14:11 14:13 14:14 14:15 14:17 14:20
25 14:27 14:29 14:30 14:31 14:33 14:35 14:37
14:43 14:44 14:45 14:47 14:49 14:50 14:52
14:57 14:58 14:59 15:01 15:03 15:04 15:06 15:0
14 15:15 15:17 15:20 15:21 15:22 15:25 15:27
15:33 15:35 15:37 15:38 15:39 15:41 15:43 15:4
:49 15:50 15:52 15:53 15:54 15:56 15:57 15:58
18:04 18:06 18:09 18:11 18:13 18:14 18:15 18:1
22 18:25 18:27 18:29 18:30 18:31 18:33 18:35
9 18:41 18:43 18:44 18:45 18:47 18:49 18:50
18:56 18:57 18:58 18:59 20:01 20:03 20:04
11 20:13 20:14 20:15 20:17 20:20 20:21 20:22
20:30 20:31 20:33 20:35 20:37 20:38 20:39
20:45 20:47 20:49 20:50 20:52 20:53 20:54
58 20:59 23:01 23:03 23:04 23:06 23:09 23:11
15 23:17 23:20 23:21 23:22 23:25 23:27 23:29
23:35 23:37 23:38 23:39 23:41 23:43 23:4